Polish Society

Polish Society

Adam Podgórecki

PRAEGER

Westport, Connecticut
London

Library of Congress Cataloging-in-Publication Data

Podgórecki, Adam.
  Polish society / Adam Podgórecki.
    p.   cm.
    Includes bibliographical references (p.   ) and index.
    ISBN 0–275–94728–9 (alk. paper)
    1. Poland—Social conditions—1980–   2.   Post-communism—Poland.
  3. Social structure—Poland.   I. Title.
  HN537.5.P532   1994
  301'.09438—dc20   93–25056

British Library Cataloguing in Publication Data is available.

Library of Congress Catalog Card Number: 93–25056
ISBN: 0–275–94728–9

First published in 1994

Praeger Publishers, 88 Post Road West, Westport, CT 06881
An imprint of Greenwood Publishing Group, Inc.

Printed in the United States of America

The paper used in this book complies with the
Permanent Paper Standard issued by the National
Information Standards Organization (Z39.48–1984).

10 9 8 7 6 5 4 3 2 1

Copyright Acknowledgment

The author and the publisher gratefully acknowledge permission to reprint material from Adam
Podgórecki and Maria Łoś, *Multidimensional Sociology*, Routledge and Kegan Paul, 1979.
Reprinted by permission of Routledge.

Contents

Acknowledgments

I want to thank my former associates at the University of Warsaw, who in 1973–1976 participated in launching a seminar on Polish society. They are: Andrzej Celiński (currently a senator in the Polish Parliament), Kazimierz Frieske (Associate Professor of Sociology and Director of the Institute of Sociology at the University of Warsaw), Małgorzata Fuszara (Associate Professor of the Sociology of Law), Beata Gruszczyńska (Associate Professor of Sociology), Krzysztof Kiciński (Associate Professor of Sociology and Director of the Institute of Applied Social Sciences), Krystyna Cygielska (a journalist in the U.S.), Andrzej Kojder (Associate Professor of Sociology of Law and a senior official in the President's Chancellery), Jacek Kurczewski (Deputy Speaker of the Polish Parliament, dean, Sociology professor), Jerzy Kwaśniewski (Professor of Sociology, and Director of the Institute of Social Prevention and Resocialization), Magdalena Jasińska (Associate Professor of Sociology), Maria Łoś (Professor of Criminology at the University of Ottawa), Monika Massalska-Dobrowolska (a researcher in the Polish Academy of Sciences), Barbara Mikołajewska, Maria Smoła (Associate Professor of Sociology), Marek Tabin (now a journalist in Germany), and Antoni Zieliński (a head of a research unit of the Institute of Psychiatry and Neurology).

I also thank my colleagues at the Department of Sociology and Anthropology at Carleton University for several useful discussions of this subject, Claire Gigantes for her editorial help, and Rena Ramkay for her meticulous work with the text. I am grateful to Professor Robert K. Merton for his help in editing chapter 2, some elements of which were added after his editorial comments. Special thanks should go to Jennifer Quaile for assistance in preparing the manuscript.

The reader is requested to read the notes; according to the author, they are often more interesting than the text itself.

1

Introduction

What is unique about Polish society and what universal truths can Polish sociology add to existing knowledge concerning social behavior?

The Polish sociological way of thinking, as it developed during the end of the last century and in the beginning of the present one, was based predominantly on speculative German reasoning. This phenomenon was not necessarily detrimental to the social sciences, since classical German sociology, as represented by George Simmel, Ferdinand Tonnies, Max Weber, Leopold von Wiese, and others, was spectacularly strong and rigorous.

Independent of this theoretical heritage, however, the Polish sociological approach might be characterized as having a clear, value-laden, anti-establishment orientation. This ideological perspective, shaped by a century and a half of defending Poland against foreign domination, was additionally reinforced by the legacy of the intelligentsia's ethos which dominated Polish sociopolitical life.[1]

In the second half of the nineteenth and the beginning of the twentieth centuries, the intelligentsia, a social stratum believed to exist almost exclusively in Polish and Russian societies (Gella 1976; Podgórecki 1979), dedicated itself to improving sociopolitical conditions in Poland. Under its influence, the roots of Polish sociological thought contained a distinctive element of the social-democratic and, in some cases, even Marxist point of view, as seen, for example, in the works of Lubwik Krzywicki (1859–1941) and Kazimierz Kelles-Kraus (1872–1905).

Paradoxically, Leon Petrażycki (1867–1931), a towering figure in Polish social science, the creator of an independent way of thinking in logic, jurisprudence, psychology, and sociology, and the individual who would occupy the first chair of sociology in Poland (1921), was virtually unknown in his own country. Petrażycki's original ideas were, at the time (after the Great War and the reinstatement of Polish independence), too sophisticated to be properly appreciated in the newly established Polish academic circles.

Petrażycki had been teaching and writing before World War I in Berlin and St. Petersburg. During this period, his principal works, which were numerous, were published in both the German and the Russian languages. He was offered the first chair of sociology in Poland under tragicomic circumstances. Known as a world-ranking authority in the area of jurisprudence, he should have been appointed to a chair in the theory of law. Since, however, this position was occupied in Warsaw by a rather mediocre but influential dean, he was "exiled," relegated to assume responsibility for the newly created branch of social science, sociology (Górecki 1974; Kojder 1985).

Before World War I, and particularly during the inter-war period, two other exceptional figures in Polish sociology, Florian Znaniecki (1882–1958) and Bronislaw Malinowski (1884–1942), were committed to the development of sociology and anthropology. Working abroad, however, limited the extent to which they could contribute to the development of Polish sociology. Nonetheless, Znaniecki was able to conduct a study on inhabitants' perceptions of the city of Poznan. His student, Józef Chałasinski (1904–1979), published a monumental study of the peasantry as well as an illuminating work on the intelligentsia, but they were released too close to the onset of World War II to gain proper recognition.

Notwithstanding these rare empirical studies, Polish sociology, as it developed before World War II, was characterized by (a) a speculative and abstract approach to epistemological issues; (b) a politically oriented tendency to attack the existing sociopolitical establishment; and finally, (c) an apparent unwillingness to analyze its own society as a whole. In general, Polish sociology could be described as marked by quasi-political attitudes of unprofessional professionals who were primarily generating amateurish criticism of the status quo.

After World War II, Polish society presented a fascinating and unique field of inquiry. It had changed fundamentally in terms of demographics since the virtual elimination of several previously existing social strata, classes, and ethnic groups. These included the landed gentry, the Jewish population, large and medium-sized business owners, tradespeople, the German, Ukrainian, and Lithuanian minorities, and those communities connected with independent political parties and organizations. In addition, the traditional intelligentsia had lost its previous influence, and the number of artisans had dramatically declined (Wyrwa 1986). New social strata emerged.[2] At the same time that virtually all spontaneous social processes and movements were being brought to a halt, new and deliberately manufactured social processes were introduced into Polish sociopolitical life.

In a society where, according to an ideologically binding dogma, the economic base should determine the content and form of the superstructure, the superstructure—by means of political pressure—shaped the processes within the base. Post-World War II Poland thus became an unusual experimental social laboratory of vast proportions. A "socialist" model of utopian society and vision of social reality that was designed a priori forcibly set in motion various sociopolitical processes in order to transform the utopian model into practice. New mechanisms of coercive social control, alien to the Polish tradition, were developed in order to monitor and enforce the applications of these predesigned social changes (the sui generis of social engineering). These coercive, "experimental," macrosocial transformations, independent of their own negative content, had, in addition, a wide range of unintended, negative by-products. This was an unusual opportunity for sociologists. For the first time in the history of humankind, a whole society was purposely and forcibly transformed into a society of a different type, while a competent group of native professional sociologists was at hand to watch how these transmutations were taking place. To what extent was this unique research opportunity seized by Polish sociologists? Since it appears that only very limited research concerning these problems was carried out, it is worthwhile to explore why this opportunity was not seized.

After 1945, not one senior sociologist joined the ranks of "official" Marxist scholars. Surprisingly enough, none of the survivors of the German and Soviet-made holocausts (the term "holocaust" was originally used by Pitirim Sorokin, a Russian-American sociologist, who was referring to the 1917 Russian Revolution and its consequences) were able to foresee the coming changes, or unmask the preplanned strategy of those who had successfully grasped political power. Despite many negative, abstract evaluations of the approaching "new" reality, virtually no one was able to predict the dynamics of these unfolding transformations.[3]

Sociologists who were re-entering academia in the aftermath of World War II did so with the feeling that they would now be able to conduct their university duties openly, free of the constant danger of arrest, confinement in a concentration camp, or instant liquidation by the Gestapo. They regarded as their main goals (1) the continuation of inquiries interrupted by the war; (2) the further investigation of nagging, pre-war epistemological questions; and (3) the learning and perfection of research techniques, such as survey methodologies, which were unknown to the new generations of social-science students.

Some sociologists jumped at the opportunity to conduct field research in the Western Territories of Poland (the so-called Regained Territories). These areas were highly interesting, not only because of the complicated migration processes that took place within them but also because of the newly emerging patterns of interaction between the small German population still living there and the Polish patriots who had survived the pressure of heavy Nazification. The process was further complicated by the interaction of these two groups with (1) the Polish population that resettled in these territories from the former Polish Eastern Provinces (annexed to the Soviet Union after 1945), and (2) an additional population that came to these territories from impoverished central Poland, lured by what was left of German prosperity.

Some sociologists quickly engaged in a battle with the rising Marxist "school." The new school did not have much in common with traditional Polish academic Marxist thought. It was founded by politically disciplined, young pragmatic upstarts, many of whom were former officers of the Polish army who had originally organized in the Soviet Union.[4]

A short discussion in professional journals between the new wave of crude theoreticians and the pre-war university professors ended with the introduction of the following compulsory administrative measures. The most prominent pre-war sociologists, economists, and philosophers were first subjected to close surveillance (certain currently well-known individuals such as the economist Bronislaw Brus of St. Antony's College—Oxford, and Leszek Kołakowski of All Souls College—Oxford, were quite eager to participate in these activities). Later, around 1949, some of these academics (Władysław Tatarkiewicz, Stanisław Ossowski, Maria Ossowska) were removed from their university posts. Sanctions of this type, independent of their immediate effects, sowed the seeds of discontent that, after a long dormant existence, began to blossom many years later.

A typical, isolated, traditional, politically decent social scientist, once confronted by a well-organized group of Marxist operators, was not merely deprived of his supportive environment, students, and co-workers; he was also compelled *nolens volens*, to develop a sui generis self-defense strategy. This strategy consisted mainly of a solipsist concentration on one's own work. Additional, unforeseen by-products of this strategy included the steady development of self-promotion techniques, indifference to the work and criticism of others, a tendency to make spurious discoveries (strengthened by the lack of instructive feedback), a tendency to translate old, well-established notions into "newly" invented concepts, and an allergic reaction to the pursuit and development of others' ideas (since this exercise both diminished one's self-image and required a wider perspective in order to oversee developments in all current work).

The end of Stalinism in 1955 produced, to a certain extent, circumstances comparable to those that materialized after World War II. On the one hand, considerable opportunities for empirical inquiries and general interpretations had opened, while on the other, there was real concern over the possibility of a return to persecution. Nonetheless, some quite serious and original studies of the lifestyles of various social strata began to proliferate. These studies used a variety of methodological techniques; some of the survey methods were quite sophisticated for their time.

The most significant among these were administratively coordinated (controls of this type were decisive not only in terms of allocating scarce resources but also in making publication facilities available as well). These studies were not, however, comprehensively researched to provide a global analysis of Polish society. The dearth of analysis resulted from a lack of vision, coupled with the far more crucial objection from the Party: that macrotheory (Marxism-Leninism), dealing with historical changes in societies, was officially regarded as binding and exclusively correct; hence there was no need to test it at any level of generalization. Consequently, a global study of Polish society was labelled "taboo."

After World War II, Polish sociologists did not have the advantage of being able to ride subsequent waves or "fashions" in social sciences that, in the West, allowed for debate of all aspects of a given issue. After the war, Polish sociologists were overwhelmed by admiration for American sociology (and especially for American sociologists whom they happened to know personally), or they remained under the regime of dogmatic Marxism. Thus, in contrast to the West, changes of mood, harmful or benevolent, were absent from Polish social sciences. In the West, dominant currents like structuralism, sophisticated Marxism (spreading "false consciousness" among scholars), monopoly of survey techniques, modernism, and feminism mobilized the "collective wisdom" of the sociological community. This mobilization gave not only American sociologists but also scholars from various other cultures the chance to explore, from different angles, the potential of the predominant intellectual paradigm. While it sometimes exerted a conformist, if not overly conformist, pressure on younger generations of scholars, on the whole this collective approach allowed participants to test whether a prevalent thinking pattern was advantageous or disadvantageous. Each paradigm had, of course, its own dogmatic enemies and supporters. Nonetheless, in the long run, these subsequent swings of "fashion" were illuminating.

Taking advantage of the 1970 economic crisis, one of the most serious Poland has ever had, a dynamic sociotechnical (Sociotechnics is social engineering from the point of view of social justice and rationality) "invisible college" transformed itself into a formal institute—the Institute of Social Prevention and Rehabilitation at the University of Warsaw—pursuing studies in social pathology and under-taking a comprehensive study of Polish society and its social problems. Upon creation, the institute was attacked by the Communist party. After some time, its structure was altered, and the scholars who had been most active in preparing comprehensive diagnoses of Polish social problems and Polish society were dismissed.

Interestingly enough, during the Solidarity period (1980–1981), when the political climate was much more relaxed, a similar research project based upon empirical material was carried out by a group of scholars who called themselves "Experience and Future." It is possible that this group was used by one of the Party bosses, Stefan Olszowski, as a tool in a desperate factional struggle for power against Edward Gierek, the First Secretary of the Communist party.[5] Nevertheless, these activities encouraged the study of Polish society as a whole. Unfortunately, they too have followed previous patterns: no study ever referred to others—each study emerged, phoenix-like, from nothing; the objective of these studies was not so much to attack evident social problems as to promote the authors of these reports; finally, none of the reports was commissioned or sponsored by a state agency or by any nonsociological organization.

The term "social pathology" was introduced early into the sociological curriculum, but was later banned from the Polish language: how could the notion of social pathology (deviance) exist within a "socialist state on its way to communism"?[6] The term started to appear sporadically in various professional magazines. It was soon discussed not only in daily newspapers and weekly magazines but also in economic journals. This was surprising. Under "real" socialism, economists were used to living comfortably in abstract, empty, normative dreams that were out of touch with reality, or, more simply, in tune with "false reality" (this does not refer to a state of "false consciousness"—social reality was far too visible for that).

Criminologists who dealt predominantly with narrow empirical issues of deviance began to place these issues into the larger theoretical framework of social pathology.[7] Even lawyers, considered as a rule to be the most conformist professionals, started, modestly at first, to ask themselves how various phenomena of social pathology developed in post-war Poland were connected to the social system and economic conditions, instead of simply analyzing family disorder, divorce, prostitution, recidivism, and juvenile delinquency.

After World War II, the Polish sociologist played the role of a sui generis esoteric in a highly marginalized profession. Sociological language was (and still is) so obscure, complicated, and full of jargon that other intellectuals, such as more sophisticated journalists, lawyers, or psychologists, were inclined to pick up few, if any, particularly outstanding sociological notions for elaboration and dissemination to the public at large.

The obscurity of sociological jargon was sometimes functional in nature; to be rarely cited served as a protective measure. Before 1989, for example, if formulated in an Aesopian manner, a critical observation concerning current problems within Polish society could escape the attention of a government censor. At the very least, it could make him think, "If I have trouble understanding this term and its context, the public, even that segment of it that knows how to read between the lines, will hardly comprehend it." Thus, an additional task for the sociologists emerged: to make their knowledge about Polish society available for general consumption, and to find an intermediary measure that would interpret and present this knowledge clearly and comprehensibly.

My own appeals to study Polish society as a whole; my attempts, both as a scholar and in my official capacity as a member of the board of the Polish Sociological Association, to focus the attention of the Polish Sociological Congress on this issue in 1977; my paper entitled "Global Analysis of Polish Society" prepared for this congress; and my other publications, including "Perspectives on the Development of Polish Sociology" (1976), were, in the beginning, noticed mainly by the security apparatus.

This remained the case until the powerful wave of awareness created by the Solidarity movement served as a traumatic eye opener. A leading Polish sociologist, Jan Lutyński, wrote, "As I tried to show, Polish sociology of the sixties and seventies was oriented (independent of its analyses of epistemological problems) towards those issues defined by the authorities and their wishes, more so than on society and its actual problems. . . . Moreover, the movement to analyse the global society is, without a doubt, a *novum* in our society" (Lutyński 1987: 135, 138).

Under these circumstances, Polish sociology became an "invisible college," unrestricted by existing establishments; a voluntary organization, facilitating and creating new ideas and disseminating them among specialists. It became an invisible college also for sociologists from other "socialist" countries. In the absence of direct contact with the West, these individuals started to learn the Polish language, travel to Warsaw, and utilize Polish sociological texts. They became fascinated with Polish sociology, its level of development, and its strong links with the Western social sciences. It is intriguing that Polish reference material is rarely quoted in their texts; their references allude directly to the original sources. Polish sociologists such as Zygmunt Bauman, Szymon Chodak, Maria Hirszowicz, and Jerzy Wiatr (all former Party members) represented Mecca to the newly emerging sociologists from the Soviet Union, Czechoslovakia, Hungary, Rumania, and Bulgaria.

A few of the more sophisticated socialist sociologists quickly went through a further "mental revolution" after visiting these Marxists. They discovered personalities and works that were really significant for Polish sociology. They encountered scholars such as Maria Ossowska, Stanislaw Ossowski, Andrzej Malewski, and Stefan Nowak. Through such encounters, many Polish sociologists became aware of their scholarly obligations towards these individuals, undertaking a sui generis liberalization mission to spread their own and original Western ideas that had not been distorted by Marxist dialectics.

Invisible colleges, which, according to the illuminating study by Diana Crane (1972), disseminate knowledge about certain discoveries in the pure sciences (especially mathematics) faster than traditional academic means, operated in Poland in a manner entirely different from that of the West.[8] Since sociology, like all disciplines in the humanities, was strictly controlled through curricula and by institutions such as universities, the Academy of Sciences, the Ministry of Higher Education, and the Central Committee of the Party, many unconventional ideas were hidden in the niches of different associations. These associations were used as testing grounds until the ideas reached scholarly maturity and, more importantly, until the proper political moment arrived. The sociology of law (not the Marxist theory of state and law), sociotechnics, and social pathology were developed through this process in Poland.

The post-1989 counter-reaction to accumulated dysfunctional phenomena did not live up to the task of building a global, empirically oriented synthesis of Polish society. Instead, it led to a peculiar "moral" purification. The purification process targeted the ethos of those engaged in scholarly research. One of the leading figures in this metamovement stated, "A university which aspires to the role of guardian and articulator of scientific ethos should be built according to the following principles: a) the organizational structure of the university should rely on the structure of the 'disciplines' . . . b) this structure should take into consideration the concept 'field structure' in order to situate the university in general academic life. . . . c) this structure should rely on the autonomy of planning research and didactic programmes . . . and d) it should base its work on small units linked by the rationales and interests of respective scientific disciplines'' (Goćkowski 1991: 32).

This approach does not attempt to comprehend, describe, or explain social reality, but instead preaches "what is proper" and "what is abominable." The escape into values is always the easiest! The former president of the Polish Sociological Association, participating in an attempt to define the ethos of the scientist in natural and social sciences, suggested that "an accusation was made here that we are using too many normative expressions, and too few statements pertaining to actual behaviour. But the central problem of our considerations deals with ethics, the prescription of what is good and what is bad, and the justification of these prescriptions through appropriate basic values" (Ziółkowski 1991: 284).

Excursions into the ethical problems of scientists are important to everyone, including those who create and disseminate social sciences. Yet these excursions are nothing more than a reminder of what is already well known. Moreover, such excursions should not hinder the basic task that Polish sociology faces. This task has not yet been systematically undertaken. Even now, when political obstacles do not preclude its accomplishment, this task remains unfulfilled.

Why is it that a global and methodical analysis of Polish society is not pursued by at least one of the many ambitious and gifted Polish sociologists? Paradoxically, the westernization of Polish sociology, invisible from the inside, plays a significant role here. Since everyone in Poland wants to be either a "Newton" or an "Einstein" (by the way, it has been shown by Jerzy Giedymin that it was Poincaré, not Einstein, who first formulated the basic equation for mass and energy [Giedymin 1984]), and when this goal is frustrated, an easy "ersatz" emerges in cooperation with those who are able to provide funds for exotic comparative studies. As a result many inquiries unrelated to Polish reality flourish in Poland. But they are comparable to the studies of the West.

In Polish sociology, two approaches to the comprehensive study of society existed: the "classical," and the "super-modern," which had been formulated by certain better-known Polish sociologists.

The classical approach asserts that the historical-economic and political situations of any society are too complicated for their global synthesis. Jerzy Szacki, using his own exhaustive and extensive study pertaining to the status of sociology in general, says, in his final judgment: "If one can draw any conclusion from this book, this book would stress mainly the impossibility of generalisations ('balancing' in sociology) which would go beyond the assessment of a sum of problems and dilemmas" (Szacki 1981: 816).

The super-modern approach tries to advance "the sociology of becoming" in connection with the concept of "agency" in order to study social problems and societies. Its starting point is the notion of becoming. That concept is presented by Piotr Sztompka in the following way: "It denotes the continuous process of society's self-transformation and self-creation as a result of incessantly repro- duced inevitable tension between the potential agency of society (ability of transformation) and its actual socio-historical *praxis* (social events)" (Sztompka 1991: 278).

Less abstract and closer to reality is Bronisław Misztal when he writes,

> Yet another hypothesis can be advanced here: that state socialist societies had changed "by default," i.e., because for historical reasons they were incapable of producing people with stable and adequate images of their own destiny that would embark upon consistent scenarios and development. Two situations of social change by default are possible. Societies can change either because they produce identity and knowledge that are incon- sistent with historical experience, thus rather than to encourage people to refocus their concerns, they instead stimulate members to undertake spontaneous activity in search of new imaginary meanings, or societies can be changing because of their inability to produce viable political infrastructural institutions (the state). (Misztal, forthcoming)

One may note that what was labelled as the classical approach has been shaped by a form of intellectual defeat ("the impossibility of generalisations"), whereas the super-modern approach outlined by postulative thinking presents too abstract a framework for advancing the theory dealing with concrete societies; nor does it provide an operative macroresearch framework for a study.

A third approach, introduced in this book, treats Polish society as a *macro- natural laboratory*. It tries to link transformations that took place in this society with the society's accumulated collective self-awareness. Between 1945 and 1992, Polish society moved from (a) a post-occupation period after the departure of the Germans in 1945, to (b) a nationalization process and a restricted free market, to (c) "real socialism," the phase of state socialism, and again to (d) the "free market" stage. Thus, in less than half a century, four crucial socio- economic and political transformations took place, characterized economically by the shift from market economy to mixed economy to "state socialism," and politically by imposed "independence" followed by an imposed totalitarian regime, and finally, independence. Although these transformations dealt a heavy existential blow to Polish society, this very blow can be treated as a unique and unexpected gift for Polish social scientists. It furnishes them with the chance to investigate the relationships between the spontaneous changes in social reality and the collective perceptions of this reality. Additionally, it provides them with the chance to observe the emergence of products and by-products of deliberate social planning, since Polish society was the macro-object of intense social transformations for half a century. This society was also, as a consequence of the accumulation of several unexpected by-products, the source of feedback that erupted spontaneously, even violently, and was directed against the "planners."

Social changes of this scope and intensity heavily influenced collective social awareness. Thus, one may hypothesize that these changes created a collective image of the global social condition. If these theoretical expectations are correct, then one anticipates that the collectively elaborated and perceived image should be the most precious target for sociological study. Therefore, in order to extract the cumulative sense of this image, it becomes methodologically advisable, if not necessary, to combine two perspectives, the study of social stratification and social change with the inquiry into people's consciousness and collective societal self-awareness, and regard them as organically intertwined.

The first perspective deals with typical sociological problems such as social processes, social change, social stratification, élites, the social background of normative ideologies, and power. This perspective is mainly based on findings of systematic sociological, or semisociological, investigations.

The second perspective deals with the realm of public opinion, actual attitudes, commonsense and widespread understandings, and newly generated factual ethoses. From one perspective, this inquiry reveals the manner in which common people construe diagnostic images of various societal problems. From the other point of view, it is connected with a cognitive elaboration of these constructs. Cognitive processing in Poland was for a long time a by-product of an official institutional outgrowth of the Communist state. Yet the official scholarly approach was constantly challenged by independent Polish sociological thinking (which was rarely parallel to official thought; rather, it was pursued underground).

The Western reader, who is not familiar enough with the "exotic intellectual subculture" existing within many professions and organizations, should be reminded that inside the sociological profession an additional, hidden ideological war was going on. If this war, not exclusively intellectual, is not considered in the whole picture, then the portrait of Polish sociology and the diagnosis of this society become vastly distorted.

Generally speaking, the duality of this analysis allows for the concurrent investigation of the influence of social processes (as an independent factor) on the collective social perception, and the study of how the society in question was shaped by a new, alien ideology (as a dependent factor). Finally, this duality enables the scholar to discover to what extent imposed values and institutions have been assimilated by various societal groupings.

With this methodological framework, it is clear that both the factual and epistemological questions that appear when a given society undergoes a macro-transformation cannot be separated. It is also clear that this framework will not lead to an invention of spurious notions, notions which pretend to be self-explanatory.

In studying Polish society empirically and presenting the findings in English, one has to remember one important point. As a rule, English-language publications of empirical data concerning Polish society and generalizations gleaned from them are lagging far behind the fast pace of events. A good example of this was the publication in 1992 of a study on attitudes of the Polish population carried out in mid-1984 and reported in Polish in 1988. According to the study, which was conducted by a prominent Polish sociologist, the most common sources of dissatisfaction were connected with macrosocial conditions of life.

The external circumstances (at that time the author of the study could not openly disclose that it was an anxiety related to a possible Soviet "intervention") were repudiated by 91 percent of the respondents, whereas the domestic situation (again, worries connected with the political repression of the Solidarity movement could not at the time be openly stated) was selected by 92 percent of the sample; respondents could choose more than one answer from a list of eighteen items (Sarapata 1992:197).

Antoni Kaminski wrote a book on an institutional theory of Communist regimes in 1988 and 1989, but published it in 1992. The main thesis of this book, which attempted a synthesis of sorts, follows:

institutions that demonstrably serve broader social interests, whatever their virtues, can be defended only when the institutions are considered fair, fairness being the prime condition for their legitimacy. When institutions merely serve the interests of a particular social group, or a narrow set of such groups, popular realization of this fact makes them vulnerable and short lived. The thrust of the argument is that, as long as the Communist party was a social movement permeated by a sense of mission, its crimes and abuses served the mission, helping to maintain the depersonalized image of the Party and keep society in a state of strict submission. Only when state terrorism subsided did the party-state complex become the preserve of informal groups oriented towards the realization of their private interests. This proliferation of special interests has gradually made the system ungovernable and contributed to its present demise. (Kaminski 1992: 24)

To discover why Polish society was not studied as a consistent whole, or why it was studied only as a by-product of research that covers a mosaic of unrelated issues, it would be appropriate to analyze scholarly models that appeared on the Polish scene after World War II. It would be even more illuminating to examine the ideal model of a Polish scholar working in the social sciences, given the scholar's links to ideology.

2

The Socialist and Post-Socialist Scholar in Social Sciences

A sociological analysis of the misfortunes of sociology under socialism still remains to be written. (Kłoskowska 1991: 258)

The main thesis of this chapter is that the traditional model of the Polish scholar was developed under the influence of two somewhat contradictory models: the Polish intelligentsia, to which it owes its amateurish flavor, and the Austro-German university, from which it acquired its feudal-bureaucratic character.[9] This model has been successfully challenged recently by the two variations of a socialist scholar: the instrumental and the spectacular.[10]

THEORETICAL INTRODUCTION

In his well-known classification of the roles played by men of knowledge, Florian Znaniecki (1965) distinguished the following categories: technocrats, sages, religious scholars, discoverers of truth, systematizers, contributors, fighters of truth, historians of knowledge, and disseminators of knowledge. He also tried to consolidate these roles into discoverers of facts, discoverers of problems, and theoreticians. This classification is instructive, but it does have some shortcomings: it is too abstract, it does not directly connect the roles of various scholars with corresponding social realities, and it does not identify the recent meteoric appearance of a new type of scholar—the instrumental scholar.

An instrumental scholar is one who injects into academia values that do not rightly belong to the ethos of the community of scholars and scientists. When these considerations are limited to the social sciences, two types of scholars are distinguished: the instrumentalists, who operate predominantly by manipulating science in order to achieve nonscientific gains, and "spectacular" scholars, who operate mainly through symbols and appeal to the "second," hidden life of society in order to become the "governor of souls" in that society.

Johann Galtung's classification of scientific roles (1981) is oriented more towards social reality. He classifies modern social sciences into the Saxonic, Teutonic, Gallic, and Nipponic approaches. The Saxonic approach offers a relatively weak analysis of paradigms, but it is strong in description and in commentary on other intellectuals. The Teutonic and Gallic approaches, both weak in description but strong in explanation, paradigm analysis, and commentaries on other intellectuals, differ from each other only in their style of scientific work. The Nipponic approach refers to the acceptance of scientific authorities (masters) and is irrelevant to the present analysis. Galtung, like Znaniecki, overlooks the specificity of the "totalitarian" scholar and provides no theoretical background that could describe or explain this phenomenon. The existing literature does not give a detailed description of the infrastructure of scientific institutions that have been influenced by instrumentalists.

This lack of description is due to several factors. First, the socialist scholar served as a convenient screen for hiding the latent power structure in the period from 1945 to 1989. Second, socialist scholars force colleagues who did not agree with the imposed ideology into endless and exhaustive administrative battles. Third, among the socialist scholars are real scholars entering into dangerous, ongoing, ideological wars with those who act to preserve and strengthen the existing power structure (this warlike engagement gives the socialist scholars-manipulators additional strength for developing their skills in attacking those engaged primarily in scientific inquiries). Fourth, as a result of these instrumental activities, real scholars are presented to the public as politically dangerous; hence, owing to the increasing fear of repression, they become isolated, not only officially but also socially, which results in an ultimate paralysis of their official activities.

Totalitarian sociopolitical systems chiefly breed this particular type of socialist scientist "personality." In such systems, the ruling party exercises a crushing dominance. The party monopolizes the culture, economy, social life, law, state, and police. Generally speaking, two facets of totalitarian systems appear in scholarly life. First, official life in a given society is ruled by the directives of an exclusive dogma, and second, social life also follows the directives of an exclusive dogma. The more the society is molded by official and social totalitarianism, the more likely it is that the dominant scholarly personality will become an instrumental type.

It is quite interesting that German sociology (especially the branch that labelled itself "critical," the so-called Frankfurt School) was not eager to elucidate the informal processes that led, under the Nazi regime, to this type of cognitive erosion. The peculiar phenomenon of a fascist scholar has not yet been fully described, but the brotherly model of a socialist scholar is still readily available.[11]

Why then has an analysis of the ideal type of socialist scholar remained so elusive? Although such scholars may be easily visible to an outsider (owing to their aggressive participation at international organizations and conferences and their inflated rate of publication), they are, for various reasons, not easily accessible for thorough scrutiny.

This relative inaccessibility has several causes. To begin with, some of the East European scholars, currently in the West, who could provide an accurate inside picture would have to disclose their own hitherto concealed involvement in the development of the socialist scholar. Furthermore, several former East European scholars who are now in the West, and who might provide an understanding of this new scientific role, are unable to do so because they operate intellectually within the categories developed by their political "trainers."

Some former East European scholars who have attacked "socialist" countries both emotionally and indiscriminately to justify their opportunistic departures have revealed some interesting facts. On the whole, however, they cannot be regarded as reliable, balanced diagnosticians. Moreover, many who have relocated in the West prefer to engage in actual research, rather than attempt to unmask their own (or others') fictitious scientific activities. Some of the scholars who have remained in Eastern Europe and who could readily disclose relevant facts about their societies choose not to provoke the authorities (usually their former colleagues). Instead, they prefer to work quietly at home, maintaining their contacts with Western academia (these contacts can no longer be as abruptly cut off by an administrative decision as they could before 1989). Finally, some of the Western scholars who could have elucidated this type of "scientific" personality before 1989 have had an interest in cooperating with their Eastern counterparts, who virtually control all access to data that is vitally important for scholars interested in the affairs of "socialist" countries.

Since Poland was (and is) the most liberal country in the former Soviet bloc with respect to the development of social sciences, all comments and generalizations about restrictions in Poland are all the more true for the other former socialist countries. The study of Polish academic life thus provides an entrance into the unique processes operating inside the hidden infrastructure of "socialist" academia. The Polish situation can be regarded as a focal example.

After World War II, four semi-independent official institutions existed in Poland. Their inception, development, and eventual destruction proceeded according to the same pattern. The Research Center of Public Opinion at Polish Radio and Television was created after the Polish October in 1956 as an arm of a sui generis invisible college, the political-discussion club called *Krzywe Koło*, or Crooked Circle. The main organizers were Czeslaw Czapów (who was almost always behind actions of this type), Jerzy Kubin, Wacław Makarczyk, and Andrzej Rażniewski. The center was "recognized" in 1962, when Crooked Circle was closed and Anna Pawełczynska, then a Party member, became its new director. Later, all of its cofounders died of heart attacks.

The main objective of the Psychometric Laboratory at the Polish Academy of

Sciences was to adapt various psychological tests (mainly American) to Polish conditions, using them in subsequent inquiries. The laboratory was closed in 1969. Its founder and director, Mieczysław Choynowski, now lives in Mexico.

Praxiology is the science that examines possible practical actions and tries to specify the conditions under which these actions are effective. As a result of the activities of Tadeusz Kotarbiński, the creator of this scientific perspective, and those of his followers, a Center of Praxiology was established at the Polish Academy of Sciences in 1958. Many interesting theoretical ideas were developed at this center that were able, to some extent, to inspire socioeconomic life in Poland. It was "reorganized" in 1973. The last director before its reorganization, Witold Kieżun, now lives in Rwanda, Africa. He has completed a book that provides a penetrating analysis of management methods in the Eastern bloc (Kieżun 1991).

The main empirical focus of this chapter, the Institute of Social Prevention and Resocialization, of which I was a cofounder, was larger than the other three institutions and often trespassed on the activities, theoretical and practical, that they pursued. Thus, anything said about this institute can also be applied to the other institutions.

To grasp the specificity of the socialist scholar in Poland (and in other socialist countries), it is important to remember the point made at the outset of the chapter: that the traditional model of the Polish scholar was originally influenced by two somewhat contradictory models, the Polish intelligentsia and Austro-German universities. The traditional Polish model of a scholar exercises a strict dedication to science (a vocation, in the Weberian sense), insisting that a science be treated as if it were a spring, to drink from which one must kneel. Generally speaking, this traditional model is founded on a principled attitude, an attitude that accepts a given norm without conditions or reservations.

Since World War II, university professors in Poland have enjoyed remarkable prestige. They are consistently ranked, in numerous studies, as the most respected group in society (see chapter 3). Under real socialism, such high regard has had its own consequences. Universities have been used by ambitious individuals to acquire social visibility and esteem. Perhaps more importantly, the ruling party has tried to capture and control university chairs, profiting from the prestige of its scholars, while maintaining support for the legitimacy of its own dubious élite.

The traditional model of the Polish scholar provides a context for understanding the impact of instrumentally oriented scholars on the life of scientific institutions that operated under the terms of a traditional Polish scholarly ethos. The following case study may also furnish a fairly good diagnosis of the situation encountered by social scientists who, against all odds, tried to preserve intellectual independence under politically oppressive conditions. Such a study may also be treated as an attempt to single out the instrumental factors that introduced "dark" social engineering to Poland. Paradoxically, this twisted form of social engineering stood in direct contrast to efforts to develop genuine social engineering, based on the idea of social justice and the use of rational social engineering, to solve acute social problems (Podgórecki 1991: 21). The case study may also show, in a picturesque way, the clash between the new "exotic" instrumental scholar, who recently entered the world scientific stage, and Polish scholarship based on the intelligentsia's perspective.

THE POLISH SCHOLAR: A CASE STUDY

The Inception and Development of the Institute of Social Prevention and Resocialization

During the sixties, the Sociotechnics Section of the Polish Sociological Association (an "invisible college"), a small group of social scientists interested in sociological theory and alert to the political overtones of their individual interests, developed the idea of "sociotechnics."[12] This was a practical social science concerned with the rules defining efficient social action and social justice. The founders of the Sociotechnics Section believed that social policy should be grounded in the basic values of the intelligentsia and consistent with the results of social research.

When sociotechnics became a widely known discipline towards the end of the 1960s, it was vigorously rejected by officials who claimed that only the Polish Communist party was truly expert in these matters. The dramatic events of December 1970—the workers' riots in Gdańsk and Gdynia—discredited this official opinion. The academics who formed the sociotechnics circle, particularly Tomasz Kocowski and, to a lesser extent, myself, had predicted some months before the riots that public outbursts of dissatisfaction would occur. After these nation-shaking events, uncoordinated, even desperate, official efforts at trying to deal with urgent social problems created an opportunity for establishing a new body that could institutionalize the sociotechnical method of social intervention. The concept of sociotechnics, still unacceptable to the officials, was replaced by the notion of "social prevention," "resocialization" was added as a legal counterbalance, and the Institute of Social Prevention and Resocialization was born in 1972. It retained its original mandate for four years.

The institute was established as an independent faculty at the University of Warsaw. The director's position was equivalent to the position of a faculty dean. The institute offered a full range of courses and a degree program. Its basic teaching methods did not differ from the methods of other university faculties, although it carried an additional burden. Extramural students came monthly from different parts of the country for three- or four-day periods. These students also attended full time during the summer holidays. Several staff members at the institute held only research appointments, although they were free to engage in teaching.

The institute launched a periodical entitled *Prace Instytutu* (*Works of the Institute*), 500 copies of which were published by the Warsaw University Press.

Staff members were the only writers allowed to submit their work to the periodical. Three volumes were prepared between 1972 and 1976 and published in 1976, 1978, and 1979. The first systematic publication concerning the global analysis of Polish society was published in this periodical.

Research, consultation, and teaching began with great momentum. Although the basic idea and design of the institute were neither widely known nor advertised, the number of candidates wishing to pursue degrees and diplomas there soon greatly exceeded its capacity to accommodate them. Applications for available places were more numerous than in other social-science departments at Warsaw University. The institute enrolled about 100 students, excluding extramural students, by its third year. In 1976, 600 students from both categories were studying at the institute.

From its beginning, an energetic effort was made to clarify the basic sociological ideas implied in the outlook of the institute's founders. This involved, in part, a series of scholarly lectures, some of them given by foreign scholars. One of the most important goals of the founders was to study practical social problems through empirical research and theoretical analysis, preparing recommendations for practical action based on these studies. Although there was not much demand for specific studies—one diagnosis of various types of social and institutional pathology was prepared for the governing council of the Polish Academy of Sciences, and another dealing with the reform of resocialization programs was prepared for the Ministry of Education—the academic staff of the institute decided to focus on the development of sociotechnics.

The institute decided to undertake a project involving almost its entire staff: "The Diagnostic Analysis of Difficult Problems in Polish Society and Sociotechnical Recommendations." The most distinctive feature of this study was the systematic and synthetic integration of results accumulated in sociology, social pathology, criminology, and economics. The report, revised in successive discussions held at institute meetings, was mimeographed in 1974 (in 100 numbered copies, to avoid the censor's intervention) and sent to various government institutions, academics, and interested research workers.[13] The institute undertook another major study that was later cancelled by the university rector (the infamous Zygmunt Rybicki), despite strong protests by Professor Czapów, then vice director of the institute. This study dealt with the following issues: (a) For which problems of socioeconomic life do parliamentary and governmental institutions seek the advice of experts? (b) Who are identified as "experts" by these various institutions? (c) What is the typology of experts? (d) Which rules should experts observe to ensure that their findings are recognized as having practical value? (e) How are differences of opinion among experts resolved?[14]

Along with these two research undertakings, the institute also committed itself to conducting more narrowly defined research into various aspects of organizational and individual misconduct. These studies were undertaken by small groups of researchers who were expected to prepare comprehensive diagnoses of social problems such as the "double life" at schools, theft of tonnes of cargo from the railroads, and the pathology of state institutions.

The institute's main theoretical tenet was a new approach to social deviance in Poland by which it claimed that the primary causes of social pathology were institutional (for example, oppression by the state apparatus, the effect of living in a peculiar type of "limbo," leading a life based on spurious activities, and the lack of authentic work force representation). According to this point of view, structural factors played a primordial, pathogenic role in the life of Polish society. In connection with this, Jerzy Kwaśniewski launched an institutional study into "positive deviance" (pro-social behavior, which is directed by an altruistic motivation), regarding it as a force that should be carefully cultivated to promote social justice.

Relying on previous teaching experience and general pedagogical principles, the staff of the institute prepared, under Kwaśniewski's guidance, new programs for study and teaching, one type for students in residence and another for extramural students. It soon became clear that the students, usually residents of the institute, were strongly attached to social ideals. They were committed to learning about society and the practical applications of their knowledge. They also wished to bring about changes in Polish society.

A new image for the professional role of institute graduates took form. Graduates were considered to be capable of using knowledge in order to suggest or initiate action that would practically resolve hitherto unresolved social issues, irrespective of official views. The graduate of the institute was to become a "social planner," an expert in recognizing problems and proposing means of dealing with them. He was not to confine himself to particular issues within institutions, but rather to see the problems of society in a more general context.

The leading role in the institute's intellectual life was played by the Center of Sociology of Social Norms and Social Pathology (at the time, the largest center in sociology in both Poland and all other so-called socialist countries, with seventeen scientists employed in one "chair").[15] The report on "The Diagnostic Analysis of Difficult Problems in Polish Society and Sociotechnical Recommendations" was mainly prepared by members of the center.

By the fourth year of its existence, several books inspired by the "spirit" of the institute had been published. Among them was Jacek Kurczewski's *Prawo w Społeczeństwie*, or *Law in Society* (1975), summarizing recent developments in the sociology of law in Poland. Others included *Sociotechnika w Zakładzie Pracy* (*Sociotechnics in Enterprises*), by Czesław Czapów (1977), and a collective work (Podgórecki 1976b) entitled *Zagadnienia Patologii Społecznej* (*Problems of Social Pathology*). This last work, the first of its kind in Poland, was a synthesis of empirical and theoretical knowledge, embracing both "socialist" and "capitalist" research into the sociology of deviance. It described and explained the various types of spontaneous and organizational disorders in a socialist society.

An extensive, two-volume manuscript entitled "Sociological Concepts and Sociological Theories," the unpublished result of a two-year seminar on this subject, was a synthesizing work unlike any other found in Poland. It gave evidence of the interdisciplinary and intellectual potential of the teaching and research staff at the institute. The manuscript was never published, although a few copies of it were circulated in Warsaw. Another theoretical work written by two members of the institute was submitted for publication, but rejected on the strength of unfavorable Marxist reviews. It has since been published in English (Podgórecki, Łoś 1979).

The Destruction of the Institute

The intense life of the institute was strongly attacked by the Communist party. The Party charged that the institute's macrodiagnostic activity far exceeded its terms of reference. Research on the competence and reliability of officials comprising the state administration was considered an intervention into state affairs, thus contradicting the Party's monopoly. A Party cell, like those existing in every other university institute, was formed in 1975. At secret meetings, the cell devised a new, reformed structure for the institute, as well as new programs of research and teaching. When the cell's activities became widely known as a result of "leaks," it became clear that a majority of staff members did not wish to change the institute into a "technical school" that concentrated on "resocializing" criminals, teaching the staff of penal institutions, and training staff for employment in the Ministries of Justice and Internal Affairs.

Similarly, another program concocted by the Party cell, to expand the extramural services of the institute in order to train these students for police and other penal occupations (at the expense of resident students), was wholly rejected by the institute staff. Advocates of the proposed changes were officials who, until then, had dominated the informal spirit of the institute. They were Stanisław Jedlewski, the director; Adam Krukowski, vice director; Ewa Tochowicz, the first secretary of the Party cell; Stanisław Walczak, the former minister of Justice, a shadowy member of the board of directors who held a part-time position at the institute (which allowed him to keep his full retirement salary); and Marek Kosewski, vice director.[16] This group was condemned by almost all the student body and ostracized by its forty colleagues. Nevertheless, since all five of them held positions in the Communist party and key administrative posts at the institute, they were quite effective in destroying the work of the institute. Urged on by the rector of the university (Professor Zygmunt Rybicki), they brought about the dismissal of ten highly qualified staff members who were not members of the Communist party by making use of the government's campaign to reduce the size of the academic "workforce." Five of the ten were Members of the Center of Sociology of Social Norms and Social Pathology. Not a single sociologist appeared among the Party representatives who had decided to "reform" the Institute.

The rector of the university, in conversation with a professor defending the staff members about to be dismissed, asked, "What can you tell me about Maria Łoś?" The professor answered, "Maria Łoś is a very intelligent and talented scholar. She has published one book on her own and is a coauthor of some others. She has had articles published in English, Italian, French, and Russian. She has given lectures at many universities, among them Harvard, Oslo, Milan, Moscow, Yale, and California." The rector then asked, "How old is this person?" When told that she was around thirty, he said, "There you are, Professor. You yourself give me enough reason to fire her. If Maria Łoś is so active and also so young, then the sooner Maria Łoś is fired, the better. She could do us harm for a long time to come."[17]

On another occasion, the rector asked me, "Why, Professor, do you cling so steadfastly to this university? We have heard that Wroclaw Polytechnic is interested in you. We shall not oppose your transfer to Wroclaw. We could probably even cover your moving expenses. Apart from that, there are some vacant administrative positions in the city. You could also utilize your legal education by working somewhere as a legal advisor. We do not have anything against that. Why do you cling so stubbornly to your work at this university? There are many other occupations in Warsaw." The rector also said, "In your center, with its seventeen members, not a single one is a Party member. Is this your way of telling us that Party members are duller and less intelligent? Do not underestimate us, sir!"

The rector also complained that "three of your staff signed the protest against constitutional changes. This is the highest percentage found in all academic centers, not only at this university, but also in the whole country. It is a symptom of a highly poisonous political atmosphere. How can I—as someone responsible for the socialist profile of a university in the capital of the country—accept it?"

The normally neutral trade union came to the defence of the staff members who were about to be dismissed, moved by the disjunction between the outstanding academic professional achievements of the staff members, and the arbitrary and unfounded charges made against them.

Students who were completing their work for the master's degree were forbidden, despite their protests, to continue work under the direction of supervisors who had been chosen for dismissal. The protests of the students were either ignored, evaded, or met with threats. At a meeting with student representatives demanded by the students, the rector of the university replied to questions about the proposed reorganization before they were even asked. He had received the list of student questions beforehand from an informer. He said:

Do not let yourselves be taken in by professors who are more actors than scholars. Know how to distinguish self-proclaimed professors from real ones! The authentic criterion is their membership in the Polish Academy of Sciences [a few weeks later, he himself failed to receive the required number of votes from his Party colleagues in the Academy], or honorary doctorates from foreign universities, especially those in socialist countries. Some professors imagine that some research centers or institutes can conduct comprehensive analyses of a society as a whole, or can study social problems in terms of organizational pathology. Marxist learning condemns and rejects such nonsense out of hand.

The student participants prepared a record of their meeting with the rector for the other students and posted it on a wall at the institute. It was immediately removed and a search for its anonymous authors was launched.

In June, 1976, the institute was reorganized on the strength of the rector's decision after his consultation with the minister of Higher Education and the Central Committee of the Party. Dr. Adam Krukowski became its new director. He was the personal assistant of the criminal deputy minister of Internal Security (Różanski) in Stalin's time, and also a deputy colonel in the Security Forces. Later, he was made a member of the university's political ruling body, the Komitet Uczelniany.

Professor Czapów, a cofounder of the institute, learned that he was discharged from his post as vice director when he received his monthly salary without the supplement ordinarily accompanying this executive position. Later, he was transferred to another institute within the university. After all the "reorganizing," only two professors were dismissed from the institute and the university. This probably resulted from the inefficiency of the bureaucratic machinery.

The Center of Sociology of Social Norms and Social Pathology, in its original form, was abolished. The head of the center and cofounder of the institute was transferred, against his will, to the Institute of Philosophy. He was given the position of a faculty member with a professorial salary, but deprived of the privilege to teach. Five other members of the center were dispersed within the university. They were placed in positions surrounded by faithful, or at least conformist, Party "scientific workers." A few others were transferred elsewhere.

The new deputy director was Dr. Marek Kosewski, one of the main agents assisting in the destruction of the institute. (He was later removed from this position when it was revealed that the dissertation that he had submitted for habilitation—a degree higher than the Ph.D—was largely a copy of his doctoral dissertation.)

The spirit of the original academic staff was expressed in a letter condemning the reorganization of the institute and demanding that the reasons behind the change be revealed. It was signed by almost all staff members and sent to the rector of the University of Warsaw, the minister of Higher Education and the Department of Education of the Central Committee of the Communist party. It remained unanswered. The members who did not sign the letter were later rewarded through promotion.

A paralysis of all serious intellectual activity during the reorganization set in and lasted several months. Members of staff who did not welcome the changes were persecuted, blackmailed, misinformed, incited against, ridiculed before students, and vulgarly and angrily abused by the director. A few illustrations of this abuse are outlined below.

During a staff meeting, when Professor Czapów informed the director of the institute, Professor Jedlewski, that he had been invited to Gdańsk to deliver two lectures and that he intended to go, the director demanded that he be shown the written invitation. When Dr. Czapów handed it to him, he read it carefully and then shouted, "You will not go! You are a thief! I will go, she [pointing to somebody on his right] will go, he [pointing to somebody on his left] will go. You, never. You are a greedy, rapacious monster. You only want money. You treat the scientific profession as a gold mine." A later inspection of the letter revealed that the secretary of the institution that issued the invitation had forgotten to sign his name on the official letter. Professor Czapów subsequently fell victim to partial paralysis. When he died in 1980, the same Professor Jedlewski wrote in his obituary in the popular Warsaw newspaper *Życie Warszawy* (*Life of Warsaw*):

He died in his fifty-fifth year. Until 2:00 A.M. he worked on his last book, which will not be finished. It is difficult to find someone who so deeply loved science. He was an outstanding scholar, an uncommon expert on the literature of his subject. This and his own research contributed to his impressive heritage: a dozen books, hundreds of articles, monographs and essays . . . He was indefatigable; his industry was exhibited in his teaching . . . He was able to find time for social workers, teachers, prosecutors, police, army, parents . . . We watched him on TV and listened to him on radio. Czesław Czapów was a humanist in the full sense of this term and so he will remain in our memory.

In another example of abuse, during a meeting of the Scientific Council of the institute, the representative of the trade union, Ms. Wanda Kaczyńska, was unexpectedly ordered by Professor Jedlewski, the director of the institute, to analyse and report on certain issues since he was unable to interpret the data relevant to these issues himself, despite the fact that his own center had prepared the data for him. She asked for a fifteen-minute adjournment in order to prepare her statement. The former minister of Justice, criminal-law professor Stanisław Walczak, called out indignantly, "I urgently demand that it be written into the minutes of this meeting that Ms. Kaczyńska has declared that she wished to terminate her work at the institute. I demand that it be written in these minutes that she openly refused, in our presence, to carry out the instructions of the director of the institute." Ms. Kaczyńska was soon dismissed.

The foreign exchange programs, which had already been arranged, were revised after the reorganization. The official responsible (Adam Krukowski) would say things like, "It is pointless to send A to the Sorbone; I could not find anything there except pretentious and showy trash"; "B should not be permitted to cooperate with the Institute of Criminology in Cambridge. When I was in England, I was told by the most competent scholars that it is an obsolete and reactionary institution"; "Since all the directors have already been to Canada and the United States, C should go to Prague in order to keep things in balance."

During the entire course of the reorganization, the director did not allow institute staff to hold any organized general meetings, nor did he allow meetings of the trade union, despite the many petitions he received claiming that such meetings were required under the circumstances. One of the directors ordered a graduate student to turn over the empirical data she had gathered for her doctoral dissertation.

Eventually, even the idea of a semiautonomous institute was destroyed. The institute's program was abolished, and its students were forced to complete their studies at a new, and very different institute. All research projects were dismantled or fundamentally revised.

The defence of the institute was regarded as an astonishing phenomenon in both Poland and other Communist countries. Yet its destruction was witnessed with a complete and puzzling indifference by the Polish academic world. Not a single faculty, committee, or association in the entire Polish scientific community protested the destruction of the institute. As an independent, innovative body, it had neither official sympathizers nor allies. As a task-oriented institute, it had never conducted propaganda on its own behalf. Consequently, it was left alone to its fate. Later, gradually, the institute rebuilt itself.

THEORETICAL REFLECTIONS

Before 1989, it was practically impossible for an independent academic institution in Poland, or any other socialist country, to exist within an officially authorized system. The Communist party and its affiliated organs were unwilling to accept analyses and recommendations that were not prepared under their direction. They were determined to suppress all organized intellectual activities that were not initiated and interpreted by the Party. Yet it was clear that the Party and its auxiliary institutions, along with their commanding power of government, could not achieve control over all intellectual activities if the instrumentalists did not collaborate with them. Nor, additionally, could they possess this control without the help of persons who were neither Party officials nor members of government. Thus, the Party tightened its controls, appointments, promotions, and resources desired by persons who were, more or less, politically neutral.

Therefore, only with the assistance of these compliant "neutrals" could the Party attain such success. Control over the distribution of social rewards, according to administrative or political rank and compliance, must be supplemented with a willingness to do the bidding of the powerful. On the other side, the compliant neutrals were "socialized" to remain in anomie and to look at one another with suspicion and, at best, indifference. Generally speaking, they were kept constantly insecure. As a result, even the few individuals who had ideas requiring the cooperation of others did not express them. They were discouraged in advance, knowing that they would incur the enmity of their colleagues. The latter calculated that if they became associated in the minds of their superiors with an unconventional activity, they would lose whatever advantages they had gained through past compliance and hamper the chances of gaining more advantages in the future.

The fact that, before 1989, none of the original, semi-independent academic institutions was able to operate according to its founding design supports the "pocket hypothesis" developed by Carl Friedrich and Zbigniew Brzeziński. According to this hypothesis, "islands" of independence and resistance do exist in totalitarian systems. "In other words, the totalitarian, like other authoritarians before him, finds it impossible to penetrate the invisible walls that surround the haven of scholastic enterprise, even though he can reduce the number of men and women belonging to it" (Friedrich, Brzeziński 1965:325).

"Invisible walls" can be interpreted as "invisible colleges" in Poland. If the invisible college is perceived as a "network of productive scientists linking separate groups of collaborators within a research area" (Crane 1972:54), then it is feasible to claim that innovative, independent scholarly work is only pursued inside these colleges. In the socialist context, invisible colleges occupy quite a different position than in a liberal-democratic society. They are not so much instruments or means for disseminating new scientific information more easily, quickly, and effectively; rather, they create a certain type of "survival-niche arrangement." These niches allow scholars to hide themselves from the watchful eyes of various conformists, to see intellectual problems that have not been generally recognized as such, to examine issues using a variety of paradigms (not merely the official, obligatory one), to come to conclusions that may challenge the constraining ideology, and, above all, to be innovative, at least intellectually.

During the early part of the institute's operation, its innovative spirit and initiative were able to merge under the integrity and serious intellectual and moral attitudes of its scientific staff. Its ruin was precipitated by morally weak members who were successfully "instrumentalized" through Party techniques of "domestication."

The founders of the institute waited for the right political and social moment to establish it. They were later able to achieve a great deal in a relatively short time. They followed the logic that, if scholars are to develop new sets of scientific ideas, they must do so faster than the officials under whose surveillance their activities are taking place, and faster than these officials are able to detect the innovative and nonconformist significance of their activities. This could be achieved by using deliberately obscure language, articulating findings through unexpected sources, revealing messages at unexpected moments, or spreading information by osmosis. Under repressive conditions, one must act unconventionally and unexpectedly in order to launch a new line of institutional intellectual activity.

It is very difficult to establish a direct link between an innovative idea and its products in social life. Still, it is possible to look for interrelations between the institute's legacy and certain sociopolitical events that took place later in Poland. The original idea for the institute was defeated because it did not have a tangible, influential constituency behind it. In short, it was premature. Nevertheless, the main idea of the institute—to spread an expertise—represented a potential strength that could be put in motion by the spark of a dormant thought. If the institute's sociotechnical plan to carry out effective, macrosocial activity contributed in any way to the spectacular, yet dignified, behavior of the Polish workers and their consultants—representatives of the Church, experts, and members of the Workers' Defence Committee (later known as the Social Self-Defence Committee), or KOR, and the Solidarity movement—then the institute's existence prior to its reorganization may have had significant meaning. The lessons from this case study can be summarized as follows:

1. Under totalitarian regimes, *official* academic structures in the social sciences are petrified by Party control and cannot find the space for innovative ideas, creative scholars, or open-minded students.

2. If innovative ideas emerge nevertheless, they enter the academic system through bodies located outside the universities, such as "invisible colleges."

3. If these innovative ideas have the potential to materialize in society, particularly when society is in an intense general crisis, they are at once counterbalanced by Party watchdogs who invade academic bodies as self-perpetuating cancerous cells.

4. If these innovative ideas can initially gain notable momentum, they operate only as long as their esoteric contents are not transformed into messages comprehensible to the mediocre (conformists, obedient followers, instrumentalists, those without moral standards).

5. Even if the initial messianic spirit of these ideas transforms conformists into temporary innovators, conformist attitudes will likely surface again, encouraging conformist-innovators to join those who represent the power élite.

6. Although academia in democratic social systems can be "poisoned" by the "dark residua" (envy, negative competition, intrigues) of human nature, these pressures are incomparable to the organized scientific oppression that is systematically produced through ideological instrumentality (in the totalitarian East, a scholar banished from one place is finished everywhere).

7. From the beginning, a group of innovators should be aware that if they at first succeed, they will have some supporters and associates. But when their activities eventually collapse, few or none of these supporters will risk their own positions to defend them (Machiavelli made this same observation five centuries ago). Later, in order to justify their cowardice, those supporters may even blame the innovators for their precipitate, irrational behavior.

8. Different social systems generate different scientific personalities that have yet to be thoroughly analyzed. Both the fascist and the socialist scientific personality await adequate analysis.

9. Although socialist scholars treat their peers as a primary reference group, only a few would resist the recommendations of those holding political power in conflict-laden situations. To hide their dependency, these scholars tend to construct picturesque legends and sophisticated myths to explain the existential "uniqueness" of their situations.

10. In sum, the social sciences, as cultivated by Party members, have had very little innovative analytical or explanatory value in socialist countries. This discipline was interesting only as an absorbing object of the sociology of science, with one exception: some Eastern scholars tended, during the worst period of totalitarianism, to shift their interests to abstract problems of logic and general methodology. Such ideologically neutral inquiries could be pursued with relative freedom. These scholars might even have found some encouragement if their inquiries were of potential use in mathematics, physics, or chemistry.

While these conclusions are self-evident, some points require additional elaboration. After World War II, the Polish population, including scientists and especially social scientists, underwent a rapid and accelerated process of instrumentalization. An instrumental attitude is one that treats norms as a means to achieve something alien to these norms. On the basis of a subjective cost-benefit assessment, an instrumentalist accepts patterns of behavior that appear, in a given situation, most beneficial for the attainment of the desired goals and rejects all others.

The opposite of an instrumental attitude is a "principled" attitude which requires that one behave in accordance with the contents of a valued norm (Podgórecki 1974:75–90). Yet the cognitive training received by scholars fosters the instrumental attitude. It gives a much better overview of available options and develops logical methods for evaluating these options. An empirical study of the ethos of Polish scholars concludes that, "in reality, scientists adhere to the scientific ethos only to a very limited degree" (Post 1985:221).

An overwhelming majority of social scientists living in totalitarian systems develop their own personal legends and myths in an attempt to mask the emptiness and vagueness of their ideas behind misleading, yet colorful, screens. They perceive themselves as political martyrs who deserve assistance and support, or rescue. They often demand that their research and teaching assistants write eulogistic reviews of their books. While they claim that their books or articles were rejected by state censorship, quite often they were dismissed by publishers as incompetent. These scholars may invoke administrative measures in order to create around themselves "scientific schools" that elevate their low scholarly standing. They tend to use assistance from the Party (or the security apparatus) to project themselves onto an international circle of mutually supporting mediocrities. Finally, they may curse the ideology that catapulted them from nothingness into "prominence," usually after skillful negotiations with the West (once they are guaranteed a "better deal" surpassing all their previous salaries combined and enriched by additional fringe benefits).

The instrumental scholar does not care about truth: scientific inquiry is only a means to nonscholarly goals. The instrumental scholar strives primarily for material, career, and power gains. He does not consider himself to be bound by established standards of scientific inquiry. Such standards exist only for pragmatic use. He does, however, know enough about these standards to demand that they be met by others. They are, consequently, used to attack others. This scholar also knows these standards well enough to pretend that he has applied them. In his opinion, the instrumentalist is "working in science," yet his primary objective is to exploit the "operational habitat" to the fullest extent that others will allow. At any given moment, the instrumental scholar turns in the direction that appears most advantageous. Instrumentality can be oriented towards either the individual's gain or the gain of his interest group. The latter case is, as a rule, screened by ideology that refers to a "higher cause."

Another crucial characteristic of the instrumental scholar is his tendency to analyze social reality *as it ought to be*, disregarding social reality *as it is*. This value-oriented style is not shaped by epistemological convictions but by the requirements of a constantly shifting official ideology. As a consequence, instrumentalism in the social sciences is weak in terms of description and explanation, but strong in paradigm analysis and commentary on other intellectuals. Such an orientation narrows the focus of description to include only the empirical data that complements its dogma. Subsequently, the instrumental scholar fabricates diagnoses that correspond with its normatively projected social reality.

Social sciences guided by an instrumental mentality are based on normatively constructed data. Hence their explanatory models become metafabricated generalizations. Under such conditions, scholars who are interested in studying the existing social reality are driven from the arena of scholarship.

Traditional scientists, pressured by instrumentalists, try to adapt to this situation, developing a split-personality syndrome: for domestic publications they produce studies in accordance with the ruling ideology; for external publications, they adopt generally accepted scientific standards.

The schizophrenic duality of Polish life (official and unofficial) that flourished until 1989 has precipitated the rise of another type of socialist scholar: the "spectacular" scholar. Socialist systems have a tendency to create personalities characterized as the "governors of souls." The mechanism for manufacturing these personalities is relatively simple. Since in a totalitarian society the government is alienated from society, all those who represent power (the state and the government) enjoy little, if any, informal respect. This creates a confusing official void. Ordinary citizens search for an authority who can tell them what is true and false, right and wrong, just and unjust. Those who are able to fulfill the task of trusted guardian acquire status as informal leaders.

Although they are at odds with the official ideology and state apparatus, these leaders do not necessarily support one another. Competing among themselves, they tend not only to gather their own followers but also to capture them from other leaders. After a time, even they become convinced that they are governors of souls.

In totalitarian societies, many scholars have been pushed into the position of governor against their will. They often feel obliged to accept this role for patriotic reasons. Authorities in totalitarian states are well aware of these processes. Consequently, they seek to break potential governors of souls in every conceivable way. Should the authorities succeed in demonstrating that someone is controversial as a scholar, he will have trouble becoming an academic leader. Should it be revealed that someone committed small illegal acts or indecencies (like financial irregularities or sexual perversions) or, better yet, that a scholar secretly sides with those in power, then the scholar, considered to have a "broken spine," will likely not be elevated to the position of a governor of souls.

The ruthless activities of the instrumental scholar thus contribute to the creation and maintenance of the spectacular scholar. The spectacular scholar can play many roles in society. Intentionally or not, he may refuse to change his views even under the pressure of current political demands; for example, he resists social pressure when in public he makes only banal statements about social facts. In another role, this scholar pronounces and defends his interpretation of disclosed social facts. The truth that he proclaims may, in fact, be trivial. It may be stated, for example, that a given phenomenon is the result of various interrelated causes (and not of dialectical processes), or, in a more controversial thesis, it may be claimed that the people's ethos plays a primary role in shaping socioeconomic relations. When official ideology declares something to the contrary, statements of this type require considerable, or even formidable, civil courage. Even greater courage is required to make statements that apply directly to current political issues.

The pressure that instrumentalists place on the spectacular scholar, especially when their instrumentality supports a "higher cause," often generates strong resistance. While the spectacular attitude may not arouse any special interest among scholars (it may even be ridiculed) under normal circumstances, it is likely to be seen in totalitarian settings as a direct challenge to the system. Consequently, scholars who have nothing theoretically significant to convey are often suddenly transformed into defenders of academia's main bastions.

Scholars who do have something ideologically important to say are launched into positions of political, as well as academic, importance. They acquire a form of charisma, catapulting them to national visibility. The more highly developed the informal structures that are antagonistic to government in a given socialist society, the stronger the tendency to breed scholars of the spectacular type. This does not mean, however, that noninstrumental, authentic, real scholars dedicated to science ceased to exist in Poland. Instead, they were marginalized by the internal life of the socialist academic community. As a consequence, they were not likely to play any significant or visible role.

The intent to defend truth and the posture that provides a scholar with social "nobility" are essential ingredients for the public perception of the spectacular scholar. It is true that intellectually limited morons who are dogmatic and publicly martyred are sometimes blessed with wide social recognition. A few shrewd manipulators, aware of their own shortcomings, occasionally climb to respectable public positions. Sometimes an obvious "nobody" is exalted to this station by accident.

Yet if someone is labelled a spectacular scholar by informal public opinion or through government harassment, he automatically becomes a member of a peculiar category. The authorities begin to treat the scholar quite cautiously. They usually attribute much greater influence to him than he actually has. Paradoxically, he often becomes invulnerable through this process. Defended by indigenous informal circles, he eventually becomes a "pet" of international opinion as well. Consequently, he starts to enjoy his position as a recognized opposition leader. Finally, this scholar no longer has time to pursue scientific endeavors; eventually, these activities are dropped altogether. Thus, while genuine in the beginning, the spectacular scholar often becomes a fictitious, albeit spectacular, scientific star.

A scientist under the socialist model directly and dramatically violates the essential features of the scientific ethos, which, according to Robert Merton, comprises four sets of institutional imperatives—universalism, "communism," disinterestedness, and organized skepticism. Science is universalistic since its generalizations do not depend on the personal or social attributes of its protagonist and are verified on the basis of objective procedure. Science thus has an international, impersonal, and virtually anonymous character. Since democracy is tantamount to the progressive elimination of restraints upon the cultivation of socially appreciated capacities, and since it is essential for the development of impersonal criteria that determine accomplishment (there is less of a fixation on status), it provides the proper scope for the exercise of universalistic criteria in science.

Merton also stresses the element of "communism" in science. Communism in this sense emerges when a society ensures that a scientific law or theory does not remain in the exclusive possession of the discoverer and his heirs, but rather becomes a common heritage of the society. In this context, Merton refers to Newton's well-known remark "If I have seen further, it is by standing on the shoulders of giants."

Although Merton does not directly identify disinterestedness, he proposes that "it is rather a distinctive pattern of institutional control over a wide range of motives which characterizes the behavior of scientists." Absolute disinterestedness does not exist; disinterestedness at best is tempered by various supervisory arrangements that serve as checks on one another.

According to Merton, organized skepticism involves, among other things, a latent questioning of certain bases of established routine, authority, vested procedures and the realm of the "sacred" in general. It follows that the totalitarian state, closing itself against the penetration of scientific inquiries, tends to limit the scope provided for scientific activity (Merton 1968: 614–15).

From this characterization of the scientific ethos, it is clear that a socialist scholar, susceptible to influence when presenting facts and using scientific procedures, emerges as a polar opposite to the model of an ideal scientist.

Why was a global analysis of Polish society impossible under socialism?

A totalitarian social system creates unique types of scientists: socialist instrumentalists and spectacular scholars. Both categories engage in pseudo- or actual scientific activities, yet with nonscientific objectives. The instrumental scientist uses science as a means to achieve pragmatic and opportunistic ends. The spectacular instrumental scientist attaches himself to the symbolic values of a governor of souls.

In the current period of transition from socialist to free-market values, three types of scholars are visible in Poland: the rapidly disappearing traditional (authentic) scholar who represents the scientific ethos, the instrumentalist (who has maintained his momentum), and the spectacular scholar, who remains the idol of the former informal structures. This general statement seems to be true, with some modifications, for other socialist countries as well.

The earlier characterization of predominant types of scholars, who emerged under the socialist regime in Poland and then set official restrictions on scientific inquiries, clearly reveals that a global analysis of Polish society was outside their realm of competence.

POSTSCRIPTUM

The difference between the socialist-instrumentalist and the Western scholar is, quite often, a very subtle one. The socialist scholar is the agent of dogma, which is formulated by the ideology existing "above" him. It gives him mandatory, albeit general, guidance. In short, he is employed according to his ideology. He works for it, receiving praise for obediently performing his job. The more vigorously he introduces this ideology into the usually hostile academic and social lives, the more lavishly the power centers reward him.

He is instrumental because he is regarded simply as a tool, a means to an end. He is used by the very ideas, or, more precisely, by the political machinery, that he accepted without any visible reservations. He is an obedient, intelligent, and creative slave. But he is, nonetheless, working for somebody else. He is a serf of his lord, the dogma founder. The direct and indirect gains he collects become the primary goals of his actions.

In contrast, the Western scholar is not concerned with authority centers existing outside of himself—he is his own agent. He need not work for a particular doctrine. His objective is purely self-promotion. If he is able to develop ideas, he does not necessarily develop them to support his own ideology. Neither is he developing ideas in order to come closer to *truth*; he generates ideas simply because he understands that the idea-generation process is his professional *job*. As he understands his task, his main goal is not to create, but to produce ideas ("I was *doing* some thinking"). He has several additional duties that are more significant for his career development.

The Western scholar's main task (which his skills match) is to repeat the ideas of others ingeniously. Yet these repetitions should not appear mechanical. It is also useful to support his ideas with empirical data taken from the current sociopolitical context. Often, these ideas are exemplified by current events in socioeconomic life. It appears that these repetitions are even more rewarding when performed in a lively, joyful, if not farcical, manner. This manner is most enjoyable for Western students who view their studies largely as a task of memorizing and digesting the ideas that are served to them. In some respect, they are right: the more familiar they become with this manner, the higher the marks they receive; the higher marks they receive, the more rewarding the job they receive.

Another, more sophisticated, skill of Western scholars is to translate previously generated ideas into currently fashionable language, attributing these ideas to themselves. One way of doing this is not to deal with the ideas of one's own teachers (some of whom could still be alive), but to reach for the ideas that belonged to one's scholarly "grandparents"—the ideas of one's teachers' teachers. Since they are usually dead, they are not able to claim these ideas as their own property. The stolen ideas, which were often originally presented in the obscure language of foregone generations, are usually rewritten in a polished and clear form. Only a few shrewd specialists can recognize the similarities between old and new layers of thought (and there is not much to worry about anyway, "since everything has already been said by the Greeks"). Scholars who are able to detect these similarities are usually not courageous enough to disclose them, and they may be right: a scholar is not only a scholar but an object of administrative pressures as well.

Since the obligatory rule in the West is "publish or perish," another imperative is to sell, or market, ideas. At the present time, given the limited number of journals and publishing houses, the rapidly multiplying number of branches (and sub-branches) of various disciplines, and the enormous and constantly growing number of scholars in universities, colleges, and institutions, this is not an easy task. It becomes practically impossible to say something imaginative, original, and outstanding in a form that is recognized as such. It is thus much better to present a conventional text in a well-elaborated, digestible form, instead of proclaiming something new. This appeals to the already-formed preferences of the boards, readers, assessors, and "peers" of the publishing houses. A text with an unconventional content would only confuse them. Conforming to the conventional virtue of reiterating ideas does not challenge the iron rule of the evaluating mediocrity.

This creatively conformist skill is closely connected to another one. In order to gain recognition, it is not good enough to publish in the specialized magazines or journals at hand: one must target the journals that are regarded as "universally" visible and prestigious. Thus, it is necessary not merely to understand their editorial subcultures but also to have some sort of access to them—a much more complicated requirement. Of course, one could send one's article directly to a distinguished magazine or journal, but this only decreases the probability of a nonconformist idea being published. A good scholar has to know these methods and put them to use if he wants to be recognized.

To display empirical and comparative data, and to write books or articles at the same time, the scholar has to receive grants. Consequently, he must know how to ask for grants. In the bureaucratic environment of modern universities, this ability above all others enables him to conduct research. Once his research is completed and published, he must begin to woo the attention of prize-giving bodies. Although reviews are, as a rule, invited by the boards of magazines and journals, he may try to "organize" these reviews in advance. A good scholar is not only scientifically competent but also, and more importantly, good at self-promotion.

The scholar must also know how to ask for travel expenses if he wants to attend conferences. He has to know which conferences are treated as "seed" oriented, introducing him to significant scholarly *networks* and assuring subsequent publication.[18] He should know whether to present a paper, act as a panellist or rapporteur, or be a session organizer. He should know with whom he should have dinner, with whom lunch, with whom breakfast, and with whom merely a coffee. He must carefully evaluate whom he should invite to a party (if he is to organize one), whose parties he should avoid, whose parties he should attend, and at which parties he should "impose" his presence. All these factors are precisely recorded, evaluated, and synthesized. In social sciences, the lack of measurable, objective criteria has produced a computerized, achievement-oriented decision-making process by which outstanding scholars are labelled.

How far is this model from the ideal of a scholar who is supposed to be a "fountain of truth"? A direct answer seems to be inappropriate here: the current conditions of Western scholarly life create a *sly* type of scholarly individual.

If scholarly models like the instrumental, spectacular, and sly grow so rapidly, is there still room for the traditional scholar who is interested in truth and not directed towards subsidiary gains? Does he become an endangered species? To what extent does the psychological factor of sheer curiosity transform itself into a *clean* pursuit of knowledge? Is there still a place in modern society for pure reflection, not guided by gain, utility, or pragmatic considerations? To what extent is the pure comprehension of reality and the cultivation of long chains of deductions still treasured as the basis for scholarly work? Since many of the so-called "think tanks" designed to encourage the uncontaminated pursuit of truth seem to have been transformed into nothing more than super-niches for "sly" scholars, where can *pure* knowledge be created?

These are not easy questions to answer, particularly since they are closely related to one another. To what extent, taking into consideration the present complexity of social sciences, can problems within these sciences be digested, analyzed, and resolved by a single individual, rather than a task-oriented, problem-solving group? It is possible that the perplexity of social textures discourages the individual thinker from familiarizing himself with the matter at hand, and that this confusion pressures one to find a new synthesis-building mechanism. Such a mechanism might consist of a team, working together (not working "for" somebody, or "with" somebody) in a complementary manner, without fixating on the dominant role of an individual scholar. It remains to be seen if this type of team will survive in the social sciences, not as a glorious exception, but as an ordinary enterprise.

Pessimistically, it can be expected that the crucial sociometric position within the "synthesis-building center" will be targeted by the instrumentalist and sly scholar; those who profess authentic joy at scientific discovery will likely not be willing to engage in a dry fight over the priority of the discovery. On the other hand, the whole matter could be misleading since "the discovery of discovery" is often made by the same group of peers authorized to label a discovery as such.

The gap between the socialist-instrumental academic model and the Western sly academic model thus narrows rapidly. This gap is small indeed when it is taken into account that the spectacular scholar, who emerged in the East as a result of political protest against the oppressive political establishment, bears some resemblance to the self-promoting scholarly *arriviste* in the West. In addition, certain scholarly figures have already lost their contact with social reality and academic thought in the West. These figures, mentally tired and worn-out thinkers, still serve as glamorous individuals pursuing positions such as chairs, heads of foundations, and presidents. As conservative gate-keepers in fact but as symbols of science in fiction, they contribute, in these posts, to the development of new ideas. What kind of ideas are these?

The mixture of socialist instrumentalism and the Western-oriented self-promotion drive is now *in statu nascendi*. The seeds of it were clearly evident in Sztompka's work in 1986. This relatively young, modern, jet-set scholar and former Communist party activist ends his meticulous, insightful, and illuminating work on Merton, dedicated to Merton himself as "my master-at-a-distance turned friend," with this sentence: "The way to strive for a better sociology of the future is to stand firmly and confidently on the shoulders of sociological giants: such as those of Merton" (Sztompka 1986: 261).

3

An Analysis of the Social Structure of Polish Society before 1989

THE PROBLEM

The social history of most European countries is marked by considerable stability and continuity. Recent Polish history sharply contradicts this general observation. World War II and the subsequent "sovietization" of Poland introduced several important social processes. The most significant among them has led to the disappearance of many traditional segments of Polish society.[19]

The Polish Jewish population (around three million) has been annihilated. The landed gentry has been destroyed. Tradespeople have virtually disappeared. Big and medium-sized business owners have ceased to exist. Independent cooperatives have disappeared. Several influential minorities including Germans, Ukrainians, and Lithuanians have vanished. Independent political parties and organizations have been outlawed and crushed. The "traditional intelligentsia," who regarded civil service on behalf of their own society as their duty and mission, have lost their decisive influence. Likewise, both the number of artisans and their level of skill have dramatically declined (Wyrwa 1986: 41–42).

The development and maintenance of an informal social structure are especially significant for understanding the complexity of contemporary Poland. This informal structure exists in conjunction with the infrastructure established by the nobility. It was largely developed when the country lost its independence, between 1795 and 1918.

In carrying out a comprehensive analysis of a society, it is advisable to pay special attention to the historically determined informal system of relations between the established, official social structure and the types of personality that function within the framework of this structure. It may appear as if the historically formed personality of a given society reflects its current social structure; on the other hand, it might appear that a society's social structure is shaped by its personality characteristics. In order to clarify causal direction, one should attempt first to present a comprehensive analysis of the social structure in question and then to consider the ways in which the basic elements of this structure are linked with the basic personality features of its societal members. Such an approach requires the comparison of existing empirical knowledge of social structure with the knowledge of various ethoses of different social groups in question.

SOCIAL COMPOSITION

The numerous studies of Poland's social structure conducted after 1945 present a rather complex and obscure picture. On the one hand, it is claimed that the country's social structure is relatively homogeneous; on the other, various processes of social decomposition and recomposition are stressed. Some researchers claim that Polish society is characterized by a relatively low differentiation of incomes. Yet it has also been shown that the factor of individual subsidiary earnings is an important variable in secondary economic differentiation (the "hidden economy").

The second economy and social phenomena connected with it constitute an essential, but often overlooked or unrecognized, element of social life. Some writers claim that, in Poland, social mobility affects individuals, classes, and strata, whereas upward and downward mobility affect only individuals in capitalist countries. These last observations concerning Poland originated in the research of Adam Sarapata. A study by Stefan Nowak (published in 1966 but carried out in 1961) confirms Sarapata's initial findings. According to Nowak (1966:89), "If we accept that the transition from countryside to town is a social advancement, as well as movement from the ranks of unskilled to skilled, manual workers to nonmanual, and, for the children of administrative employees, from their parents' rank to the "intelligentsia," . . . then forty-two percent of the population . . . occupy [after the Second World War] positions higher than those of their fathers." (Here and later, unless specially noted, all translations are mine.)

Generalizing from this research, Jan Szczepański reiterates the ideas of Stanisław Ossowski, declaring that "whole social classes may be mobile when, for example, they change social position after a revolution" (Szczepański 1970: 497).

Research on the hierarchy of occupations and prestige in post-war Poland offers interesting data on social stratification. The research conducted by Wesołowski and Sarapata in 1958, once classic in Poland, specified three crucial features relating to social position: its stability, the material benefits derived from it, and the prestige attached to it. Their research showed that, in Polish society, the features most highly esteemed fell under the category of "knowledge and skills" (especially those of professors).

The importance of prestige explains the unusually high position occupied by skilled workers during the Solidarity period. This was indicated by the high prestige ratings accorded to the learned professions and skilled workers and by the low ranking of unskilled workers. The decline in prestige of the "private sector," despite the relatively secure financial position held by people in this category, is further evidence of the importance of the prestige factor. Wesołowski and Sarapata also concluded that changes taking place in Poland before 1958 "did not lead to particular demographic and social categories forming different ways of assigning social prestige to occupations and positions. To a certain extent, at least, a system of common values emerged" (Wesołowski, Sarapata 1961: 107–08).

Wesołowski and Sarapata's research sets out a comparative framework for the analysis of similar hierarchies of various groups and socio-occupational positions in other societies. In the late fifties, the first four positions on the scale of social prestige were occupied by the following social groups in West Germany: (1) capitalists, managers, higher administrators (members of the government), university rectors, land owners; (2) intelligentsia (university professors, opera singers, teachers); (3) nonmanual employees (accountants, draughtsmen); (4) small capitalists, craftsmen. In Poland, however, the first four positions were occupied by (1) intelligentsia (university professors, doctors, teachers, mechanical engineers, lawyers, agricultural engineers, journalists); (2) skilled workers (iron and steel workers, lathe operators, foremen); (3) nonmanual workers (accountants, heads of administrative units); (4) small "capitalists" and craftsmen (Wesołowski, Sarapata 1961: 107–08).

Research carried out during 1964–1967 in Lodz, Szczecin, and Koszalin, based on a more complex technique, led to the conclusion that:

in terms of earnings, skilled workers have overtaken clerical-manual workers, in terms of prestige, they have overtaken office workers, compared with the pre-war situation. Foremen and brigade leaders have higher average incomes and higher average prestige than office workers. Yet the two groups differ little with respect to the general evaluation of their positions. Although shifts in social positions can be considered new phenomena, the substantial difference in the position of the intelligentsia and technicians or blue-collar workers also indicates the persistence of old forms of allocating rewards. (Słomczyński 1972: 268–69)

These findings were indirectly supported by a random national sample of the adult population based on 2,468 interviews conducted in 1975. According to Wacław Makarczyk, the author of this inquiry, the Polish population believes that scientists ("men of science") and artists ("men of art") contributed most to the prestige of the country in the past, whereas now the main contribution comes from "statesmen" (Kościuszko, Pułaski, Dąbrowski, Poniatowski, Piłsudski, Sikorski, Świerczewski, Gierek, Wyszyński, Gomułka) and "sportsmen" (Makarczyk 1979: 30–37). The high prestige of scientists and artists in the past can perhaps be explained by the fact that education became a

socially recognized virtue during the period of partition (1795–1918). The traditional culture of the Polish nobility, which imposed its patterns of social life
on all other strata, was based on appreciation of the ethos of a leisurely life, an
ethos enjoyed and respected among equals. Other research suggested that the
Polish social structure was, in the period of real socialism, perceived as open,
and that "the level of openness is very close to the model of equal opportunity"
(Janicka 1973: 61–100). Kazimierz Słomczyński, the ex-party sociologist quoted
above, expresses this idea in the following way.

The inquiry, which considered clusters of related professions, found that the difference
between manual workers and other social categories is probably smaller now than during
the pre-war period. Nevertheless, the distance separating non-manual employees from
the working class is still sufficiently large to be considered an inheritance from capitalist
society which has not yet been eliminated. (Słomczyński 1972: 268–69)

Interestingly enough, the hierarchy of prestige appeared to be stable. In 1991,
the Institute of Philosophy and Sociology at the Polish Academy of Sciences
conducted a study based on a representative sample of the Polish population. It
brought the following results (Domański 1991:30): "The highest levels of prestige are still occupied by the intelligentsia: university professors (83), physicians
(75), engineers (71), teachers (70). Prestige is shared with those professions that
have institutional power at their disposal: ministers (77), directors of factories
(72), bishops (72), chief engineers (71), judges (71). Relatively high prestige
belongs to highly skilled workers-miners (68), steelworkers (63), and locksmiths
(61). This stratum is valued more than clerks and administrative personnel. (In
this research: 100 = the highest level of prestige; 0 = the lowest level of
prestige.)" Another 1991 study also places professors at the top of the occupational list (Karpowicz, Lelińska 1991: 41).[20]
Research conducted in the early 1970s found that the perceived "openness"
of the Polish social system was related to political and social position and did
not necessarily reflect the social reality of the time. "It has been shown that,
although we do not find the emergence of impassable barriers or great distances
in social interactions, we can observe visible tendencies restricting of social life.
Characteristics such as the nature of one's work, one's socio-occupational position, and one's level of education play a key role in this instance" (Worzywoda-
Kruszyńska 1973: 24). Indeed, people may be pressured into working together
at various sites and institutions, but they do not necessarily associate with those
whom they reject ideologically, for example, Party members.
Despite its intriguing results, the unpublished work of Ryszard Dyoniziak has
been unacknowledged in the largely unrevealing literature on social stratification.
Dyoniziak asserts that a clear relationship exists between social position and
attitudes towards egalitarianism, consumption, and social needs, as well as so-
called "false consciousness." "We can see that the strength of egalitarian demands is inversely proportional to perceived consumption needs . . . Thus, as

consumption needs increase, demands for egalitarianism within individual occupational groups decline'' (Dyoniziak 1967: 211–12).

It could then be said that appetite not only comes with eating but also tends
to restrict the eating of others. Consequently, does this mean that if ''real socialism'' (socialism as it appeared in reality) was persistently spreading the idea
of equality, it would begin, at the same time, to work against itself?

Some generalizations about social stratification in Poland are found in a work
edited by Jan Szczepański. He tried (unsuccessfully) to present a synthesis of
the social structure in ''socialist'' society. He makes various abstract observations, rarely providing concrete assertions. One of the few that has empirical
meaning concerns the position of manual workers: ''The contradiction of their
position is based on the fact that, according to the ideology and the legal principles
of the system, they are the co-owners of the means of production, while at the
same time, they are hired workers subject to the technological constraints resulting from their relationship to machinery, which also has repercussions in
legal work regulations'' (Szczepański 1969: 488).

Another observation that has some empirical meaning examines administrative
personnel: ''On the one hand, there is a contradiction between the importance
of this category and its qualifications, and on the other, between the significance
of its functions and its work, and between its responsibility and its prestige''
(Szczepański 1969: 480). According to the same author, the social strata are,
on the whole, planned and designed in advance.

Here we also come to the conclusion that the role of spontaneous processes is limited,
although they cannot be completely eliminated or regulated. Nevertheless, their effects
are directed by plans, laws, and regulations. It seems that this channelling of spontaneous
processes—processes of change and social transformation—this mutual interaction between spontaneous tendencies and processes of planned change in the social structure
through the planning of education, employment, wage policy, etc., is sociologically the
most fascinating aspect of the development of industrial society in our country. (Szczepański 1969: 492)

This issue is also treated, if somewhat differently, by Winicjusz Narojek.
Having analyzed various processes of social change and various, more or less
consciously conceived, social techniques of economic and social transformation,
Narojek comes to the conclusion that ''in socialist society, two kinds of dynamics
coexist with each other: on the one hand, the dynamic of sociosystemic transformation and on the other, the dynamic of adaption and praxeological [effec-
tiveness-oriented] thinking. This results from the fact that [this society] is
simultaneously a political movement that promotes social goals on the basis of
a given scale of values, and a system or organized activity, a 'planned society' ''
(Narojek 1973:294–95).

This dilemma has been treated more thoroughly by Jadwiga Staniszkis, who
claims that, under special conditions inherent to the system, spontaneous social

processes take the upper hand over the general and more centrally planned socioeconomic strategy. Subsequent strategy is designed to overcome these spontaneous conditions, transforming the social process into a "normal" (planned) one. Consequently, strategies that are designed to deal with extraordinary situations such as conflicts, tensions, and riots in fact regulate ordinary social life (Staniszkis 1972:145–46).

THE RURAL SOCIAL STRUCTURE

Analyses of Polish society that deal mainly with industrialization and urbanization would be deceptive if they were not supplemented with data on the social structure of the countryside.[21] It is generally estimated that just under half of Poland's population live in rural areas. The rural social structure is complex and differentiated. According to Boguław Gałęski (Gałęski 1966), one can distinguish the following types of farms: (1) farms that provide an additional or marginal source of livelihood for the family (there are about one million farms of this kind); (2) farms that constitute the main, albeit insufficient, source of livelihood for the family (less than twenty percent of the total number of farms); (3) farms that are the sole source of family support (less than eighty percent of the total): (4) family farms that employ outside labor (not more than 50,000); (5) agricultural cooperatives such as multifamily peasant farms (in 1962, these numbered 1,342 and contained 26,000 families); and (6) large-scale farms, nearly all state owned (over 8,000, employing 370,000 people). Gałęski's data, which are now obsolete, nonetheless made some attempt at synthesis. Paradoxically, more updated data have been provided by an outsider. "The Polish agrarian structure is quite remarkable in contemporary Europe . . . More than 60 percent of Poland's individual farms are smaller than 5 hectares in size (all holdings greater than half a hectare are counted as farms), and few of those provide the sole source of income for their owners . . . there is no doubt that, with more than one quarter of her active labour force employed in agriculture, Poland has not advanced as far along the roads of industrialisation and agricultural modernisation as her socialist neighbours" (Hann 1985:5–6).

A governmental publication (*Rocznik Statystyczny* 1991: 315) provides the following typology of farms (with occupied hectares):

governmental farms	3,490,000	(18.6%)
co-operative farms	696,000	(3.7%)
private farms	14,228,000	(76.0%)

Recent studies on the situation of Polish agriculture have revealed an increased activization of rural workers, apparently due to the crisis of the early seventies. "Research indicated that the situation of crisis pressed peasants even more [than others]. This led to an intensification of rural production and, in conditions of individual farm work, added an extra work load. In 1982 the average [work] time of an individual farm worker (7 hours and 27 minutes) was 1 hour and 17 minutes longer than [that] of a worker not in the agricultural sector. With exception of living owners of private enterprises, peasants were the only professional category whose work time increased by more than half an hour, in comparison with 1976 data'' (Beskid 1987:232).

Because of its normative context (the impact of modern values that weaken traditional social bonds), and because of the influence of modernization processes (especially the impact of the mass media directed mainly at urban populations), the complicated agricultural structure is influenced by cultural models originating in the towns. Indeed, according to research carried out by Wacław Makarczyk and Zdzisław Szpakowski in 1959 and 1969, about one-third of the rural population would like to change their place of residence, from countryside to town, all things being equal.

This study is all the more valuable and unique for its follow-up study conducted in 1969 (Makarczyk, Szpakowski 1972). In his earlier research, Makarczyk writes that ''trends towards stabilization in the countryside and in the occupational status of a farmer become stronger as the economic status of the farm increases, [and] the social position of the farm owner increases as his own subjective evaluation of his social position increases in terms of prestige, income, and security'' (Makarczyk 1964: 161). This particular study reveals that urban culture has had a levelling effect on the culture of the countryside.

A 1983 conference dedicated to the study of industrialization processes as they affect peasant life came up with several interesting generalizations. Among them were the following:

uncertainty concerning the future of individual farms connected with the belief that the possibility of influencing one's future is minimal . . . the loss in value of traditional rural culture . . . the decreasing capacity of the cities to absorb immigration from the countryside . . . depopulation of the agricultural regions in the northern and western parts of the country . . . the increasing flow of younger women to the cities and, connected with that, the diminishing chances for young men to establish a family . . . the gradual decline of a patrimonial approach to the land . . . the instrumentalist treatment of individual farmers by various institutions . . . the disintegration of rural culture . . . an increase of the suicide rate . . . the maintenance of a low standard of living among rural workers. (Janik 1985: 285–86)

Tadeusz Łepkowski discusses the meaning of social changes that took place in Poland after the Second World War, particularly between 1944 and 1956, concluding that these changes ''contributed to the promotion of entire social strata, changed society for a long time to come, and transformed this society structurally and intellectually (including dissidents of different types), influencing behavior, and even imposing Stalinist phraseology'' (Łepkowski 1989:6).

IS A SYNTHESIS POSSIBLE?

The task of presenting a comprehensive synthesis of Polish social structures based on the results of existing studies is thus still an open-ended one. The picture produced by current attempts to furnish a preliminary synthesis is full of contradictions. On the one hand, Polish society appeared to be homogeneous (this was due to the relative similarity of centrally distributed earnings for the bulk of the population), yet on the other hand, this society was strongly affected by nomenklatura (and its vestiges, the "new" nomenklatura) and the secondary, unofficial system of economic differentiation—the second economy (Łoś 1990). Of course this picture is further blurred by current, ongoing processes of privatization and by the lack of systematic data describing these processes.

Although the decomposition of previous class distinctions has resulted in the lessening of differences between town and country and between manual and nonmanual work, the gap that still divides nonmanual from manual workers is substantial enough to constitute a visible sign of inequality, or an "inheritance from capitalist society." Although "downward" social mobility was perceived as insignificant and "upward" mobility as vivid, the downward mobility of defenceless individuals has led to a systematic destruction of traditional reference groups and to the weakening, or even elimination, of formerly "natural" agents of social control.

The process of social and economic growth leading to urbanization and a relative increase in the standard of living in the seventies, coupled with the rapid decline of these processes in the eighties, has generated various processes and phenomena of social pathology. Yet in Polish research on social stratification, these processes and phenomena are surprisingly and paradoxically absent.

Although the decomposition of traditional class structures leads to an erosion of social and economic differences, it often results in alienation from traditional norms without at the same time creating sufficient premises for the emergence of positive mechanisms to help regenerate the disrupted social bonds. These processes lead to the formation of new patterns of individual and social life that tend to carry out this recomposition at a "lower" level—the level of mass culture. However, when mass culture starts to act as a catalyst for recomposition processes by providing ready-made stereotyped models of attitudes and behavior, it simultaneously blocks the processes that lead to an affiliation with the traditional "higher social values" of the intelligentsia, depriving these values of the respect previously accorded them. This new homogeneity of values does not lead to the cementing of traditional, local ties that were disrupted by vertical mobility.

The "peasantization" of towns can still be felt in another form, although in the seventies and eighties, it lost some of its previous momentum and intensity. The traditional and neighborly ways of life in the peasant community, where business and service were mutually rendered, have now been taken over (at least in principle) by the rational, pragmatic, and impersonal state administration. The Communist administration encouraged success on the basis of other criteria. One of these criteria may be the utilization of privileges achieved through the occupation of a particular social and political position. Consequently, a move can be observed towards a situation in which social positions are considered attractive in so far as they constitute a means of obtaining access to social stations with attractive social rewards and privileges.

Nevertheless, a peculiar three-tiered pyramid emerged as the diagnostic picture of Polish society. At the top was a powerful and economically well equipped social stratum, which has yet to be recognized sociologically even though, or perhaps because, some Marxist sociologists, as members of the power élite belonging to this stratum, devoted the bulk of their time to studying it. This stratum was called the "nomenklatura" (Voslensky 1980).

Some of the population was situated in the middle; it was this group that constituted the main target of sociological inquiry, such as it was. Finally, a relatively large proportion of Polish society consisted of those who were at, or rather, below, the "minimum" social level. This lowest social layer was almost exotic, yet few economic studies gave reliable insight into its existence (Tymowski 1973).

Since all significant private property was liquidated in 1945, and since the private property that emerged after 1989 is still not organized as a political unit, old political power or new political networks of connections determine the composition of Polish society. Despite ongoing privatization, eighty-five percent of the existing property belongs to the state, according to a 1991 estimate. Thus, a preliminary consideration of the Polish social structure leads to the conclusion that an analysis of political structure and personality patterns encoded into a specific ethos, and not into the means of production, are crucial. Such an analysis alone has the potential to cope with changing types of social reality.

An analysis of stratification determined by purely political factors has led some ex-Communist scholars, like Leszek Nowak, to present a stratification theory that is supposedly adequate to the reality of socialism, but that is built on strange assumptions. In their understanding, Polish society was "owned" by those who had at their disposal (1) the means of social oppression, (2) the means of production, and (3) the mass media. According to this totalitarian vision, economic factors did not play a decisive role. Of utmost importance was the constant fight among players to grasp power. Although these threefold owners of society treated their "possession" as a field for dangerous manoeuvres or open war, they were aware that they could not stretch their games too far, since this same society supplied them with their only source of livelihood (Nowak, L. 1991). In Nowak's words:

The system of triple power is modelled in non-Marxian historical materialism as the pure power. Triple power means that power which has eliminated its rivals—private property and religion—and has been embodied itself in them. It is thus power in its pure form, which maximizes regulation. In the theory of such power it is assumed that a given society is isolated from all other societies, that it consists of two classes only (the rulers and the ordinary citizens), that in society there are no intellectuals who would devise ideologies for both parties of the conflict, etc. (Nowak, L. 1991: 292)

Nowak does not, however, understand the role played by "civil society" in the creation of Polish society during the Communist regime.

Some similarities may arise between the situation that existed under the Communist regime and the situation that emerged after the Solidarity period. This point of view was presented by the general government ombudsman: "Communists governed as usurpers, their arrogance was apparently a psychologically understandable self-defence mechanism, which, of course, does not justify anything. But, they had a bad conscience, and they were aware of that. Post-Solidarity politicians now have the full social mandate, but the lack of bonding with society is the same as it was before. I speak with responsibility, and I have grounds to maintain it" (Łętowska 1992: 143).[22] These statements indicate how confusing the image of the existing social stratification is, at the present moment. Lack of systematically collected and verified empirical data lends additional impulse to this confusion.

This lack of understanding of the actual and potential role of "civil society" has been further blurred by some respectable scholars, such as Stefan Nowak, who stress that certain socialist values have been successfully implanted in the social infrastructure. "In sum, from these postulates [on Polish society] emerges a pattern of a rather egalitarian society of a socialist character, a society that accentuates, in its social structure and in its way of functioning, the principles of democracy, the rules of law and order, and citizen control over efficient operating power; power that should be appreciated and that should fulfill the material needs of its citizens, respecting them appropriately" (Nowak, L. 1989: 108).

Kazimierz Frieske's analyses contrast sharply with Stefan Nowak's speculation. In 1987, Frieske inquired into the management techniques and ideologies of more than five hundred Polish high officials (directors of government departments—executives at the nomenklatura level). He found that officials of a nomenklatura type use knowledge (professional or scientific) most often to "solve practical problems," whereas those who enter into high positions after long professional preparation stress the educational functions of knowledge and expect from it a "new look at the problem" (Frieske 1990: 244). Andrzej Kojder reflected that

everyone who wants to function in public life (and science is a part of it) must, in one way or another, co-operate with the system; must enter into a "symbolic" relation with the system, must establish a more or less "dirty togetherness" type of relations. Making use of [Vilfredo] Pareto's "circulation of élites law," nomenklatura tends—*per fas and nefas*—to neutralize and, subsequently, absorb some conciliatory leaders of the opposition by signing less significant agreements with them, making minor concessions, and even offering them symbolical official functions, often accepted. (Kojder 1990: 150)

Of course, after the 1989 revolution, the defeated nomenklatura underwent a remarkable transformation, at least on the surface. Hence, a note of caution should be kept in mind:

It is obvious that these changes in social consciousness [regarding the new perception of social problems] are impossible without a radical reorientation of the attitudes of social-policy decision makers. It is hard to expect that this will happen spontaneously, because of the fear that disadvantages may affect this group. This is a factor constituting a major barrier to the introduction of the program of rationalizations aimed at solving social problems in Poland. (Kwaśniewski 1991:169)

It therefore appears that the values imposed on society by the legitimacy of its social structure and by those who occupy executive positions in government could be regarded as essential links between social stratification and the cluster of accepted life ethoses.

In order to clarify the functions and legitimation of the Polish legal system as it surfaces, it is necessary to take into account the background against which respect for the law was established. When Poland was deprived of its independence between 1795 and 1918, law, and especially that part of the legal system connected to the state, was treated as a symbol of the invader's power. Lack of respect for the law was then seen as an act of patriotism. The national independence uprisings (the most important of which were in 1830 and 1861) were rooted in an armed, underground struggle that contained elements of contempt for organic work based on procedural systematic and legal achievements.

The short period of pre-war independence (1918–1939) failed to produce a good sociolegal school of attitudes because there were no traditionally accepted or sufficiently prestigious structures that could strengthen or incubate acceptable types of legal attitudes. The period was spent consolidating the country, constructing a new industrial base and state administration, and dealing with the social and political contradictions of a "reborn" state.

German occupation (1939–1945), characterized by Kazimierz Wyka as "pretence living" (limbo life), relied to such a degree on the suspension of social, moral, and legal norms that this relatively short period encouraged the accumulation of considerable deviant potential. The psychological characteristics that arose from constant bribery, black-market activities, and strategies devised out of the biological necessity of survival sustained their value long after the condition that had created them disappeared. Additionally, the Polish Jewish population, which had filled an effective vacuum in trade (as a sui generis middle class since Polish knightly tradition forbade its members to engage in business), was liquidated by the Germans. As a consequence, other segments of the population, less capable in terms of trade and organization, emerged to undertake the task of conducting trade (Wyka 1957). The post-war struggle after 1945 between old and new authorities, traditional values, and newly imposed institutions led to such far-reaching refutation of the notion of prestige in social life that an almost complete social nihilism emerged.

LIFESTYLES—THE POLISH INTELLIGENTSIA

These processes should be taken into account when considering the actual, rather than the normative, model of the lifestyle or ethos of Polish intelligentsia. In a classic work, Jozef Chałasinski presented the normative profile of pre-war Polish intelligentsia, which was the general "procreator" of the Polish social ethos. He attributed the following characteristics to this social stratum: a fear of being declassed again, a code of correct behavior, a feeling of superiority that carries only spurious social justification, a ghetto subculture, elevation of a lack of productivity to the status of virtue, and a view of education as largely decorative (Chałasiński 1946: 37–95).

In the context of the analysis of Polish social stratification presented earlier, it is interesting to attempt a synthetic picture of the ethos of Polish society. To investigate problems of ethos in a society or nation, at least three approaches are possible. The first, the *phenomenological* approach, attempts to penetrate into the so-called spirit of a nation or society. It aims to reveal a society's characteristic feature and essence. This approach is used fairly often since it is perceived as the most attractive and easily justified (Barzini 1983), yet by its very nature, phenomenology may produce a false picture by jumping onto the wrong track.

A more reliable method for analyzing the national character of a society is the *historical method*. This method relies on the collection of various facts and historical data from which generalizations are derived. However, the methodological procedure used to arrive at historical generalizations can be misleading. Political opinions accepted a priori ideological values, and subjective factors are found in a largely unrevealed framework; hence historical data and facts are all too easily collected as convenient illustrations. An analysis of ethos (or, as some would say, *Zeitgeist*—national character) traditionally utilizes these two methods.

Another approach is also possible. *Anthropological and sociological methods* provide, at the present stage in the development of the social sciences, reliable empirical data from which an initial synthesis of the given society or nation can be derived. This approach has the advantage of being based on data collected systematically and inductively. It does, however, have certain weaknesses: generalizations based on these data often far exceed their legitimate scope; the reliability of recorded answers depends on many circumstances; and several questions are considered taboo and cannot be asked.[23]

In her anthropological study based on a three-year stay in Poland, Janine Wedel came to several interesting conclusions. One of these revealed the role of the spiritual life in Poland. She says:

Duchowe life is the emotional and spiritual fibre of the private world. It allows one to escape from the psychological weariness produced by the realities of *zalatwianie spraw* [fixing problems]. Far removed from material concerns, *duchowe* life gives Polish culture its true flavour. A crucial component of *duchowe* life, regardless of social status, is

intellectual pursuit. Slavic countries have strong literary traditions—people *read*. That which is expressed verbally in political and social life in the West is put on paper in Slavic countries. That which is aired in the United States is published in articles in Poland. Talented writers—of plays, films, novels, poems and nonfiction—are involved in social and political affairs and deal with these problems in their works. Theatre almost invariably focuses on historical or current political themes. Poland's film idols are not glamorous screen stars but political-moral heroes. There is little tradition of "light theatre" or "light films." As one writer put it, "Polish writers want to be saints—the voice of the nation."
. . . In Poland every social group aspires to intellectual accomplishment. People read not merely as a pastime, but also to compare their life experiences with those people they are reading about and to participate in intellectual discussion. Hence, one can understand the disappointment of a secretary in my institute when I was unable to shed more light on the characters in *Gone with the Wind*, which she was reading for the third time, or the disappointment of my seamstress, a Hemingway fan, when I could not tell her much about Hemingway's life. One can also understand the utter disbelief of several friends that I had not read Karen Horney's books on neurosis in modern society; that I had read only two of Dostoyevski's works; that I could not remember the details of Joseph Conrad's *Lord Jim*, which Poles say depicts the moral complex of being Polish. One friend gave me a reading list so that I could better participate in *duchowe* life on my next trip to Poland. (Wedel 1986: 156–58)

Although this anthropological insight does indeed give an interesting, and apparently correct, snapshot of the ethos of the modern Polish intelligentsia, it does not necessarily describe the ethos of an average Pole. Nonetheless, it provides some clues for understanding general Polish snobbishness.

Several studies deal with the basic attitudes of the Polish population. Substantial research has been carried out on the moral and legal attitudes of society— five national surveys between 1962 and 1970 (Podgórecki 1964; Podgórecki 1966; Podgórecki et al. 1971), a study of the ethics of young people (Kiciński, Kurczewski 1975), and an examination of sociopolitical attitudes (Nowak 1966). It is worth remembering that some of these studies used representative samples of the whole society and have been systematically repeated over more than a decade (1962–1975).

In order to systemize this material, a conceptual differentiation among attitudes can be made. *Declared attitudes* are generally the social values that have been installed in the individual's psyche through various educational methods, socialization processes, and ideological appeals. Declared attitudes are not always identical with *approved attitudes*. Past and present experiences have taught the Poles to conceal every possible divergence between declared and approved attitudes. Approved, or internally accepted, attitudes are not always externally declared, and they do not always constitute the basis of actual behavior. They might be "suspended" under pressure from some ad hoc need (a decent person may steal for his hungry family) or the stress of long, harsh, and intensive constraints (someone may be silent about his true political opinions out of an awareness of political repression). Attitudes that constitute the basis of actual behavior—*motivational attitudes*—are, from a sociological point of view, the most interesting. These, in fact, are responsible for social interactions.

Material collected from studies of the Polish population suggests that attitudes of an even more complicated nature exist. These are called *meta-attitudes*.[24] Certain kinds of meta-attitudes are especially characteristic of the Polish ethos. They are: a "fiddling" attitude towards survival, an "instrumental" attitude, a "ubiquitous insecurity," an attitude of "spectacular principledness" (principled heroics), an attitude of "individualism as imperative," and the "all thumbs" attitude.[25]

Meta-attitudes are not directly manifested in actual behavior. They do, however, influence other attitudes. They operate as hidden forces existing outside the sphere of perceived opinions and values that determine how these opinions and values are to be manifested externally. A meta-attitude can thus be defined as a disposition towards a certain type of stable reaction that does not manifest itself externally, but structures from inside the motivations that are consecutively expressed in behavior. Meta-attitudes are hidden and petrified attitudes.

The "Fiddling" Attitude of Survival

The most important meta-attitude, arguably, is *the fiddling attitude of survival*.[26] This meta-attitude constantly intervenes in the individual and collective life of Poles, allowing for tremendous flexibility since it is constantly being tested. Lech Wałęsa once said:

A communiqué was issued on the subject of my meeting with the Holy Father. I can add only one thing to it. I noticed at one point that the Holy Father looked tired, troubled. I decided to cheer him up, since I saw that he wanted to cheer me up. So I said to him, "Holy Father, I think Poland is a chosen nation, the most fortunate nation in the world." The Holy Father looked at me and asked why I thought so. I told him that every day, many times a day, we can define ourselves. We live helplessly, things which are evident elsewhere are not evident here, black is white for us. We are constantly testing ourselves. That is why we are able to go back to the basics. At the same time, we look at rich Americans and ask, "What tests do they measure themselves by? Well, they can pick up a new girl, get a new car . . . " (Committee 1983: 8)

The fiddling attitude of survival leads Poles to accumulate material possessions in order to gain security (more psychological than economic) in the face of uncertainty. This particular Polish attitude has an *autotelic* character, a purpose unto itself. Thus, the tendency to acquire relationships (enlarging the association of equals) loses its *heterotelic* origin as a means of ensuring the conditions for survival. Envy then becomes "envy for its own sake," losing its original force as a negative regulator that peeps into and undermines the skills and strategies of others, in order to prevent them from threatening one's own options.

The current Polish strategy of survival seems to be based on two discrepant factors. The first is reliance on strong links with the family (mainly nuclear) and carefully selected friends. Some quite sophisticated studies indicate that at the forefront of values respected by the contemporary Polish population are the welfare of their own children and marital success (quite often understood as a mutual-defence union). Acceptance by others and good health are also highly placed (Podgórecki 1964; Kocowski 1975). Children in Polish families are beginning to be treated as "idols" (in China, "small emperors"), symbolizing the closeness of the small group and the kind of emotional humanism specific to the world of values that is confined within the framework of narrow communities. In situations of uncertainty due to external threat, this internal asylum is treated as having both a heterotelic (teleological) and an autotelic value: autotelic because of the rewards it provides, and heterotelic because it allows for the possibility of cutting oneself off from disturbing external events.

In a perverse way, the ability to survive gives Poles the feeling of heroism and uniqueness. As Elias Canetti perceptively observes, "The moment of survival is the moment of power. Horror at the sight of death turns into satisfaction that it is someone else who is dead. The dead man lies on the ground while the survivor stands. It is as though there had been a fight and the one struck down the other. In survival, each man is the enemy of other, and all grief is insignificant measured against this elemental triumph. Whether the survivor is confronted by one dead man or many, the essence of the situation is that he feels *unique*" (Canetti 1962: 227).

It is well known that the Polish ethos is characterized by individualism in both its traditional and modern versions. Yet this is tempered by a tendency to cultivate friendship ties. It is not always recognized that in Poland, the focus on friendship is a tendency to associate, by mutually binding decision, with *equals*. Associating with someone on the basis of an ability to make one's own decisions, often marked by *Brüderschaft* (brotherhood), is itself a manifestation of a sui generis, arbitrarily established élitism.

A comparative study conducted in Poland and Finland concluded that

there are similarities between Finland and Poland in terms of the size and occupational homogeneity of friendship networks. The same might be said about the main demographic features. For instance, in both countries married and older people are without friends more often than unmarried and younger persons. Having many friends seems to be very typical of the life style of upper white collar workers, whereas farmers and unskilled workers seem to have more ascribed relations. In both countries upper white collar workers tend to live apart from other groups, and their friends are usually of the same occupational status. (Jaakkola, Makarczyk 1978:354)

Equality is granted to those in the same status category, although not automatically. A voluntary act of internal and selective acceptance is necessary if informal possibilities are to be ritualistically transformed into concrete and stable ties. These mutual ties constitute the unusually strong and vital fabric of the inner life of Polish society.

This particular type of social relationship may transform itself or degenerate into the phenomenon of "dirty togetherness," a community of cooperation established by the mutual use of illegal means or the acceptance of illegal goals. Dirty togetherness may be regarded as the *second* component of the socialist strategy of survival. It may sometimes take the form of "socialist fiefdom." This is a tendency to create for oneself (or for one's group), inside of one's own field of discretion, a domain that enables one to oppress others. Practically everybody in a "socialist" society has his own field (fiefdom) in which he can exercise a sort of monopolistic power. On the lowest level, he may or may not sell a magazine of limited circulation to a potential buyer; it is up to him to decide whether the face of the buyer is submissive enough to grant him this favor (the majority of vendors act as agents of the government's selling firms). On the higher level it is up to the official to grant his friends (or families of these friends) the kind of privileges that are at his executive disposal (Podgórecki 1991: 176–77). A relatively comprehensive study of the recent changes in Polish society and the decomposition of the Communist party arrives at a conclusion similar to the concept of socialist fiefdom: "[w]hen the political nucleus represents in fact a coalition of various centers (even when contained within the dominant party) they find themselves lacking legitimacy. As a result, those individuals (or groups) appropriate the prerogatives of the state on their territory, treating their official functions not as a service to the society but as a *de facto* private property used for their own (and their relatives') benefit" (Dyoniziak et al. 1992: 297–98).

The only departure from individualistic orientation is manifested inside the Polish family. Here, an individual acts not only in his own interest but also represents the interests of the collective body (the family). The internal life of a Polish family is a complicated mystery. Studies conducted or coordinated by Mirosława Marody attempted to elucidate this mystery. Analyzing the subjective perception of great insecurity in Poles, she and her team distinguished the following six areas of social life: family life, social interactions, work, politics, culture, and "socialized" nature. These areas, among others, represent the hierarchy of "spheres of realization of the basic human drives." One member of Marody's team, Hanna Bojar, writes:

Even a superficial analysis of parameters dealing with the functioning of the Polish family leads to the conclusion that, in reality, family does not fulfill its expectations. Its high position in the hierarchy of values and aspirations of members of Polish society corresponds not so much to the real situation of family, as to usually unfulfilled expectations. The Polish family cannot realize its basic functions and loses its ability to situate an individual in a physical, social, and temporal dimension. Also, its organizational functions degenerate upon encountering the domineering disintegration of social life. The recompensatory model of family is visible in its overdeveloped representative functions and its domination over an individual. A family, placing all its ambitions in its children, develops a sui generis defence mechanism, thus becoming an additional source of insecurity. These processes generate additional tensions between the subjective image of the role of a parent and the objective possibilities of realizing this role. (Bojar 1991: 65)[27]

The ingenuity of socialism introduced into the fiber of Polish life the phenomenon of dirty togetherness. Under a state of dirty togetherness, elements of traditional social control, plucked from ethical imperatives, are so saturated with various erosive influences that they eventually lose their character as agents of social control, assuming instead new traits of perverse loyalty. This loyalty is additionally cemented by family ties, mutual fiddling services, and private transactions. These transactions open up opportunities for mutual blackmail should the reciprocal code of collaboration be violated—for example, should one hitherto trusted partner disclose certain behaviors of the other. These ties, both manipulative and instrumental in character, serve to establish stronger links than impersonal, rational relationships and, in turn, create their own superstructure, which dominates the social system in which they prosper.

Indeed, the fact that dirty togetherness is usually publicly perceived as an influential superstructure with an uncertain center of decision making evokes various attitudes of social insecurity. It also leads to the strong conviction that only public programs are able to materialize without counteraction from the superstructure of the community of dirty interests. When there is a reason to expect counteraction, or even retaliation, the agents of the community will extinguish any attempts to threaten them.

Various clusters of dirty togetherness, linked (or perceived by the public as interrelated) to a developed frame or superstructure, may have very important consequences. These clusters may bond the entire social system together as a whole. In order to understand this effect, it is necessary to connect the notion of dirty togetherness with the concept of "legitimacy" as it was established under conditions of "real socialism." It is possible to distinguish the following types of legitimacy:

Legitimacy based on normative grounds. According to this type of legitimacy, only those regulations and institutions that are derived from the legal norms of the higher order have legal validity. At the top of the hierarchy of all norms is the ultimate norm, the Kelsenian *Grundnorm* (a norm that renders validity to all subordinate rules), which is regarded as the final source of normative power. Avant-garde élite legitimacy may be regarded as a subcategory of this type. Wlodzimierz Wesołowski, using a form of double talk, formulates this point in the following way: "The Polish people live in a system that has been trying to implement some of the exceptional missions of the vanguard élite. The political élite attempted to gain legitimacy by referring to its superior knowledge of the course of history and of the interests of rank and file. One doubts, however, whether this attempt at gaining legitimacy has been successful" (Wesołowski 1989:46).

Legitimacy based on the democratic support of the population. This includes legitimacy that is valid according to official law, but rejected as unjust, reactionary, and oppressive by the majority of the population; in the eyes of the population, it is devoid of legal authority.

Legitimacy validated through the rejection of all other possible options (negative legitimacy). The legal system that does not have support from the majority of the population and is not derived from a legally valid constitution may still be regarded as legitimate if all other options (such as war, absence of sovereignty, or total destruction) are considered to be even worse.

Legitimacy based on the superstructure of "dirty togetherness." If, behind the given legal system (which is rejected by the population as unjust and undemocratic), a complicated infrastructure of mutually interdependent interests is operating, the legal system may become accepted, not on the basis of its own merits, but because it creates a convenient cover system for the flourishing phenomenon of dirty togetherness. Each institution, factory, and organization serves, independent of its own production tasks, as a formal network establishing a stable frame of reference for mutual semiprivate services and reciprocal arrangements. For example, the daughter of a highly placed person may be accepted into medical school in return for the offer to buy cement to build a house; or the privilege of immediately buying a car may be exchanged for admitting an elderly aunt into a well-equipped hospital. In this situation, the formal legal network, irrespective of its own questionable efficiency, becomes a very precious cover scheme. It is clear that individuals who operate inside this system will, after a while, start to support this legal matrix, not because they accept it as a system of normative validity or for its own inherent virtues, but rather because they become familiar with it, with the rules of its game, with its "who's who" foundation, and with its conditions of efficiency. The community of dirty togetherness is thus defensively directed. It tries to defend itself against the "hostile official system" in which it operates and which it perversely supports.

Spectacular Principledness

Spectacular principledness (principled heroics) refers to the attitude that not only approves of a given norm or value for its own sake but also celebrates certain norms or values because they are considered sacred and symbolically significant. Poles have a clear tendency to accord respect to everything connected with the Fatherland, political independence, and the suffering of the nation throughout its history (martyrology). Also impressive is their organic skepticism towards everyday systematic work, their apotheosis of historical events such as the "Gallant Rescue of Vienna" (1683), the Charge of Semosierra (1808), and the Polish participation in the Battle of Britain (1940), the tendency to see themselves as the Messiah of the world, and their celebration of even the most minor social, religious, or state holidays. Ordinary everyday integrity is alien to this attitude.

These virtues are treated as autotelic values. Poles are unable to profit from their heroic accomplishments. Practically no one knows that Enigma (a German code machine) was captured and decoded by Polish and British mathematicians. Yet almost everyone competent in this matter knows that the ability to intercept German messages sent by this device was crucial for the Allied Forces' victory in the Second World War. Hardly anyone is aware that a German V-missile was captured by the Polish underground army and sent to England. This operation, too, had tremendous value for the Allied military forces. The Poles, when compared with other nations, are unable to translate their own sufferings into political, or even economic, advantage. Their spectacular principledness has become an almost sacred value.

Data suggest that spectacular principledness has been maintained in Polish society through its traditional attachment to religion. Survey data from 1964 reveal that approximately 86 percent of the urban and 90 percent of the rural population define themselves as "believers" (Podgórecki 1966a: 197, 204). Subsequent research carried out in 1966 (studies based on a representative sampling of the Polish adult population) shows that 72.5 percent of the urban and 82.8 percent of the rural population claim to be believers (Podgórecki et al. 1971: 274, 278). Research conducted in 1971 that queried the middle-level intelligentsia (young people undergoing occupational training in supplemental-education institutions, teachers and local government employees—a total of 1,115 people), indicates that 64.8 percent defined themselves as believers (Ciupak 1975). Women claim a religious faith more often than men. A lower level of education is more frequently associated with declared religious faith. Rural respondents define themselves as religious more often than urban ones. This is also true of older people more often than young.

The residue of religious belief may support attitudes of spectacular principledness. It may also constitute the basis for strengthening status that is traditionally ascribed. Thus, religious attitudes may constitute a link in the chain that connects the attitude of spectacular principledness with traditional acceptance of ascribed (as opposed to acquired) status; both religious attitudes and the notion of ascribed status are currently being challenged by modern or post-modern thought.

After the election of a "Polish" pope and the revolution of 1989, Polish religious faith displayed its mysteriously complicated character. It became clear that this character had been blurred during the Communist regime. Its essence was the unique union between allegiance to the opposition and loyalty to the Church. A popular joke might best display the complexity of this situation: during Mass, when all faithful have to kneel, a single person fails to conform and towers visibly over the crowd. His neighbor whispers, "You should kneel!" The person bows down and replies in a low voice, "No. I am not a believer." When asked, "So, why did you come here?" he replies, "I am also against the government!" Janine Wedel comments on the problem of Polish religiosity in this way. "For many Poles, the Church is a refuge: it provides personal solace in times of economic and political upheaval. As one friend put it, 'The Church is the only place where I feel safe' " (Wedel 1986: 161). The joke explains why the prestige of the Polish church declined significantly after the 1989 revolution. The common enemy disappeared, and a collective front against this mutual enemy was no longer required.

The Polish political situation (dependence on the Soviet Union) so clouded the religiosity of Poles that it was difficult to distinguish responses that were declaratory from those that were real. Even more complicated was the fact that faith in the rural areas as it manifested itself after 1989 declined considerably—30 percent (in rural areas located more than sixty minutes from the city). This decline was accompanied by a drastic drop in the prestige of priests. One-quarter of the priests maintained that the faithful did not approach them for advice or help (Nosowski 1991: 57). Yet the religiosity of Polish youth was a remarkable phenomenon. In 1988–1989, 95 percent of high-school students and 88 percent of university students declared their allegiance to the Catholic church. Nonetheless, research conducted in April 1991 showed that the Church as an institution enjoys the trust of only 69 percent of the total population, as compared to the army, which is trusted by 75 percent overall (Nosowski 1991: 58). Other research conducted in March 1991 indicated that 23 percent of the population approves of abortion on demand (Nosowski 1991:61). The whole situation becomes quite complicated. Nonetheless, at least three general conclusions emerge: (1) the religiosity of many has a declaratory character; (2) it manifests itself more visibly in the cities; and (3) authentic religiosity is not always associated with approval of the institution (it can coexist with anticlericalism).

In order to clearly understand the essential features of spectacular principledness, it should be noted that, in Polish society, the value of a gesture is greater than the value of a more mundane action, however effective. More specifically, in Polish culture, an attempt to do something that requires spectacular demeanor and an impressive confrontation with the problem is more highly valued than a pragmatic, logistic, practical, or economic solution. The worth of a given position is not evaluated in terms of the actual qualifications it demands; it is evaluated for the potential ''show'' that can be put on by the person holding that position when approaching a problem.

Symbolic values certainly surpass real ones. Informal evaluations are more significant than the tangible, socially and objectively recognized effects of actions. Legends and myths become the critical factors. The subjective aura of an intended social action and the capacity to transmit this aura in a social performance (for a relevant audience) seem to be more important than the actual consequences of the action.

In relation to moral and legal norms, the meta-attitude of spectacular principledness expresses itself as rigorous. This rigor is manifested in relation to others, in keeping with the human tendency to blame others rather than oneself. However, it does not remain only at this level of expression. Research reveals that sanctions from the Polish Communist legal system are applied with a degree of harshness that is consistent with these rigorous general attitudes (Jasiński 1963).

Random journalistic data suggest that this generalization may hold true in post-Communist Poland as well.

The tendency towards social punitiveness can be explained in a number of ways. It may be the expression of ambivalence towards the law. On the one hand, it may express respect for the law (linked to the demand for its widespread application), while on the other, it may reflect the fact that the law is not consistently applied and followed (as indicated by demands to strengthen the law through the application of its own sanctions). More convincing is the supposition that social punitiveness constitutes an expression of accumulated social frustration. (It should be noted as a comparison that Finnish society, supposedly because it possesses historical frustrations comparable to those of Poland, also demands and applies the sanctions of criminal law on a large scale.) When informal social rigor (pressure towards conformity) produces expected results, it manifests a genuine respect for the law. In general, an informal legal rigor seems to be more effective when law is perceived as just and fair.

Instrumentality

Another meta-attitude common to Poles is *instrumentality*. As the principled attitude accepts or rejects certain norms for their own sake, the instrumental attitude is selective and calculating. On the basis of a subjective calculation of profit and loss, this attitude accepts norms that are convenient for the achievement of desired goals and rejects all others. It would be a fundamental mistake to perceive this attitude as socially destructive. It may even form the basis for carrying out various tasks beyond one's individual interest. But often, in fact, this attitude is oriented towards *private* goals. Research reveals that it is currently found to a greater extent in the younger generation than in the elder.

We can discern various types of instrumental attitudes in the financial sphere, sexual lives, personal relationships, political options, and institutional arrangements. These instrumental attitudes may appear isolated from one another, or they may constitute an entire instrumental personality.

A summary of research carried out in 1964 (Podgórecki 1966a,b,c), 1966 (Podgórecki et al. 1971), and 1970 (Podgórecki, Kojder 1972) on principled and instrumental attitudes suggested the following:

1. The principled attitude rises in frequency with increases in age.

2. The scope of available instrumental attitudes increases with the level of education, but respondents with higher education (completed or not) are nevertheless more disposed to compromise.

3. Private farmers are more disposed to the principled attitude than members of other occupational groups.

4. The principled attitude is associated with living in a big city.

5. The principled attitude is linked with a lack of insecurity, while the instrumental attitude is associated with a strong feeling of insecurity.

6. Proper adaptation to life is essentially linked with the principled attitude, while maladjustment is associated with the instrumental.

A comparison of these findings leads to some modifications in earlier generalizations. The hypotheses regarding the relationship between age and acceptance of a principled or instrumental attitude (the rise in frequency of the principled attitude with age) and the relations associated with subjective social traits (like insecurity, maladjustment, pessimism) are reinforced by these findings. The instrumental attitude is thus linked with insecurity and maladjustment, according to earlier and later research, while the principled attitude is associated with both proper adaptation to life and a feeling of security.

The instrumental attitude may be regarded as a sui generis consequence of the fiddling survival attitude. It should also be cautioned that it contradicts all the principled approaches to interpersonal relationships. Thus, while instrumentality has some roots in the Polish national character (even if fiddling was directed mainly against governments imposed by foreign powers occupying Poland throughout a century), it is a calculating, teleological life perspective (even if traditional spectacular principledness can rationalize common, everyday breaches of the law). But it was real socialism that encouraged instrumental attitudes to blossom.

The tension between contradictory hierarchies of values, the constant tendency to suppress traditional attachments to institutions and organizations generated by Polish society through its history, everyday inefficiency that departs markedly from norms otherwise regarded as healthy and valid, an erosion of trust between close friends and even members of families, the distribution of rewards based on political flexibility towards changing ideological programs, and private goals assembled by "radar oriented" instrumental attitudes: taken together, these factors lead to a new type of anomie combined with social nihilism.

Ubiquitous Insecurity

Historically, due to its geographic location between two aggressors, the Polish population has had a deeply rooted and permanent feeling of insecurity. This feeling was recently reinforced by the insecurity generated under a totalitarian sociopolitical system. The Polish reality presented many opportunities to study this problem. Fear could have many faces, private or communal. Krzysztof Nowak stated this vague generalization in the following way. "Formerly, by telling the truth, one could offend some vague, dark forces, whereas now, assuming a stance on a concrete issue, one runs the risk of conflict with a concrete person" (Nowak, K. 1988: 189).

According to several reliable studies that will be analyzed in this chapter, the Polish population had firmly entrenched feelings of insecurity after World War II. Research based on a nationwide sample in 1964 yielded the following results: 68.4 percent of the urban population clearly possessed insecurities, while 74 percent of rural respondents concurred with this outlook (Podgórecki 1966a: 194, 202).

More detailed data revealed that those with lower levels of education, including unqualified workers, exhibited a higher level of insecurity (Podgórecki 1966: 47–48). A subsequent study conducted in 1966, also based on a nationwide sample, supported the previous findings: 76 percent of the urban population and 69.7 percent of the rural population were insecure (Podgórecki et al. 1971: 283, 273). Jacek Kurczewski, in analyzing this data, came to the conclusion that "these findings can be interpreted as a symptom of the relation between low social position and insecurity, and high social position and a lack of insecurity" (Kurczewski 1971: 207).

It is interesting to note that a study conducted in 1978 (sampling 1,557 members of the urban population) revealed contrary results. According to this study, "in 1978, the Polish intelligentsia was more psychologically weakened than workers, the latter had at their disposal more psychological strength. This situation manifested itself in a lower level of insecurity and less fear among workers; workers also characterized themselves as having more faith in their opportunities and a higher evaluation of their potential" (Koralewicz 1987: 99). In a different text, interpreting the same findings, Jadwiga Koralewicz disregards the differences between unskilled and skilled workers, comparing only the insecurity of the workers and the intelligentsia. She says, "Only the intelligentsia's authoritarian attitude is supported by insecurity. . . . The workers' authoritarian attitude, determined mainly by their cognitive perspective, is connected with a relatively lower level of insecurity and a greater belief in themselves" (Koralewicz 1987: 224).

These findings contradict a different inquiry that was included in a complex study directed by Koralewicz. Thus, according to Anna Potocka-Hoser, workers as a rule had a negative opinion of their interpersonal relations at the workplace; feelings of friendliness, justice, and honesty were absent on the job, whereas feelings of insecurity were high (Potocka-Hoser 1987: 148). These contradictory findings might be explained, at least partially, by the fact that the ethos of highly skilled workers reached its peak during the 1980–1981 Solidarity events, when workers, and especially skilled workers, started to believe in themselves on the wave of the approaching Solidarity victory.

Kojder's research on the attitudes of the young intelligentsia (students) also finds that "the system" is one of the most oppressive elements of Polish social life. He quotes a typical statement from one of the respondents. "After forty years [of socialism], a large army of decision makers was established (at various social levels), by people morally small, corrupt, afraid of their bosses, and therefore eager to be involved in any wicked action to defend their position and connected privileges" (Kojder 1989: 151).

It is interesting to note that insecurity is not an entirely urban phenomenon. The most important finding of a study by Maria Łoś was that "awakened ambitions and motivations cannot, at the present moment, be fulfilled in the countryside. Therefore, the fear of defeat equals the anxiety of one's own environment'' (Łoś 1972: 263).

According to a tentative synthesis suggested by Marody and her team, a feeling of widespread insecurity is currently endemic in Polish society. "Feelings of insecurity, so characteristic at the present moment for the Poles, are generated not so much by the slowness of newly introduced institutional change produced by the present government, as by the lack of social transparency. Transparency is most important for the average human being in his action in everyday affairs'' (Marody 1991: 267–68).

Aleksander Matejko presents a more suggestive and profound perspective on the role of fear in Polish society. He says, "Poles enjoy the *illusionary* world in which they feel safe and successful as long as there is no direct danger of facing reality. The clash of declarative values with actual behavior is one of the major obstacles to an effective transformation of the Polish society. For example, friendship is a mixture of love and competition, religion is a contradiction between manifested conformity and the daily violation of declared norms, marriage coexists with unfaithfulness, the education of children is also full of inconsistencies (for example, the tendency of parents to project their own irritation on children). All these attitudes *impoverish* Polish daily life and are reinforced by *inconsistent* behavior. And those tendencies that existed before were magnified by communism'' (Matejko forthcoming).

Generalizing from these findings and ideas, one can elaborate three levels of social fear: (1) fear that a given person may represent the sociopolitical system (informer, security officer, prosecutor); (2) fear of possible danger (riots, investigation by security agents, discrimination against intellectuals); and (3) fear of some obscure, dark political force: fear of the surrounding inquiry, "inescapable" victimization by the totalitarian political system, or an inability to demonstrate one's own innocence.

On this basis, the following generalization seems to be appropriate: the further away one is from a concrete situation and the closer to a feeling of surrounding danger, the likelier it is that one will fear all concrete situations, and the closer one will be to the crushing sense of ubiquitous insecurity.

All Thumbs Attitude

The *all thumbs meta-attitude* is characterized by the inability to perceive a means of achieving desired goals (Podgórecki 1987: 601). Again, Marody deftly reformulates this idea: "Characteristic of Polish society in the eighties is the lack-of-sense attitude. This attitude creates a belief in the deficiency of links between effort and effect, goals and the appropriate means of realizing them, desire and its fulfillment. This attitude did not appear in immediate everyday experience, but rather was a result of the accumulation of various experiences at different levels of generality'' (Marody 1991: 222).

A meta-attitude of this type thus leads to a partial realization of a socially accepted goal (realization of a part of the goal that is not necessarily the most essential one), or produces some additional by-products that undermine (or even mock) the goal itself. It may also create, during the process of realization, side-effects that divert attention from details, thus changing the entire task-oriented process into a farce.

Many factors generate this particular meta-attitude. They include an inability to work in a disciplined way, a disinclination towards cooperation (an offshoot of the individualism of the nobility), a disproportionate sense that antagonistic circumstances are working against an established plan, and a bifurcation of effort into contradictory streams tending towards opposite targets, so that overall control is lost. In general, the unexpected but structured dissonance between rational expectations and their results constitutes the essence of the ''all thumbs'' meta-attitude. Although this attitude has always been an ingredient in tragedy, a substantial degree of inadvertent folly is inseparably connected to it.

The all thumbs attitude may intervene as the most important ingredient of nation-building sociopolitical movements. For example, the KOR had a decisive influence on the triumphant emergence of Solidarity. The end of the KOR reflected the spirit of the ''all thumbs'' meta-attitude.

Even after this final act [the dissolution of the KOR] another small chapter in the history of the KOR closed. In itself, it was rather minor, but it was widely noticed and variously interpreted, affecting both nerves and health. On the day of Lipiński's speech [Sept. 28, 1981], a delegation from the Radom region of NSZZ Solidarity introduced a motion to the effect that Congress should pass a resolution thanking KOR. The chairman of the Radom region explained why that particular region was introducing the motion, which— given the events of 1976 and the enormous work that the KOR had accomplished in Radom—was rather obvious. Late in the evening, after the conclusion of the plenary meetings, Paweł Niezgodzki suggested that the delegation of Mazowsze introduce a counter-motion. This was a long and affected statement containing a number of formulations from the preface to the project of the program of Solidarity, as well as many other statements, such as that Poland has been Christian for a thousand years, that the Church and the Pope have played an enormous role in creating the situation that made this congress possible, and so on. The motion also contained a single sentence—positive—about the democratic opposition, without any specific mention of the KOR (although it was not the democratic opposition, but the KOR that was dissolving) . . . The motion was withdrawn. (Lipski 1983: 389–90)

And is this silly episode to serve as a conclusion to the history of KOR? It must, since the organization no longer existed. Much was left behind, and much will survive for a long time to come: in the people who participated in its work, or those who benefitted from it, in the effects that will last for many years, and also in the books and periodicals that constitute material proof that all this was not just a dream. (Lipski 1985: 454–56)

The all thumbs attitude is also produced by a dissatisfaction with spurious words and empty concepts. All dogma were so misleading during the period of real socialism that, in the post-communist period, it became impossible to believe in any. Bronisław Misztal states that "The movement known as the Orange Alternative emerged in Poland in the early 1980s, and it continues to operate, even though the original conditions of socialist reality have changed. From a relatively small and vanguard form of street theatre it grew to form the manifestation of one's discontent with the world of symbols" (Misztal 1992: 55).

Thus one may conclude that the social roots of the all thumbs attitude are as follows: if one is unable to solve the problems at hand, one might, consciously or unconsciously, transform the task-solving attitude into a theatrical show. Gratification does not then come from the desired effects, but rather from the spectacle involved. If the ethos of farce and social entertainment reigns supreme over the task-solving attitude, the gesture takes the upper hand over the tangible results.

GENERAL REFLECTIONS ON THE STRATIFICATION OF POLISH SOCIETY

Although existing research on Polish society was, despite its relative sophistication, scattered, accidental, and fragmentary, it showed very clearly that this society was undergoing fundamental change. These transformations consisted of a tendency to flatten the social structure by increasing its homogeneity (the planned decomposition of the classes and strata of the presocialist social structure). Yet this went hand in hand with the emergence of new, unplanned, heterogeneous strata based on a *secondary distribution of incomes*, drastically changing the officially proclaimed equality. These kinds of processes first gave rise to an imposed or "planned" social composition in accordance with the ideological measures undertaken to implement the principle of egalitarianism. Secondly, they led to a recomposition that ran contrary to the expectations of the decisionmakers. It would thus be useful in the Polish case, an almost purposely designed societal laboratory, to distinguish between functional recomposition (consistent with expectations) and dysfunctional recomposition (giving rise to unexpected side-effects that are negative from the planners' point of view). It would also be useful to distinguish between spontaneous recomposition processes and those that are guided. After 1989 the situation suddenly reversed itself: ennobling the negative side-effects ("second economy") became the main societal target, whereas the market economy started to transform the remainders of Communist failure into the triumphant building of capitalism. These fascinating transformations will be seen more clearly when an appropriate amount of systematic research has been accumulated.

One of the crucial problems concerning society as a whole before 1989 was the distance between "functional" and "dysfunctional" changes inside this society, and the extent to which these processes ignored the question of general psychosocial deviance, which amounted to a special type of societal schizophrenia. These processes led, as was mentioned before, to a reversed pyramidal triptych. At the pinnacle were (and possibly still are) the top dogs, the instrumentally oriented stratum of operators; in the middle was the mixture of those corroded by instrumentality, as well as the mass of those escaping into principal orientation (the middle dogs); and on the bottom, there was a large stratum of less successful fiddling-survival strategists—the underdogs.

The dualist nature of the processes taking place in the heart of Polish society has its equivalent in lifestyles expressed in sui generis social ambivalence and, disturbingly, the most excessive vodka consumption in the world (the former USSR did not publish such data about itself). This lifestyle is maintained by the constant pressures created, on the one hand, by the fear of authority, which comes from pragmatic and practical sources (if a given government, Communist or post-Communist, possesses legal and factual power, one seems well advised to comply with its regulations), and, on the other, by the "mission" attitude of the traditional Polish intelligentsia.

The watch-dog pressure exerted by the intelligentsia involved constant reinterpretation of all regulations issued by the government. Even after the abolishment of the Communist regime, those vigilant watch-dog eyes are eager to spot all official movements and actions that establish real, or imaginary, new nomenklatura. Thus, according to these ambivalent pressures, a member of Polish society is always under the scrutiny of official control and the stress of an invisible peer group and receives contradictory guidance from both. It is not difficult to see that these two sets of factors (official and informal) reinforce the continual growth of a schizophrenic personality based on ambivalence.[28]

The assertion that the ethos of Poles, accumulated through many historic events, trials and errors and elaborated by a few outstanding thinkers, is an outcome of the nation's past history would be merely banal if it were not for the fact that the modern structure and stratification of Polish society seems to be molded by the personality patterns discussed above. More concretely, the specific type of underdevelopment in Polish society—lack of a developed middle class—has shifted the trend of societal development towards the ethos of "higher social classes," thus giving these classes almost direct access to the process of designing basic patterns of life for the "lower social strata." The emerging middle class seems to be interested in instrumentally handled education, material prosperity copied from Western patterns, the computer culture, a skeptical, if not cynical, attitude towards the traditional intelligentsia's values, a ritualistic religious ornamentation, and a decisive retreat from deeply developed Polish patriotism.

In the historic process of amalgamating the structure of Polish society, positive economic motivation did not gain enough momentum for development, compared to that in Western Europe. This, in effect, led to a situation where socially established patterns of behavior (meta-attitudes) became decisive. If these generalizations are correct, then Polish society directly contradicts Marxist theory.

It presents a situation where the Marxist "superstructure" is more influential than the "base." And this is one of many interesting similarities between Poland and Israel.

In any case, the explanatory potential of meta-attitudes seems to not be exhausted. The functioning of the sociopolitical élite may be explained through the shift of instrumentally oriented social members towards the positions of power. The persistence of these institutions, which before 1989 were hated by the overwhelming majority, may be explained not only by the use of force but also, to a large extent, by the phenomenon of "dirty togetherness," and by the functioning of the greedy "half-intelligentsia," which is motivated by a desire to compensate for its low social origin. The vast public economy and administration (even after 1989) operates as a product of the perverse support gained from the fiddling-survival and instrumental attitudes. Fiddling-survival attitudes seem to be responsible for the "miraculous" transformation of the existing institutions and organizations into a hidden economic system ("second economy"), which supports them. The very simple rationale for this is that, when "second life" activities are allowed to shelter under official institutions and organizations, practically all who participate in these activities have some vested interest in keeping the formal system going.

On the grounds of negative historic and collective experiences, the meta-attitudes described here have been selected, through repeated trial and error, as the most suitable. In consequence, meta-attitudes such as fiddling survival, instrumentalism, ubiquitous insecurity, spectacular principledness, and "all thumbs" represent unique historic products in the life of Polish society. Since recent Polish history was shaped by unequal duels with imposed foreign regimes and upheavals in the effort to regain independence, these attitudes may be regarded as the most crucial elements of Polish social life. They structure the social structure.

4

Theory of Polish Society

IS POLISH SOCIETY PECULIAR?

Small or large social groups should not be the only objects of a *comprehensive* sociological inquiry; rather, it should embrace the entire society. Since various social groupings exist within different social contexts and occupy different positions within the framework of social structure, the whole society designs and shapes their composition, dynamics, ideology, and "internal life," sometimes even transforming them into their own antitheses. Thus, society as a whole establishes the ultimate framework for its substructures. Only a scrupulous examination of several societies lays the requisite foundation for a more abstract, general study of the concept of society and, ultimately, humankind.

Polish society presents a most interesting object for such an inquiry. To begin with, it is an old society (it has existed for more than one thousand years) with firmly entrenched social features. While it played a prominent role in the political and economic development of Europe in the sixteenth and seventeenth centuries, it is currently of less than secondary importance. Until recently, moreover, Polish society was understood theoretically as a substructure of the Soviet Union's ill-conceived Marxist regime (Szczepański 1970), rather than as a society in and of itself. Yet its longevity has made of this society a unique social entity in which the civil society has definitely outgrown the state. Polish society underwent a peculiar, collective experience (the loss of independence in the eighteenth, nineteenth, and early twentieth centuries) that altered the relationship between state and citizen. It has a history of substantial emigration, with roughly one-quarter of its population scattered around the globe. Within this society, a group of very competent historians exists, and an adroit group of social scientists who have conducted numerous empirical studies (albeit fragmented and of uneven quality) that provide many insights into its rapidly changing sociopolitical and economic life. Finally, the uniqueness of transformations in Poland lies also in deliberate attempts by officials to halt the spontaneous processes of sociopolitical development and mold the society into a "planned," predesigned, ideological model. For the first time in the history of humankind, a society of this size, with its historical traditions and very clear national identity, went through a process of deliberate transfiguration.

Paradoxically, social scientists have not been able to devise a comprehensive theory that grasps and analyzes the specific identity of Poland.[29] This is likely because of the Polish inclination to see everything from the self-centered perspective of the traditional nobility ("an elephant and the Polish question"). Such analytical attempts are often developed emotionally, entangled in Polish martyrology, or a nonaggressive, ethnocentric, self-centered desire to build an image of a peaceful and unimposing nation.

It would be a mistake to expect that any single theory could provide an adequate explanation of Polish history and a clear understanding of its current sociopolitical situation. In order to elucidate the uniqueness of Polish society, it is necessary to examine different theories that help to reveal its multidimensional nature (Podgórecki, Łoś 1979). Several perspectives and levels of analysis (political, economic, social, and cultural) must be engaged to achieve as comprehensive a theory as possible. Monopolistic Marxist attempts to present such an analysis are currently regarded as failures, even by those who were once official and devoted Marxists (see Kołakowski, for example).

THE GEOPOLITICAL SITUATION

According to Randall Collins, Max Weber was the first to show that the essential force behind the development of various states was not economic, but military-geopolitical (Collins 1986: 2–3, 186–209). The decline and rise of a society is thus determined by elements such as size and resource advantage, positional advantage ("marchlands"—states with fewer military neighbors—and "interiors"—states surrounded by powerful neighbors), integrated or fragmented neighboring states, "show-down" wars, whether won or lost, integrity of internal sociopolitical forces, and overextension and disintegration of parts.

Poland, a rather peaceful society that expanded in the fifteenth and sixteenth centuries through unions and mutual agreements (Horodło's union with Lithuania in 1413; the incorporation of part of the Ukraine into Lublin in 1569) was almost completely surrounded by powerful neighbors with imperialist tendencies. The northern frontier, the Baltic Sea passage, was open to Swedish aggression against Poland's weak naval forces. The western frontier was shifted, step by step, towards the heart of Poland by the military expansion of the German Ost-Politik in its attempts to find more political *Lebensraum* in eastern Europe. The growing Russian Empire pressured Poland from the East, attempting not only to establish a secure passageway, or corridor, between itself and western Europe but also to transform Poland into a subservient state that could be economically exploited and utilized militarily. Although the southern frontier had historically been relatively secure, the rise of the Austrian Empire in the eighteenth and nineteenth centuries changed this situation dramatically.

Poland is thus well suited to the Weber-Collins thesis. In terms of its geopolitical location, the only consolation that the Poles possess is the knowledge that they are protected against possible Chinese attack by a small buffer state.

AN HISTORICAL PERSPECTIVE—
THE BROTHERLY NEIGHBORHOOD

Prior to its loss of statehood in 1795, the most characteristic features of Polish society were political, religious, and social tolerance. This tolerance was a product of the ethos of the Polish nobility, a social stratum that was unusually large in Poland, constituting approximately eight percent of the population in the sixteenth century. All processes introduced by the nobility have had a very strong impact on the entire society. A most imaginative historian, Andrzej Zajączkowski, claimed that the basic societal values and patterns of behavior of this stratum were generated by a "neighborly circle" (Zajączkowski 1961; 1962). Everyone who belonged to this circle was, as a rule, regarded as an equal.[30] "In neighboring communities of nobles, all members were considered equal since all belonged to the nobility's stratum. Nobility—good nobility, of course—was a condition of membership. But they were equal only in principle, because each community had a certain internal structure, based upon a pyramid-like design" (Zajączkowski 1961: 67).

A peasant-like nobleman who shared a border with a nationally known magnate, enjoyed the same normative rank as his powerful neighbor, according to this ethos. The notion was expressed not only as a normative recommendation; it also could manifest itself in practice. A magnate who arrogantly pretended that he was different, or that he belonged to a higher social category, would face severe sanctions—he might be ostracized by the majority of his neighbors if he provoked them enough.

All community members belonged to the local authority council (*sejmik*), a body that not only had the power to resolve all important problems of the region but also to influence opinion nationwide. Such influence contributed to a powerful ideology that cultivated and stressed the equality of all "noblemen-brothers." Although this tolerance embraced mainly those who belonged to the same status group, its general philosophy was also applicable to those outside of the sacred neighborly circle.

A Western philosopher characterizes the main features of traditional Polish tolerance when summarizing the basic ideas, formulated in 1411, of Stanislaw from Skarbimierza: "What attracts our attention here lies in his fundamental principle of universal tolerance, legitimizing not the moral duty of charity, but rather a series of positive rights: the infidels' right to enjoy peacefully organized states and institutions, the right of property rationally acknowledged as distinct from *res nullius*, and the injustice of all and any individual or collective aggression in the name of religion'' (Letocha 1986: n.p.). Tolerance was thus extended to Jews, other national minorities, those who belonged to different religions, and those differently situated on the ladder of material power.

Potentially and ideologically, every nobleman was a king. In fact, he might be elected to this position by the national cofraternity (*sejm*). Also, any nobleman, if motivated by deep conviction (or else corrupted by someone rich or influential), might invalidate the final decision of the highest national council or the assembly of delegates from provincial councils. He could use his prerogative of *liberum veto* (free veto). This prerogative imbued each nobleman with a strong sense of belonging and a powerful conviction of equality among all members of his stratum.[31]

The nobility's orientation towards equality produced an antithetical attitude of envy elsewhere in society. ''If anyone can be a king, why am I not elected to this position? Why, then, should he be?'' A poisonous envy penetrated the Polish social texture. It suffocated the essential features of *neighborly togetherness*, aptly named ''the nobleman's paradise'' by Norman Davies (Davies 1981). The social life of each neighbor was, in principle, transparent. This visibility nourished the desire to possess equally that which was possessed by a neighbor who was better off.

Within this frame of reference emerged the skill to impress and entertain friends, guests, and ''neighbor-brothers.'' As an attitude, however, it was self-destructive. It did not require that something be created or built for future generations; it was grounded firmly in the present. Its deep-rootedness puzzles many who study the history of Poland. Why was this society, so rich in talent, imagination, fantasy, and wit, so poor in terms of its contribution to constructive attitudes in universal terms?

Remnants of this attitude, reinforced by the peculiarity of ''real socialism,'' are visible in contemporary sociological inquiries. ''Observations of behavior show that people often strive for economic success, but the economic success of others evokes in them envy, rather than respect. To our question 'In your opinion, what do people in Poland most often feel about those people much wealthier than themselves?' some seventy-five percent of the respondents said 'envy,' and only two percent said 'respect' '' (Reszke 1985: 56).

Eagerly cultivated ''brotherly and neighborly togetherness'' had a tendency to degenerate into dirty togetherness, which operates through a complicated infrastructure of mutually interdependent interests in opposition to the existing legal system.[32] This system is able to create a convenient smoke-screen for the flourishing of ''camaraderie.'' Under the phenomenon of dirty togetherness, traditional social control, shorn of ethical conviction, is so saturated with erosive influences that it loses its character as an agent of social order, instead assuming a ''perverse'' loyalty.

This loyalty is entrenched by family ties, mutual ''fiddling'' services, participation in both petty and grand crimes, or even in mutually beneficial, informal, but not strictly legal private transactions that make possible mutual blackmail, in case the reciprocal code of collaboration is violated. These relationships, in turn, create a tightly knit network, which, as a new independent social factor, influences the social system in which it flourishes. Under the influence of dirty togetherness, each institution, office, factory, or organization serves, regardless of its officially declared aims, as a semiformal network establishing a stable frame of reference for an enormous number of private mutual interests and reciprocal arrangements.

In "socialist" Poland, this phenomenon appears in diverse forms. For example, someone may receive a vacation at a sea resort as reimbursement for a favorable review of another's Ph.D. thesis. In such a situation, the formal legal network, regardless of its incompetence, forms a very precious cover. After a while, individuals operating inside this system may even begin to support the legal matrix in order to secure their own vested interests. In fact, this occurred regularly under "real socialism."

A SOCIAL LIFE BASED ON LEGENDS

Independent of its immediate gains, "sociability" performs a far-reaching function. In addition to its short-term, visible effects, it develops the capacity to create legends and myths. Once a legend is socially established and recognized, it starts to function independently of its carriers, becoming "objective" and impersonal, without the need for constant personal involvement. The legend's primary function is to strengthen a nation's ability to endure adversity, while preserving its identity. This particular form of mythology gained momentum in Poland during the period of partition, between 1795 and 1918.

After 1945, an inertia set in, reinforced both by real socialism's "conscious" strategy of legend building, and by civil society's resistance to this type of socialism. As a result, even a genius who presented and discussed his ideas lost out to a skillful fake lauded by the lobby supporting the myth. A martyr, created through myth, becomes the object of compulsory social adulation and respect. He does not even need to pretend to articulate his desires, wishes, and privileges. Each citizen for whom a martyr made unsolicited sacrifices has a "sacred" duty to repay the martyr for his sufferings. The creator of myths has clean hands. He does not ask for anything; he hesitates, is even reluctant to accept any offerings. Eventually he takes them, once asked, begged, and pressed. He may finally accept these offerings to show allegiance to the "cause."

The well-developed strategy of legend construction works in its simplest form when individuals compete to establish themselves as political, religious, national, or (when fighting against their former allies) revisionist "heroes." A more advanced strategy was developed in the years between 1950 and 1962. One example of this would be a dogmatic apparatchik professor attempting to create a social "halo" around another Party scholar on the tacit understanding that the latter would reciprocate. If a legend is successfully established for an entire collective, all of its members enjoy the honors it brings. Since the market for legends is limited, and the pool of gratification attached to them even more so, each "group of heroes" has a natural tendency to discredit all other hero-pretenders and establish a virtual monopoly.

Under the traditional Polish ethos of "brotherly togetherness," myths were not widely recognized as efficient social-engineering devices; hence legends were only employed on a haphazard, individual basis. In the twentieth century, new social subgroupings emerged and developed this dormant technique in a fairly effective manner. When these subgroups started to use innovative myth building, some who were still immersed in the traditional Polish ethos became envious of these strategies and tried to develop counter-tactics to discredit opponents.

An envy-perpetuating pendulum cycle was thus established. It was linked to another, more general feature: the Poles seem incapable of perceiving social reality *as it is*. They perceive reality according to perspectives furnished by "governors of souls," visionaries, and self-proclaimed leaders. Poles seem unable to recognize social processes as they appear. Instead, they wait for someone to tell them the meaning of what they directly encounter. While members of all societies comprehend social facts largely through the eyes of those who invest these facts with preconceived meanings, the Poles' eagerness to adopt meanings concocted for them has taken on an extreme character.

People have a general tendency to live in individual cages of illusion, subjective ideas, prejudices, and cognitive fabrications that appeal to their insecurities, devotions, and priorities. Yet at the same time, those who live in complex societies tend to adapt to their social environment in a way that is predetermined by various ideological utopias. Traumatic national events, especially the loss of independence in the eighteenth century, forced the Poles, still steeped in national pride for their illustrious past, to escape into the world of fabricated dreams. They were eager to understand and explain their harsh sociopolitical reality through elaborated legends and undeserved sufferings. In part, this approach emanated from the conviction that each grief would be compensated by an equivalent reward.

The dominant Catholic religion greatly contributed to this attitude. It spread passivity, fed by the sweet belief that an intervention "from above" or "from outside" would suddenly interrupt the Polish reality and restore a cherished belief in "brotherly neighborhood." The Poles expected that either Napoleon, God, or the West would drop all other preoccupations and do everything possible to make the Poles happy. John Le Carré exaggerates, but not too much, when he writes, "Colonel Jerzy was a Pole and I have never understood why so many Poles have a soft spot for us. Our repeated betrayals of their country have always seemed to me so disgraceful that if I were Polish, I would spit on every passing British shadow, whether I had suffered under the Nazis or the Russians—the British at the same time having abandoned the poor Poles to both. And I would certainly be tempted to plant a bomb under the so-called 'competent department' of the British Foreign Office'' (Le Carré 1991: 164).

The more pristine and innocent the Poles were, the bigger the reward would be. An unexplained conviction that other influential people had their social obligation was (and is) the foundation of the *Weltanschauung* of the patriotic Pole. Of course, even a Pole has an undisputed duty to offer his life for the "Fatherland," but the causal relation between his heroism and the expected effect (the restoration of Poland) is not a matter for the patriots.

The cumulative experience of the Poles teaches them that they are unable, when relying on their own resources, to achieve anything tangible since they face two neighboring countries, both more powerful in terms of military might, more aggressive in the authoritarian management of their populations (which, however, is a different and, as far as efficiency is concerned, opposite kind), and superior in their material resources. This reality has further reinforced both the Polish tendency to escape into collective dreams, and the common conviction that help has to come from outside. In this respect, the Poles can be compared with other nations involved in desperate struggles for independence.

While legends were generated spontaneously at first, only the most convincing ones were selected and accepted as part of the natural belief system. Once their usefulness—not so much in terms of cognitive illumination as emotional appeal—was recognized, these utopian descriptions of social reality became established as socially accepted patterns of communication. Activities and institutions existing outside the boundaries of these utopias were disregarded. Czeław Miłosz, an *émigré* professor and poet who was virtually unknown (except to a very narrow intellectual élite) and overlooked by scholars, became a deity in Poland after receiving the ennoblement of the Nobel prize. The award thus generated the myth, the myth created the celebrity, and the celebrity produced an internationally known poet. The Polish greed for legend was able to personify another desperately needed poet-hero, at the right historical moment, with the massive help of the Solidarity movement.[33]

THE AUTOTELIC REFERENCE GROUP

The phenomenon of "brotherly brotherhood," as it existed in nobleman's Poland, implied that an unknown type of reference group was functioning (see Merton 1968). This was not a "normative" reference group. Within the boundaries of the brotherhood, the internal order of this group was considered natural, given with blood. Nor was the nobility a comparable reference group. Although some of its members would often try to show their superiority, they did so not to convince others of their higher status, but to indicate that they were able to perform theatrics for themselves.

This unknown reference group was also not a "membership" social group. It was closed; virtually no one could enter it, except by birth. It did not generate the feeling of belonging to an abstract body, to "us" as opposed to "them." From a social point of view (not economic, political, military) "they" did not exist. Belonging was connected to a concrete reference to brother-fellows or to a neighboring community.

It was an *autotelic reference group*, understood as valuable in itself, without regard to any outside criteria. Values from the outside were sometimes accepted or absorbed by this group. Yet the external nature of these values was always detectable. The autotelic values of the nobility were additionally stressed by the fact that this social stratum only accepted values that reinforced its integrity. Although a nobleman (or a noblewoman) cherished such values as fatherland, freedom, equality (within one's own circle), and independence, these values were treated as derivations from the basic values of one's own group, much as democracy was treated by the Athenians.

According to Aleksander Gella, the Polish intelligentsia, which, he maintains, ceased to exist as a social stratum after the Second World War, showed several important features: "(1) agreement of behavior with any professed conviction; (2) the cult of civil courage; (3) social and political nonconformism; (4) respect for the dignity of every man; (5) the moral imperative of solidarity with all people who suffer from wrong" (Gella 1988: 157). He also generalizes that an intelligentsia always emerges when "a group of intellectuals with reformist or revolutionary ideas gathers followers from among educated people who understand their social criticism" (Gella 1988: 163). Had this been true, the intelligentsia would have re-emerged in the Polish national scenery in 1989, before and after the Fall of Nations.

Why did this not happen? It seems that Gella underestimated the strength of Polish civil society, which was able to serve as a niche for the dormant spirit of the Polish intelligentsia.

It appears that the intelligentsia as a social stratum exists now only in historical libraries accumulating data on the second half of the nineteenth century and the beginning of the twentieth. Indeed, the intelligentsia never existed as a social class; it always functioned as the voice of social or political underdogs. The recent resurgence of voices demanding the establishment of a political party that would represent the intelligentsia only strengthens the original point. The traditional intelligentsia would never have articulated its own interests in order to fight for them. This would have been "beneath the dignity" of its members. If remnants of the "intelligentsia" were so molded by the processes of instrumentalization and politicization that they now want to voice certain values, it only shows that the bulldozer of communism was strong enough not only to transform the edifice of traditional forms of democracy and tolerance but also to transform the dignity of the inner self shared by Poles. Thus, instrumentalism was able to destroy the core of the traditional Polish intelligentsia, a phenomenon clearly seen in the recent distaste for nonegoistic activities (made repugnant by real socialism through its compulsory "social work"), the vivid public distaste for élites of all political factions ("political class"), the lack of recognized political leaders (including the traditional governors of souls), the revived cult of the "small establishment" (preferably settled abroad), the almost totally forgotten humanism and lack of grand, inspiring literature (with the exception of work by Jan Józef Szczepański, with his Conradian devotion to the romantic categorical imperative), and the expanding ignorance of both written and oral history. All these elements contribute to the final decline of the traditional intelligentsia. The remnants of it are effectively transformed into its own bastards.

Most social strata tend to be heterotelic in that they are functional, useful for something that exceeds the limits of their own value. Members of the bureaucracy think of ways to promote themselves into decision-making positions. Workers hope to become capitalists. Paradoxically, the Polish nobility lived in a dream world designed to keep them at the center of social life forever.

The traditional Polish intelligentsia has retained the core of this spirit. Gella gives a suggestive summary of certain, not always visible features of the Polish intelligentsia:

The Polish intelligentsia's ardent love of history also reproduced many of the foibles and faults of the former ruling class in the national mentality—impracticality, a deeply rooted disregard for manual work, frivolity, extravagance, overconfidence, conceit, and an exuberant individualism that made it difficult to achieve consensus in hundreds of important matters. Strong individualism coupled with pride and conceit often caused bursts of quarrelsomeness—a remnant of the eighteenth century. Members of the intelligentsia stood at the front of all other class parties—workers, peasants, and bourgeoisie—but they never created their own independent social force. In fact they never fought in the name of their own group interests, at least not formally. (Gella 1989: 158)

When the nobility left the historic scene, it was the traditional intelligentsia who generated respect for the attitude of spectacular principledness, probably the nobility's most striking feature.

THE FACADE-SELF OF THE POLES

In different societies, various types of "I" (self) are composed in different ways. Not only the self's composition but also its elements and structure say something about the society that generated this composition. Society, serving as the framework for interindividual interactions, plays a decisive role in designing the final content of the dominant self. One may distinguish several types of selves. The *instrumental self* can be understood as a given individual's willingness to change his attitudes according to an actual situation. In its purest form, instrumentalism is completely manipulative. In opposition to the instrumental self is the *principled self*, understood as the self that accepts a given norm and disregards all possible and probable by-products of undertaken actions.[34] For this type, nothing eliminates the validity of a rule perceived as unconditionally binding. The *looking-glass self* provides feedback on how others perceive the image of his personality. If this reflection matches its prearranged design, it may or may not lead to rearrangement. The *ideal self* is concerned with an individual's perception of himself as he should be, and not as he is. It offers a comparative personality reference point or a set of values whose achievement is regarded as the highest goal of life. The *real self* (or material self) deals with all biological and technical determinants that influence the life of an individual, the material factors that shape him. The *private self* is the one that is seen exclusively in one's own moments of truth. All one's secrets, private feelings, and most intimate, shameful, and ego-related experiences remain within the core of this self. It is the private self that furnishes the ego with its rudimentary integrity. The *facade self* is understood as the type of self that conveys a predesigned picture to others. It presents to others an intentionally constructed image. Historical and sociological data support the claim that Polish society is especially prone to developing rather exaggerated facade-self images and subsequently treating them as genuine.

In the tradition of the brotherly-neighborhood spirit, matters seem to be socially transparent, and what occurs inside one family is treated as something well known to all "equal" members of the whole community. But this knowledge is artificially tailored. The facade self suits this purpose perfectly. Equality breeds envy, and envy is fed by its very contradiction. A self-performance is designed to convince other people that the actor is, in fact, an exceptional individual who behaves as their equal only through exemplary modesty. A continuous *pas de deux* between non-authentic masks and genuine pretences is carefully arranged to make an impression on others. A common eagerness to use facade images and facade-oriented activities encourages the atmosphere that promotes legends and myths.

This fabulous environment also reinforces the everyday use of facade selves by providing a synchronic feedback. In Polish intellectual circles, appearance is much more important than essence. Therefore, those concerned with the heart of the matter, but deprived of the ability or patience to cultivate social relations, are lost a priori, even if they alone are able to grasp the essence of the matter under investigation. Traditional Polish culture is a culture of gesture.

For the Polish, an alliance of equals creates a level field for understanding the social reality. This alliance is, at least in part, united and inspired by the envy of fellow mediocrities.[35] Yet those skillful enough to overcome this barrier face a much more difficult obstacle—the united front of facade seekers. "Facts" are defined in terms of the facade, whereas the facade is determined by a predesigned legend.

The nobility's facade self has additional, far-reaching consequences. Gesture is more important than the meaning or fruits of concrete action. When individuals attempt to do something, the effect of their work and skill required to undertake the task are overshadowed by the theatrical value of the performance accompanying this activity. The performer's main concern is not the technical requirements of the task at hand or the merits of the work under consideration; rather, it is whether the agent's manner of doing, acting, or performing is impressive enough, and, above all, whether the performer is seen as a good actor.

The facade ethos apparently rests on insecure feelings. The Poles tend to overestimate everything coming from outside, particularly from the West. Praxeology—the science of how to act effectively in an efficient modern society— became attractive in Poland because it offered a chance to overcome this insecurity. In a society where people are mainly interested in the style of their performance, and where the final result is merely a by-product of superficial engagement in the work process, net results are verified clumsily and do not necessarily undergo an efficiency test.

It is interesting to note that "socialism" was largely responsible for rapidly disseminating the category of *subsidiary selves*. When people are deprived of their own selves and identify with the tasks prescribed for them by others, when they are regarded as vessels for an idea, doctrine, or ideology, then they are ready to become Party members, automatons, Communists, and anti-Semites.

FUNDAMENTAL ATTITUDES AND POLISH CIVIL SOCIETY

Closely connected with the facade orientation is the characteristic Polish attitude of *spectacular principledness*. As explained earlier, spectacular principledness refers to an attitude that not only approves of given norms or values for their own sake (regardless of the circumstances) but also celebrates certain norms or values because they are considered sacred and symbolically significant. It is worth noting that spectacular principledness, essentially different from "egoistic" nationalism, is absent from the ordinary, everyday attitudes of Poles. It is reserved for the special moments of national life.

Polish principledness with respect to the Fatherland has almost become a sacred value. Empirical data suggest that spectacular principledness has been maintained in Polish society through the traditional attachment to religion. Historically, this attachment was superficial (the nobility liked the external splendour of Catholic church), but the loss of national independence and, recently, the election of a Pole to the position of pope revitalized deep religious beliefs. Nonetheless, Polish philosophers and religious scholars can claim no conspicuous original achievements (with one possible exception—Kołakowski's underestimated but brilliant mockery of the Bible: Kołakowski 1955).

Historically, the Polish national "psyche" was composed of two souls. One belonged to the Polish nobility and was characterized by strong loyalty to the attitude of spectacular principledness. The second was shaped predominantly by the largest social stratum—the peasantry. The peasantry had been oppressed by higher social strata, Austrian, German, and Russian occupants, and nature. The mutually reinforced pressures of man-made and natural factors contributed to the development of the fiddling attitude of survival. In addition to the attributes described earlier, this meta-attitude is marked by a strong distrust of any type of bureaucracy and of those occupying higher social positions. To trust the bureaucracy means voluntarily entering into a trap set by officials. Self-reliance is an essential ingredient of this attitude. The peasant responses to bureaucratic pressures—self-reliance, extended family ties, hard work, and a planned life perspective—constitute the essence of the fiddling survival orientation.[36]

The ambivalence created by oscillation between the pressures of survival, on the one hand, and the impotence imprinted in the orientation of the facade self towards spectacular principledness, on the other, resulted in a strange phenomenon. A dramatic sense of impotence was reinforced by historical frustrations in the face of partitions of the country, the lost uprisings of the nineteenth century, and the invasion and occupation of a newly resurrected Polish state by German forces between 1939–1945 (when six million people, one-sixth of the entire Polish population, including three million Jewish citizens, were killed).

The sense of impotence was additionally reinforced by the typical all-thumbs orientation of the Poles. Characterized by a mysterious inability to achieve a desired goal, this type of orientation leads, as noted earlier, to a partial realization of a goal, or the generation of certain processes that undermine, or even mock, the goal itself. It also creates side-effects that change the whole task-oriented process into a farce by turning attention to unintended details.

It is essential to remember that Polish society is basically a closed body. It was originally composed of an impenetrable confraternity of equals linked not only by "blood" but also by gossip. Remainders of this stigma are still visible today. "Polish society may be also included among the so-called closed societies. In closed societies, the political center considers itself threatened by both rebellious messages (incompatible with those officially received), and the formation of an independent network of senders and receivers intent on exchanging information. The center's monopoly is thus challenged both as a source and gate-keeper of disseminated information, and as a supervisor of all organized forms of life" (Łukasiewicz 1988: 48).

In a dominant subculture of "gesture" and anti-task orientation, rational action is useless. Gossip, spectacular demonstration, and the highly visible, broken mean-goal paradigm are much more effective. They capture attention, augmented by the sensitivity of the closed social-networking infrastructure. The all-thumbs meta-attitude is therefore more likely to exist on a derivational rather than rudimentary level. It is fair to say that the unexpected contradictions between rational expectations and actual results constitute the most essential feature of the all-thumbs life orientation.

Some studies claim that Polish society was not divided by a generation gap (see mainly Stefan Nowak). According to these empirical inquiries, the values and attitudes of older and younger people were essentially the same. A deeper look, however, showed that this similarity was spurious. It appeared to be a product of the political union between the generation of parents and the generation of children. At the most basic level, these generations were united by a negative evaluation of the existing "socialist" regime, its practices, and its Marxist ideology. The illusion of the "generation agreement" was apparently created by the ban of empirical studies that were directly concerned with political matters.

Despite the "hard" sociological data that maintained that there was no generation gap (for example, see Nowak 1981), the actual distance between generations was quite large. In a Polish family where the father hated his son and the son despised his father, a quiet, cordial supper was impossible to imagine. The wife-mother, in order to avoid a brawl, would provoke a political discussion. A frail familial harmony appeared immediately.

The unforeseen phenomenon of Solidarity showed clearly that the differences between various age groups in terms of behavioral patterns were, in fact, quite significant. This point of view was later reinforced, albeit in a different political configuration, by the new opposition to Lech Wałęsa's centrist politics from a younger, more determined, and more rebellious generation of workers. Generational continuity is, nevertheless, a peculiar problem in Poland. After World War II, there occurred not only a process of "negative selection of individuals" but also a much deeper, more important, and longer-lasting process of *negative selection of generations*, which had been ongoing since the beginning of the eighteenth century. This process was crowned by the appearance of the Marxist power élite after the Second World War.

Those who participated in the partitioning of the country, joining the administrations imposed by Austrians, Germans, and Russians, were repudiated as traitors. They constituted the first rejected wave in the negative process of generational selection. It is well known that the cream (patriotically, intellectually, and ethically speaking) of the Polish male population joined the Napoleonic Wars (1805–1812) in the vain hope of resurrecting the Fatherland. Another generation was engaged in the uprisings of 1830 and 1863. As a consequence, they were decimated by killings, imprisonment, exile to Siberia, and emigration (especially to France).

These events deprived Poland of its most active, promising, and altruistic population. During the First World War, the younger Polish generation was politically divided against itself but nonetheless created its own fighting division, the nucleus of the future Polish army. It also took part in the Silesia uprisings against the Germans and participated in the victorious war against the invading Soviet army (1920). Although applicable, the term "holocaust" has never been used in connection with the annihilation of six million Polish citizens during World War II, nor has it been used to refer to the destruction of a quarter of a million Warsaw citizens during the 1944 uprising.

The extermination of highly motivated Home Army members (predominantly young men and women who were, as a rule, members of the secret "Flying University" and daughters and sons of the Polish intelligentsia) was almost immediately followed (1945–1946) by the cruel annihilation of another segment of the younger generation by the Soviet NKVD[37] (the acronym for People's Commissariat for Internal Affairs—the secret police). Some historians claim that these years witnessed the complete destruction of the traditional intelligentsia as an independent social stratum (Gella 1990). In any case, it cannot be disputed that all these physical and moral waves of destruction repeatedly eliminated the most highly motivated Polish élites from national life.

One of the main, but often unnoticed, reasons for the relative success of Marxism in post-1945 Poland was that it was imposed onto the psyche of the young generation that survived these waves of negative elimination. The interplay between negative selection of generations and the fiddling attitude towards survival aimed at coping with harsh sociopolitical realities was most conducive to the all-thumbs attitude.

In contrast, the instrumental attitude is selective, calculating, and manipulative. Through the subjective evaluation of profits and losses, it accepts only those norms that appear consistent with the attainment of immediate aims. It would be a mistake to think of it as a Machiavellian version of continuous cheating. It can be constructive. As already shown, it may form the basis for carrying out various tasks that go beyond individual interest. This attitude is defined by flexibility, a complete rejection of any form of fundamentalism, and the skill to find proper means to achieve goals that are regarded as important. These characteristics have been supported by empirical research (Podgórecki 1974; 1979; 1987).

It is important to note that the instrumental attitude, spreading rapidly among the Poles (especially the young), is connected to a claim-oriented lifestyle. Claim orientation refers to an incessant pretention to obtain something. It can be understood as an acrobatic disregard of the norms of logic and an attempt to legitimize newly formulated demands. If someone is quiet and does not make "noise," especially in situations of rigorous competition, nobody will notice him. If someone repeatedly presents a claim, then he develops a personality structure through which he might delude himself into believing that he is indeed entitled to what he wants. If someone presents his demands in a serious and well-elaborated manner, his opponents might be more likely to perceive these demands as substantiated by reliable arguments. Therefore, the claimant may never be asked to reveal his credentials. Additionally, if, in the event that a claim is rejected, someone manifests an attitude of righteous indignation, his opponents are then pressured into an uneasy position of guilt. Finally, someone who constantly makes claims is likelier, taking into consideration the frequency of his demands, to receive something on a purely statistical basis.

It is clear that the claim-oriented lifestyle is a natural product of the fiddling attitude towards survival. In order to survive, one often has to "make waves" and mobilize all possible resources to obtain the goods that allow one to operate at a subsistence level. Some criminologists maintain that the "lower classes," especially the youth, are characterized by spontaneity, emotional expressiveness, short-term hedonism, physical aggressiveness, and, above all, the desire for instant gratification. These classes are not prepared to defer satisfaction under the pressure of everyday needs and poverty. They are not oriented towards the extended, rationally planned future; rather, they are guided by the principle of immediate consumption (Cohen 1955). These stereotypes, which are not necessarily correct as descriptions of the working-class subculture, coincide well with the claim-oriented lifestyle of Poles who were "socialized" under real socialism. A difference exists, however, in that the claim-oriented lifestyle of Poles run through all social layers, whereas the subculture of instant gratification characterizes only the youth of the working class. In Western societies that are influenced by welfare-state social arrangements, this difference tends to be blurred since a prolonged dependency on state support results in the development of similar lifestyle attitudes.

The claim-oriented attitude is one of the special consequences of a socialist habitat. Socialist regimes, lacking in goods and services, stuff their populations with the belief that they have the right to several important entitlements. The propaganda-socialization process becomes effective because representatives of these societies, although they do not actually receive the promised goods and services, acquire the conviction that they are entitled to them.

It is difficult to find traces of this life orientation in the ethos of the nobility or in the ethos of the hard-working peasantry. It is also characteristic that not only the Poles but other societies that are products of socialist "breeding" manifest the claim-oriented attitude. This lifestyle was also characteristic of the Spaniards who stayed in the Soviet Union after the war in 1936, and of the Jews who recently left the Soviet Union to go to Israel or the United States.

Polish Civil Society

Polish society serves as an unexplored and peculiar example of civil society. The fact that it was deprived of its own state for a century and a half is pregnant with many important consequences. First, the attitude of the average citizen towards the law has been, on the whole, negative. The law and the legal system have been treated as an alien imposition. Citizens have been disinclined to feel any loyalty towards foreign legal structures. In fact, they have felt the reverse. Viewed as an imposed, oppressive force, the state was the enemy. Consequently, all of its administrative organs were considered to be elements of an organized extortion. As a rule, cooperation with these organs was seen as national treason. Abuse of the law was perceived as a patriotic virtue rather than illegitimate behavior. (This highly skeptical, if not hostile, attitude towards the law was restricted mainly to the constitutional, administrative, and, in some of its aspects, criminal legal system.) Thus, survival under the heavy burden of continuous foreign occupation had a fiddling character: all tricks that outfoxed the law and its apparatus were regarded as patriotic achievements.

Second, if the law and the state were alienated from society, mutual help, reciprocity, and community support had to flourish. This was not restricted to economic matters; indeed, culture was the prime target of these activities. The countryside estates of the gentry, despite the threat of heavy penalties, became centers of education and medical help. There, Poles were taught how to deal with the punishing hand of the state bureaucracy. Together with the Church, these centers attempted to maintain Polish habits.

Third, young people were socialized to put the interests of the oppressed nation above their own personal goals, thus elevating patriotism to a virtue of the highest order. The political, social, economic, and educational institutions of the occupiers (Austrians, Germans, and Russians) were regarded as alien, if not poisonous. Rules that existed in the occupiers' countries were not only treated as non-obligations; quite often they were turned against the occupiers. The Poles tried to manipulate the occupiers' blindness to their own advantage in order to compensate for the harm being done to their nation.

Fourth, women played an unusual role. They were not only romantic companions but also, and more importantly, the sacred centers of family life. They were hard-working "oxen" and patriotic missionaries as well.[38] While men were fighting, or in hiding, or missing, the burden of raising children, maintaining the household, and maintaining links with existing patriotic organizations fell into the hands of mothers (matrons). There emerged a particular image of the Polish woman-patriot. Interestingly enough, a special cult of the Virgin Mary—referred to in Poland as the Godly Mother—was developed. This cult evidently (but also latently) served to reinforce the strength of overburdened women. One wonders why feminism as a social movement was not originally developed in Poland. Nonetheless, it is worth mentioning that shortly after World War II a book was published in Poland that contained all the essential ideas of feminism (Schanter 1947).

Fifth, the rejection of official law pushed people to rely on their own laws—to rely on intuitive (living, unwritten, or natural) laws. Intuitive law thus became the foundation for all types of private associations. Few of these associations were perceived as contradictory to official goals or officially declared programs. They were established only as extensions of the mutually binding, informal infrastructure of intuitive law.

Sixth, the culture of "gesture" was a reminder that the existing legal and political cage would not allow the creation of anything stable and tangible; nothing that could house the hidden community forces. The culture of "gesture" served as a constant reminder that the most important social problems, independence and freedom, should always be at the center of national attention. To some extent it was also an ennoblement of the accumulated Polish stupidity whereby one tried to solve complicated problems by means of a simple "noble" gesture.

Seventh, since the centers of official leadership were not regarded as legitimate, informal circles of power became especially significant. They saw themselves as "governors of souls." Poets, writers, and even daydreamers pretended that they had the power to interpret events, forecast the future, and uphold the national spirit. There is a strong similarity here with the attitude of Irish Catholic writers. Although all governors of souls competed with each other for dignity and power, they did so in the name of the supreme mission—national salvation.

Eighth, all these features were generated during the long, dark period of lost national independence. Nevertheless, it is striking how fast they re-emerged during the post-1945 period, when the state was an alien idea (Marxism) for the overwhelming majority of society.

Polish civil society manifested itself in the spontaneous creation of the Solidarity movement in 1980–1981. This movement was characterized by the following features: (1) a mounting, daily criticism of Marxist ideology and the inherent corruption of a state guided by this ideology; (2) a tendency to reinstate trust in a social fabric eroded by the phenomenon of "dirty togetherness"; (3) a counteraction against the dominant climate of social instrumentality through the reinforcement of social principledness within various patriotic and religious bodies; (4) the rejection of fear and self-censorship generated by the excesses of the Stalinist period and sustained through repression in subsequent years; (5) a reincarnation of the traditional intelligentsia's "missionary posture" towards those who were economically and politically repressed; (6) a repudiation of the antinomy between workers and intelligentsia, and between older and younger generations (all these social strata became united in a common front against the imposed process of autopoiesis [auto-reincarnation] of the Party); and (7) a strong desire, consistent with Polish historical tradition, to spread Solidarity's ideas to all societies built on similar ideological principles.

The New Middle Class

The instrumental orientation is also visible among recently generated concepts that attempt to explain modern Polish society. The new middle class embraces two social groupings: highly qualified workers and the "new intelligentsia." Qualified workers are those who have some experience in lower-level management and possess higher technical qualifications, although they still perform manual work. The second element, the intelligentsia, is more complicated in terms of its social structure.

The traditional Polish intelligentsia is not included as part of the new middle class because as a group—with its mission to work for the whole nation, sacrifice itself, educate peasants and workers, and regain national independence, coupled with its heavy losses during World War II and large-scale emigration—it had lost its former dominant sociopolitical position (Gella 1989). It also lost ground among the younger generation when the newly created state, utilizing the power of totalitarian mass media, tried to convince its population that the country would become a paradise for those who had previously been exploited.

With the emphasis on massive industrialization, a new social stratum emerged: the technical and executive intelligentsia (see Konrad and Szelenyi 1979). This new stratum absorbed the "half" intelligentsia and its affiliate, the "string" (*szpagatowa*) intelligentsia, a sort of petty bourgeoisie, claiming to belong to the intelligentsia. Eventually, administrative technocrats and technical workers were united through their instrumental attitudes and systematically began to strengthen the widespread conviction that real socialism was an economic and social failure. This new class possessed the administrative skills and sociotechnical abilities to make independent social diagnoses. It replaced the Jewish middle stratum that had perished during World War II, as well as some meager groupings of the Polish bourgeoisie. Finally, an alliance that linked newcomers to the traditional intelligentsia was decisive in creating the Solidarity movement.

The Alienated Subsociety

Leon Petrażycki categorized societies into complementary or disparate organizations (Petrażycki 1936: 6–7). Societies belonging to the first category are able to cooperate socially on several levels. Disparate societies are so culturally alien that all attempts at mutual cooperation end in conflicts that are difficult to solve. It is also possible to extend this classification to the relations between various segments of the same society.[39]

According to Petrażycki, there are two types of basic activities within human societies: (1) those based on behavior of a physico-technical character (cultivating the soil, breeding cattle, making handicrafts), and (2) those based on behavior of a psycho-juridical character (legal activities, merchandizing, credit transactions, management). These activities can be further divided into (a) routine activities (stock breeding, grain cultivation, traditional handicraft production—all the activities that are inherited from forefathers and involve the application of customs and routines) and (b) innovative activities. Petrażycki did not, however, outline the possibility of a complementary-disparate society or such segments within a society.

The Jewish population in Poland, before its annihilation in World War II, played the underestimated role of a complementary-disparate segment of the society. It specialized in psycho-juridical and innovative behavior. The Jewish people were quite an important element in Polish society. Their community was once the largest in the world. As Norman Davies claims, "In the centuries preceding the partitions, the Polish-Lithuanian Republic had progressively attracted to itself the largest Jewish community in Europe. The Jewish state multiplied faster than any other group . . . until the great Exodus to America reached its height, [Poland] contained four-fifths of world Jewry" (Davies 1981, vol 2: 240).

A center of refuge was established in Poland because of the country's religious and political tolerance. The Jewish population was divided into several subcommunities and had limited, but separate, self-governance. The specificity of this population was based precisely on the fact that it was both complementary and disparate. Some of its representatives, as a result of the Jewish devotion to learning, entered mainstream Polish society by serving in various lucrative and socially influential positions as lawyers, physicians, professors, or bankers.

The Jewish community was disparate not only because of the problem of language. Assimilation into the Polish environment was a slow and negatively evaluated process. For Jews, any personal association with the Poles amounted to cultural and religious treason committed for opportunistic reasons alone. Nobel laureate Isaac Bashevis Singer, a Polish citizen before the Second World War, demonstrated this clearly in his sociologically revealing novels. The notion was rooted in a sense of incredulity, combined with indignation: how could anyone disregard five thousand years of Jewish culture and associate himself instead with the "primitive," self-contained culture of the Poles? Paradoxically, the Jews, usually better-off families assimilated to Polish culture, remained in voluntary self-contained ghettos.[40]

Poles had their reservations too. The Polish intelligentsia, which shaped Polish culture in the nineteenth and twentieth centuries, justified its apprehension towards the perceived invasion of foreign elements in two ways: (a) its members believed that only they were able to serve as defenders of the subjugated state, and (b) as a "declassed" stratum—a great number were forcibly uprooted from their rural estates and moved to the cities—the intelligentsia felt that it had to defend itself against any further inroads on their status. The Polish intelligentsia's anti-Semitism was, however, of a peculiar character, and it can only be understood in its actual historical context. It might be useful to recall that before World War II, Polish Jews (Jews with Polish citizenship) could be divided into five distinct groups. They were:

(1) a camp of Orthodox Jewry, with a traditional identity based on religion, a strong tendency toward voluntarily maintained isolation from the non-Jewish society, and a ghetto-centered pattern of social life; (2) the assimilationists, with a program of assimilating Jews into a general society, possibly with a complementary retention of some selected Jewish traits; (3) the Zionists, from far left to far right, who rejected the world of the ghetto and who projected Jewish national rebirth in *Eretz Israel* (the Land of Israel); (4) the Jewish Socialists (the Bund), who rejected the ghetto world of the Orthodox, the Zionist project, and capitalist society and who formulated a program for civil equality, socialism, and a secular, *Yiddish*-based Jewish cultural autonomy; and (5) the Jewish Communists, those Jews who joined the Communist project of total upheaval of the existing society and its millennarian reformation. (Schatz 1991: 338)

Polish anti-Semitism and Jewish anti-Polishness have been differently shaped towards, and by, these groups. Apart from some assimilated Jews, these who remained in Poland after World War II and several emigrations to Israel were mainly the Jewish Communists. As fierce internationalists, they entered into direct ideological conflict with Polish national patriotism.

This historic conflict had several additional dimensions. First, as already mentioned, Poland had accepted Jewish people from all over Europe and had its own interest in them. Second, in the absence of a developed indigenous middle class, the Jews were able to assume many functions of the *petite bourgeoisie* (the Polish nobility regarded trade occupations as unworthy of their children, and their example spread to other social strata). Third, the Jewish population suffered in the eighteenth and nineteenth centuries, together with the Poles, the harshness of the partitions that exposed them to the occupants' "divide and conquer" policies. As a result, the Jews' frustration with the occupants was, in part, transferred to their Polish neighbors, sometimes in more or less hidden anti-Polish attitudes. Fourth, while the Jewish population benefitted from the traditional Polish tolerance, it felt only peripherally connected to the mainstream of Polish cultural life and did not necessarily feel deeply responsible for the fate of society and state. Fifth, the Jews became very sensitive to the defense mechanisms of the Polish intelligentsia. It was not so much political and economic rejection that alienated them as the fact that this rejection was expressed in the form of gossip, a joke, or painful personal comments. Indeed, in the short run, this type of abuse was much more painful than more "objective" or impersonal "rational" political or economic measures would have been. This attitude lay the ground for future generalizations about Polish anti-Semitism. Sixth, during World War II, German "social engineers" located main liquidation camps in Poland. This appeared to have a lasting propaganda effect. Few remember German "rational planning" (setting up camps where the largest Jewish population lived), but almost everyone associates Jewish tragedy with the place where it happened. Seventh, it might be interesting to note that, after World War II, a small percentage of the remaining Jewish population became the target of anti-Jewish feelings. These feelings were evoked in part by Jewish Communist sympathizers' warm acceptance of the invading Soviet forces in 1939, and by the eager welcome festivities put on by part of the Jewish population for the puppet government (hated by the Poles) imposed by the Soviet authorities in 1945. Apparently, that same part of the Jewish population opposed the Polish defensive war against the Soviets in 1920. "In the CPP [Communist Party of Poland], we have had a high percentage of Jewish intelligentsia. Thus, suspecting the old CPP of being anti-Semitic was a lie. With Jewish comrades, we have been linked by mutual tasks, to stay in jails," said Wiktor Kłosiewicz, one of the leading Polish Communists (in Torańska 1985: 183).

Tragic Polish anti-Semitism had (and still has) one essential element that has yet to be fully recognized. After World War II, important segments of the Jewish intelligentsia "invaded" areas traditionally occupied by the old Polish intelligentsia. Many people of Jewish origin entered into academia, the mass media, culture, art, and other bastions of traditional Polish life. While Polish culture was oriented towards the cultivation of societal life and did not accentuate the role of the intellect and education (at least not until the eighteenth century, when it became an efficient weapon against the occupiers), the Jewish population placed a high value on scholarship and intelligence. This development might have led to complementary cooperation. Yet after World War II, it took a different turn. Poles of Jewish origin not only became quite successful in Polish cultural life but a high percentage lent support to the new, Soviet-imposed regime. "Yet, quite a sizeable group of those [Jews] who arrived from the Soviet Union played an important, and not very credible, role in the Stalinist power apparatus, mainly in the party and the political police. Among them were also fanatical orthodox

Communists who conducted the Stalinist 'witch hunts' with special eagerness'' (Szczypiórski 1982: 76).

Regarded as the best-known specialist of Polish history after World War II, Krystyna Kersten quotes, and accepts, an analysis by Abel Kainer (apparently a pseudonym): "The symbol of the role of Jews, during the first years after 1945, was, in the eyes of the general public, a Jewish security agent. Indeed, the highest echelons of the Ministry of Public Security, under Bierut and Gomulka, were occupied by Jews or those of Jewish origin'' (Kersten 1986: 174). Elsewhere, the same author presents an opposite point of view. "The mythologized participation of Jews in the thrusting upon Poland of an alien political system was used to set up an alibi for prejudice or even hostility leading sometimes to criminal acts'' (Kersten 1992: 8). And also: "Anyway, upon looking at this matter, it is clear that the legend about the symbiosis of Jews and Communist power is only a legend'' (Kersten 1992: 84). It seems clear that in this respect the Polish People's Republic followed its Soviet masters. But perhaps, as Lipski notes, "it is a Machiavellian recommendation elaborated at the Moscow center. It says that minorities serve that function most effectively (compare the role of Poles, Jews, and Latvians in NKVD) and, when practical, may be used as convenient scapegoats'' (Lipski 1992: 157). According to Leonard Schapiro (1961: 165),

Jews abounded at the lower levels of the party machinery—especially, in the *Cheka*, and its successors, the GPU, the OGPU and the NKVD. (In the issue of *Pravda* on December 20, 1937, there is a list of 407 officials of the NKVD, decorated on the occasion of the twentieth anniversary of the *Cheka*. Forty two of the names, or about eleven percent, are Jews, and the actual total of Jews may well have been higher, since many of them may be supposed to have adopted Russian names. How many of these Jews survived the purge of 1938 is another matter).

After World War II, despite the well-known tragedy of the Holocaust, this situation provoked the re-emergence of the traditional antagonism of the Polish nobility. This time, it targeted not Jews but "outsiders." The antagonism was deepened not only because the Marxists used the people of Jewish origin in imposing an ill-conceived sociopolitical system on Polish social reality but also because, in doing so, they surpassed the effectiveness of many ethnic Poles. It became evident that they outclassed the new breed of Polish Communists. If indeed this was the case, the previously empty engine of envy found fuel with which to revitalize itself. But before something definite can be said in this complicated area of sociopolitical reality, a well-balanced sociological study should be conducted.

Indeed, the complexities of the relationship between Jews and Poles still awaits adequate, impartial, and comprehensive inquiry. Jaff Schatz recently conducted a penetrating and competent study of the generation of Polish-Jewish Communists, those who "were born around 1910. . . . [and] joined the Communist movement at the end of the 1920s and in the beginning of the 1930s" (Schatz 1991: 3). Schatz regards them as "the last genuine millennialists of their kind, or, as they would prefer to say, the last true Communists." Again, it is characteristic that this generation, alienated from Polish culture, would say of itself that those who *"Mir hobn gevigt a toyt kind"*—"We had dandled a dead baby," or *"Mir hobn getanzt oyf a fremde hasene"*—"we have been dancing at a stranger's wedding" (Schatz 1991:322, 312, 314). These remarks may be true of some of the pre-war Polish-Jewish Communists who were motivated by ideas of social justice and messianism—justice for all, but they would be misleading if attributed to the Polish-Jewish Communists who became prominent during the period of real socialism. The lack of clear distinction between these two generations of Jews is fallacious. The post-war generation of Polish-Jewish Communists certainly did not identify itself with alien "dead babies" and was dancing indeed during the strangers' period of mourning, as the majority of the Polish population viewed the totalitarian sovietization of Poland. To be correct one should speak about two distinct, if not opposite, generations of Jews who lived in Poland after the Second World War.

The State and the Society

The situation under real socialism in the late 1980s was peculiar. The classical claim that the economy determines politics is, in reality, much more complicated. Indeed, the economy shapes the current political situation, but the economy has been politically constructed in line with Marxist ideological directives. Thus, during the period of real socialism, in the last instance politics played the role of determinant (of social and economic structures). Those who actually had power belonged to the élite center that shaped politics according to its interests (and the interests of a higher-ranking élite center—the Soviet one). At times these decision makers have been called the "owners" of Poland. In reality, their domestic interests and those of the Soviet party élite shaped, through an oversized apparatus, the underlying economy. They thus created a situation directly opposed to that described in the theory of workers'-interest representation.

This dominance was additionally reinforced by the fact that relations between various populations in countries of real socialism have been highly restricted. People depended on the position of their respective state within the Soviet bloc and its economic and military organizations. Even after the "Fall of Nations" in 1989, regardless of their position, these countries were unable to establish direct relations between their populations. They communicated only through channels controlled by their own power centers, which, in the case of subordinate states, were in turn controlled by the élites of the dominant state. This situation was interestingly commented upon by Johann Galtung (Galtung 1971). The old idea of Marx, that "workers of all countries" should unite, had thus been transformed into a theatrical farce: they may indeed unite, if they have permission from the bureaucrats who control them. This generalization, however, held true for the Soviet camp until the late 1970s. Currently, under the impact of the Solidarity ideology (Podgórecki 1987b) and the influence of the "second economy" (Łoś 1990), workers seem to be gaining some autonomy from the monolithic Communist state, and some incipient forms of international solidarity have been initiated.

GENERAL REMARKS

The first remark related to these considerations is that the analysis of human behavior with respect to a whole society should be undertaken on three levels. On the first level, activities specific to a given society must be investigated. This inquiry singles out specific patterns of behavior generated by Polish society in its historical development. It has thus been possible to identify several general attitudes or meta-attitudes characteristic of the Poles; yet they are not necessarily exclusive to them. It is the configuration of these attitudes that is unique for the Poles.

On the second level, categories of behavior that are specific to whole blocs or families of societies must be considered. Some patterns of behavior, such as a claim-oriented lifestyle, have been specified as peculiar to the whole camp of socialist countries. An additional study should be conducted to find out whether this type of orientation is also specific to those living in developing countries.

On the third level, certain activities that are common to all living human beings must be studied, irrespective of the type of culture and civilization in which they live.

The second remark is that modern, or post-modern, times are prone to very rapid social change: not only does technological life undergo rapid and fundamental transformations but, in a relatively short span of one or two generations, the dominant features of the lifestyle of a given society may change dramatically. New patterns may emerge, and others may disappear. (The dramatic rise of a new, instrumental social class has ensured the continuing development of the principled character of the Polish post-nobility culture, shaped through many centuries by the ethos of the intelligentsia.)

The third remark is that in studying a society as an integral entity, a researcher should not be deluded by current trends, perceptions of fluid characteristics, changeable public fashions, and fluctuations in opinion. The researcher should instead enter profoundly enough into social reality to seize the underlying characteristics that result from a long process of historical development. These well-established tendencies appear to be more durable than the conspicuous, but whimsical, epiphenomena targeted by most researchers.

Finally, sociology really translates into a study of humankind. Yet to study humankind in its totality, one must begin by studying those societies that have established themselves as separate sociohistorical entities and search for features that constitute their uniqueness.

5

Messianic Destiny and Inflammatory Revolution (1989–1990)

VARIOUS UNDERSTANDINGS OF THE INTELLIGENTSIA

The problem of understanding the ethos of the intelligentsia is directly connected with the hybrid nature of this social stratum. To be adequately described, this unique social category requires not only new special diagnostic notions but also a peculiar elucidation of the values that characterize it.

Although the spirit of Solidarity is usually derived from the worker's subculture, a closer look at the Polish case reveals that this spirit is instead linked to the ethos of the intelligentsia. It thus makes sense to examine the essence of this group.

According to Gella, various social strata are connected with the concept of intelligentsia. In the "classical" historical understanding, the intelligentsia is a stratum that was established in the nineteenth century in Russia and Poland and continued to exist in Poland until 1945. A second understanding links the Polish intelligentsia with its counterpart social groupings in Hungary and Czechoslovakia during the interwar period. Perhaps the most controversial view is that of a better-educated and humanist-oriented middle class of the West, which, together with professional intellectuals, regards itself as the intelligentsia. Another, clearly misleading understanding perceives this stratum as consisting of those who regard themselves as the working intelligentsia in so-called socialist countries. By a further conception, the intelligentsia are the often European-educated members of the social strata in African and Asian nations that compete for leadership with the native bourgeoisie. Or it might be the incipient groups of dissidents (and sometimes even "revolutionaries") who appeared in affluent societies after World War II. Finally, the intelligentsia can be taken to mean those small groups of dissidents in Eastern Europe that not only challenged the totalitarian establishment but also closely resemble the classical intelligentsia of the nineteenth century (Gella 1976: 23).

Misconceptions connected with the unique sociological notion of intelligentsia are disseminated by historians and sociologists alike. Prominent Polish historian Stefan Kieniewicz proclaimed, "To begin, and to avoid any misunderstandings, I would like to present a definition. . . . I shall use 'intelligentsia' to indicate the social stratum that lives by its own mental work" (Kieniewicz 1982: 13). The well-known works of George Konrad and Ivan Szelenyi (which were useful to them in their own attempt to reject Marxist jargon and ideas) spread similar misconceptions. They say, "It was Gramsci who quite properly drew from the work of Marx and Lukacs the conclusion that every social class needs its own intelligentsia to shape its ideology, and that intellectuals must choose which class they are going to become an organic part of" (Konrad, Szelenyi 1979: 5). Without empirical data, they maintain that the intelligentsia is nothing more than a newly created stratum of administrators and technocrats hired to work for the Communist regime. It is difficult to find a more misleading concept.

These definitions not only blur the distinction between intellectuals and clerks (who support themselves through their own mental capacities) but also completely miss a particular feature which is unique to the intelligentsia.

Berlin's and Gella's Potent Understandings of Intelligentsia

The best description of intelligentsia comes from a letter of March 28, 1978, that Isaiah Berlin addressed to me. His understanding of the intelligentsia was situated in an elaborated historical framework.

Thank you for sending me a copy of *Oficyna Poetów* with your article on the intelligentsia, which I read with great interest and attention, and, in particular, of course, the note in which you refer to my attribution of intelligentsia. You may well be right, and, in consequence, I may be mistaken; but I am not clear about why you think this. I think that my concept of the intelligentsia is perhaps somewhat different from that which you indicate in your article. The fact that it refers to writers, artists, thinkers, academics, intellectuals of various kinds, critics of society, is far wider than the group to which I wish to refer. In your sense of the word, it goes back to the French philosophers in the eighteenth century, to the German *Aufklärer*, perhaps to the libertine skeptics in France in the seventeenth century, perhaps even to the humanists of the Renaissance. I wish to speak of something more specific and narrow: *a self-conscious group of thinkers who see themselves as directly opposed to an oppressive and irrational regime, united not only by opposition to it, but by a belief in, and a deep respect for, the methods of natural sciences, the dedication to such values as civil and personal freedom, personal integrity and the pursuit of truth no matter what the consequences—and therefore in opposition to the established government, established churches, tradition, prescription, reliance upon uncriticized intuitions, and irrationality of every kind.*

In this sense, to take the English, neither Dickens, nor Carlyle, nor Ruskin alone can be regarded as members of the intelligentsia. Besides which, in England the very notion of intelligentsia is thin and unconvincing, inasmuch as there has not been a modern, powerful, clerical establishment to be attacked, nor an arbitrary government, at least not in the nineteenth century. In Russia, neither Gogol, nor Dostoevski, nor Tolstoy, nor even Chekhov would have thought of themselves as members of the intelligentsia— Tolstoy is very hostile to it, the same applies to the nationalist school of Russian composers and painters—but the term, in my sense, does apply to countless doctors, schoolmasters, agricultural experts, and economists, who regarded themselves as disciples of the central oppositional Fronde, on which they looked as leading in the war against obscurantism, despotism, bureaucratic rule, and philistinism. I do not know if Poles used this word before the Russians—I should be very interested to know whether they did—I had always assumed that it was used by someone in Russia in the 1860s, whether Boborykin (to whom it is usually attributed) or someone before him. I do not believe, for example, that a Polish poet like Mickiewicz would have identified himself with a group of this type, no more than would his contemporaries, Silvio Pellico, Byron, Pushkin, or the Decembrist poets—they may have fought against despotism, but they were not committed to the idealisation of natural sciences and scientists, nor to a faith in material progress. The major values of the eighteenth-century Enlightenment certainly formed a sine qua non of the Russian intelligentsia in the sense in which I wish to speak of them.

My intelligentsia had a powerful sense of internal loyalties, in terms of how they could regard men like Katkow, and even at times Turgenev, as traitors or backsliders, and Slavophiles, however intelligent, intellectual, pure-hearted, brilliant, and influential, would not be regarded as members of this movement.

If it is not a Russian phenomenon or Russian word, I should like to be corrected.[41]
[Emphasis added]

Gella proposed a short definition that captures very well the requirements of Berlin's exposition. He said, "The old intelligentsia was a culturally united, though not homogeneous, social stratum of educated people, characterised by a charismatic sense of calling and a certain set of values and manners" (Gella 1988: 132–33). Berlin's description and Gella's definition stress the *missionary* attitude that was common to both the Polish and Russian intelligentsia. The Polish intelligentsia also stressed the essential prerequisite of manners. In Poland, a member of the intelligentsia had not only to be motivated by a desire to help his country (and all other countries that had been oppressed) but also to behave in a certain ritualistic manner.

It is quite easy to show the possibilities indicated by Gella's definition. One could ask a naive, or perhaps in fact an artful, question: were Hitler or Stalin themselves members of the intelligentsia? The question is not an easy one, since one can argue subjectively that both Hitler and Stalin wanted to devote themselves to the improvement of German, Soviet, or international society. If the missionary component is regarded as decisive, the answer would be "yes." Fortunately, Jozef Chałasiński and then Gella both stress the feature of *manners*. From this point of view, and in accordance with prevalent intuitions, neither Hitler nor Stalin could be regarded as members of the intelligentsia because they would never have been socially accepted by any judge of etiquette. Although an insistence on the criterion of manners may be regarded as much less significant, it is cognitively useful.

As Chałasiński indicated, an emphasis on manners was introduced by the disinherited nobility in defense against the possible influx of others who did not belong to the same social stratum. In his classical work on the normative profile of the pre-war Polish intelligentsia (whom he regarded as the general "procreator" of the Polish societal ethos), Chałasiński outlined the following characteristics.[42] (1) An essential feature of the intelligentsia was its fear of being further declassed (the already downgraded gentry, uprooted from its land, feared further downgrading). (2) The code of correct behavior constituted a barrier separating the intelligentsia from the lower strata, thus safeguarding its shaky social position. (3) The intelligentsia had a feeling of superiority that was only spuriously derived. Therefore, it was concerned with its so-called "good" reputation, and with social respect. (4) The intelligentsia was characterized by its own ghetto subculture ("The ghetto does not like outstanding individuality: the ghetto is especially negative towards young talented people"). (5) The intelligentsia elevated non-productivity to the status of virtue; it was also oriented towards consumption and dependent upon those in authority. (6) Although the intelligentsia should be considered the main creator of Polish culture, it was basically an amateur creator.[43] (7) The educational achievements of the intelligentsia were largely decorative (Chałasiński 1946: 37–950).

The value of Chałasiński's analysis is primarily historical, not so much because of rapid social changes as because of the devastating impact of real socialism. Societal barriers (questions such as whom one invites to one's home, whom one invites to a private party, with whom one goes on vacation) seem to be the last trenches still (frantically) defended by the intelligentsia.

THE INTELLIGENTSIA IN SOCIALISM

A Polish economist recently said, "After the [Second World] War in our country, the influence of the intelligentsia steadily declined. This situation was generated by several causes; I am going to mention some of them. The Polish intelligentsia existing between the wars was decimated[44] by Nazis and Bolsheviks, and a considerable part of it was dispersed throughout many continents. The continuity of its culture was brutally disrupted; the processes of translocating various segments of society on higher social ladders were not supported by the reinforcement of proper patterns of social behavior" (Steczkowski 1991:9)

Not only was the intelligentsia brutally oppressed; its very concept was modified. Under the influence of Communist government, and with the support of highly placed sociologists like Jan Szczepański, this social stratum was officially redefined so as to be seen through the prism of officially accepted Marxist ideology (Szczepański 1959). Marxist ideology recognized the working class, the peasant class, and the "working intelligentsia." Contrary to these cognitive restrictions, the true character of the intelligentsia contradicted the official understanding. Thus, according to Kwaśniewicz,

there is the study carried out under the supervision of S. Widerszpil [an official Marxist] in 1989 . . . it concentrated, among other things, on the hierarchy of values connected with various spheres of activity (power, prosperity, creative work, altruism). Each type of value can be regarded as a determinant in the way of looking at the intelligentsia. Thus, the dominant type of orientation directed towards creativity, knowledge and innovativeness (the "Appollonian" orientation) was represented by 33.3 percent of the respondents. The next in hierarchy was the orientation towards material well-being, consumption and comfort (the "Dionysian" orientation)—24.3 percent. These orientations can be regarded as being compatible with the interests of the intelligentsia as a professional group. But his study points out the existence of an orientation towards altruism and empathy (the "Promethean" orientation—25.9 percent) which may indicate the intelligentsia's readiness to undertake activity for the sake of society. The remaining types of orientation were rare: orientation towards power, domination and recognition ("Herculean")—2.1 percent—and towards self-knowledge and self-development ("Socratic")—5.3 percent. (Kwaśniewicz 1989: 222–23)

The fact that the Promethean orientation was held in such high regard means that the historical legacy of the intelligentsia still left its mark on the spirit of Polish society, despite the systematically implemented devastation wrought by the Asiatic-Soviet mode of life and thinking.

It is important to remember that the missionary (Promethean) attitude of the Polish intelligentsia during the Solidarity period "infiltrated" the minds of Polish workers quite deeply. In September 1980, members of the Solidarity movement in Gdańsk sent the following message (quoted in Ruane 1982:232) to workers in other 'socialist' countries:

The delegates assembled in Gdansk at the first congress of the independent self-governing trade unions, Solidarity, send the workers of Albania, Bulgaria, Czechoslovakia, the GDR [German Democratic Republic], Rumania, Hungary and all nations of the Soviet Union greetings and expressions of support. As the first independent trade union in post-war history, we are profoundly aware of the fact that we share the same destiny. We assure you that, in spite of the lies disseminated in your countries, we are a genuine, ten-million-strong representative body of workers, created as a result of workers' strikes. *Our goal is to struggle to improve the life of all working people. We support those of you who have decided to embark on the difficult path of struggle for a free trade union movement.* We believe that it will not be long now before your representatives and ours are able to meet in order to exchange experiences as trade unionists as formulated by Tadeusz Diem. [Emphasis added]

This clearly reveals that the missionary attitude was not altogether extinct. Earlier, the Polish nobility had fought to help others. The watchword then was, "For our freedom and yours!" Recently, Polish workers repeated the same idea.

THE INTELLIGENTSIA AND ITS SUBCATEGORIES

It should be noted that, under real socialism, the concept of intelligentsia was manipulated into different meanings and variations. Some spoke of a "creative" intelligentsia, others of a "half" intelligentsia or "provincial" intelligentsia, "string" intelligentsia, "first generation" intelligentsia, and "traditional" (*tradycyjna*) or old intelligentsia.

The concept of creative intelligentsia was similar to that of the working intelligentsia. From the Marxist point of view, this was a subcategory that was professionally and educationally equipped to serve the dominant ideology. It assembled talents that were willing (not eager) to contribute to the development of the ruling culture. Thus, the term creative intelligentsia would encompass writers, poets, composers, sculptors, professors developing their disciplines, painters, and all those who generate new ideas that contribute to the officially binding Marxist culture.

Half intelligentsia referred to those who pretended to be members of the intelligentsia, but who were neither intellectually nor psychologically equipped for it. This label was representative not so much of the socially oriented drive to obtain a certain social position as the psychological facade that was intended to place someone in social circles evidently inappropriate to them.

First-generation intelligentsia described those who pretended to belong but who were not eligible for membership—not for lack of intellectual or artistic abilities (in fact some of them were extraordinarily creative), but for lack of manners (and appropriate social background). Behind the label was an assumption that one had to be at least two generations away from one's humble social origins to acquire appropriate manners. Manners were a vestige of the intelligentsia's origin in the nobility, and they were a sui generis defense mechanism used by the intelligentsia against the invasion of upstarts.

String intelligentsia referred to a variation of the same security tactics. It was a humiliating label for those who had no proper portfolio in which to carry their belongings and had to wrap them instead in paper and string.

Why was the intelligentsia so defensive and suspicious of outsiders? To begin with, it still celebrated the past ethos of the nobility. It was also deeply influenced by its unique missionary spirit—only members of intelligentsia could properly respond to a spiritual, political, or social calling. Next, it was alert to potential informers of any kind. Finally, the intelligentsia was somewhat snobbish.

These labels were inimical to and frustrating for the Communists (whose social origin was low, as a rule), since the traditional intelligentsia unconditionally rejected Marxist ideology.[45] This was an additional, if not decisive, reason why Communists were so keen on eradicating any intellectual and habitual reminders of the old intelligentsia. Indeed, historically, the traditional intelligentsia transmitted, from one generation to another, this precious missionary spirit, as well as the standards of proper etiquette. This definitely represented a "class conflict."

Social Hypocrisy

Theoretically, the provincial intelligentsia appears to be the most interesting. The historian Lesław Sadowski conducted a study on this subject, using the ethos of the Polish intelligentsia in the nineteenth century in the eastern regions of Lomża, Suwałki, and Białystok (parts of Poland previously under Russian occupation) as his example. He understood the intelligentsia as a "heterogeneous social stratum, open to various political and intellectual influences; a stratum that does not have only one face, and is unique for it" (Sadowski 1988: 300). Despite his controversial assumption, his own meticulous study of social reality led him to a conclusion that revealed the weakness of his understanding. He concluded, "Provincial members of the intelligentsia, physicians, teachers, lawyers, clerks, the pioneers of civilization acting in solitude, 'Pharisees' of democracy, were unable to bear the load imposed on them. Either they were ingested by the world of the middle bourgeoisie with its philistine hierarchy of values and ambitions, or, if they were able to withstand the oppressive climate of provincial life, they became frustrated, and like starving loners, absorbed by despair or rebellion" (Sadowski 1988: 31).

The ideological degradation of a member of the intelligentsia guaranteed that this "warrior" was unable to respond to the call of the intelligentsia's missionary imperative. Although previously a hero animated by the "holy" spirit, he fell, defeated, into self-depreciation and self-deception. Unable to fulfill high expectations, he started to eat at himself in his despair and hopelessness. This metamorphosis, implicitly contained in the analysis of the life of a nineteenth-century provincial member of the intelligentsia, is interesting since it can be translated into a principle of more general validity. When aspirations are directed at goals too highly positioned, and when the holder of these aspirations still cherishes the ideas that inspired him, he finally realizes, once thwarted by the impossibility of accomplishing his goals, that he was put into an existential trap. He then becomes his own worst enemy, or starts to play the role of a well-shielded *social hypocrite*.

This phenomenon, born in the nineteenth century, blossomed spectacularly in the twentieth under the Soviet occupation after World War II. The successor to the Polish traditional intelligentsia, aware of the binding force of categorical imperative and, at the same time, of the inherent impossibility of executing this imperative, was pressed to concoct, invent, or design a myth on the spot, or any other useful cover story explaining his inability to follow this imperative. He would thus be able to argue skillfully that a special type of duty of a higher order unconditionally demanded his instant services; that he could not be engaged in any hazardous activity since he was the custodian of a sacrosanct mission; that he was engaged at that very moment in a perilous operation that might jeopardize the assignment entrusted to him. Like a young delinquent who claims that he did not commit a crime or that the crime was committed by somebody else, that he is a victim of false accusation or was intimidated into participating in the deed, a member of the intelligentsia, under the pressure of real socialism, would try to clean himself up in the eyes of others, and in his own. As a consequence of such rationalizations and justifications, social hypocrisy developed and was elaborated under real socialism in a skillful manner, becoming the most highly sought-after commodity.

The duality of official and private life constitutes a well-recognized form of schizophrenia among Poles. Modern Poles are able to operate deftly in both spheres, undertaking complicated tasks within their interrelated boundaries, performing many crafty operations in each without collision and without trespassing on other people's competence. In comparison, the phenomenon of social hypocrisy has been, until now, completely protected by silence. Recently, ground that has been well fertilized for the development of social hypocrisy has created the base from which legends and myths, both personal and related to groups, can grow. Personal fairy-tales are one of the most striking and unique phenomena of Polish society. Women use their natural charms, and men employ (sometimes reluctantly) a real or imaginary martyrology to convince themselves and others, including outsiders, of their political dignity. In a peculiar way, the "ordinary" ethical decalogue ("Do not lie," "Do not steal," and, especially, "Do not commit adultery") was regarded as a set of secondary demands by some Poles who belong to the political opposition. Fear of the oppressive political system was so real and imminent that its defeat was regarded as critical. Therefore, transgression of the rules of the ordinary ethical decalogue could be justified on the grounds of maintaining a high level of public decency. Typically, a planned or accomplished transgression would be justified thus: "It would be impossible to sustain so costly a level of concentration without some side-stepping rewards."

In real socialism, social hypocrisy manifests itself in a peculiar, topsy-turvy way. With unusual perception, Timothy Garton Ash was able to describe the subvariant of hypocrisy that compels someone to condemn his very self by pretending that he is someone else.

Yet, his profound contempt for those men from lower classes who made the Polish revolution, the "peasant-natured" worker Walesa, the "little shit" Bujak, is all part of his social position as a prominent member of (what he himself calls) "the Warsaw Establishment" and Poland's Communist ruling class. Thirty-six years previously he was himself, like Walesa and Bujak, a peasant's son: blond, well-built, energetic, free of religious prejudice—the perfect human material for a new élite. Once recruited, like half a million other peasant sons, he prospered through the system. He studied journalism, history and political science; he acquired knowledge and some sophistication; he had position and influence as Editor of *Polityka*; in the 1960s he began to travel, was feted as the coming man in America and West Germany; his clothes became smarter, position, authority and influence was added . . . power. And now these peasants, these "little shits," wanted to share it with *him*, Mieczyslaw F. Rakowski, the toast of Washington and Bonn, he who spent "exquisite nights" drinking vodka with his friends in Moscow. (Garton Ash 1984: 200)

THE INTELLIGENTSIA AND CIVIL SOCIETY

The intelligentsia played a unique role in both Russia and in Poland. Each of these societies, although different (Russian society was oriented towards liberation of the illiterate and the oppressed, and Polish society towards the regaining of national dignity and independence), were characterized by a clear gap between the state and civil society. The role of poets and writers ("bards") was prominent in Poland. In the absence of a legitimized state, there was an urgent need for national and societal leadership. Since 1795, when Poland had been deprived of her independence, formal, official, and state representative leaders had not been recognized by the society as authentic and genuine symbols of authority.

To inject some authority into this sociopolitical vacuum, the institution of "governors of souls" was created. In this historical framework, where non-criminal social visibility was reserved only for literature and poetry, the governors of souls alone had the potential to reach the national peak of spiritual power. Poetry thus developed a peculiar double meaning: from one point of view, it was an expression of feelings and ideas, but from another, it was a peculiar code, containing a deep political message. Not only was the intelligentsia constantly engaged in the process of encoding and disseminating these messages but it was also preoccupied with the task of decoding "clandestine" data. Even now, people are coming up with new revelations about the meaning of the symbol "44," the mysterious name of the "Governor of Freedom on Earth" taken from the vision of the priest Peter, in Adam Mickiewicz's famous poem *Forebears*, written more than a century ago.

Polish civil society thus defended itself against the impetuous invasion of the state, its impersonal rationality, its depersonalized justice, its hidden exploitation, and, above all, its denationalization. Paradoxically, the sharpest sword the intelligentsia could raise against the state was the verse of a poet.

Civil society had a different meaning in Poland than in Western countries. In the West, civil society maintained operations parallel to the state. It supplied the state with additional resources or undertook tasks that were not appropriate for the state. In the West, the state and civil society not only tolerated one another, respecting the boundaries of each other's activities, but also supported one another. In the Polish situation, the two were open enemies.

At the end of 1970s, the Solidarity movement became an open enemy of the state. It was the spirit of traditional intelligentsia, combined with the activities of various agencies of civil society—especially the catalytic interference of the KOR—that provided the necessary foundation that gave rise to the power of the Solidarity movement.

THE SOLIDARITY MOVEMENT

To understand properly the activities of the KOR in 1976, one has to return to Cracow in the years just after the end of the Second World War. Andrzej

"Adi" Ciechanowiecki, a young Cracow intellectual, established the Club of *Logofagi* ("Friends of Wisdom," so named by Tadeusz Chrzanowski) in 1947. Every week, they held meetings at the YMCA.[46] This independent, exclusive group (exclusive both for security reasons and from sui generis snobbishness) consisted of a cluster of friends or young intellectuals connected by the urgent need to change sociopolitical reality in Poland. The club was closed when it became obvious that the coming tide of Stalinism made any public life with a non-Marxist orientation highly dangerous.[47] In 1957, some members of this group were able to establish an independent journal, *Przeglad Polski i Obcy*, ("Polish and Foreign Review"—I was one of the editors of this magazine), which tried to continue the activities suspended at the end of the eighteenth century and examine and develop political ideas in weekly discussions. This journal, which owed its existence to the events in Poznan in 1956, was dismantled by the authorities after a few years of publication. Nevertheless, several members of *Logofagi* moved to Warsaw and established three independent groups: *Pomidor* ("Tomato"), "Keep Smiling," and *Pawiany* ("Baboons").

It is necessary to add that these groups represented only a small part of the enormous variety of political, semilegal, or illegal associations that existed in Poland after the war. They were unique, not because they undertook organizational and military preparations in the face of an approaching third world war (between Western countries and the totalitarian Soviet Union), but because they collected intellectual data that described and explained what was going on in Poland (and in Eastern Europe) and prepared a political and, where possible, scientific analytic diagnosis of the situation.[48] They also hoped to design an adequate and useful political program for Poland, if permitted by the geopolitical situation in that part of Europe.[49]

Jan Józef Lipski and Stanislaw Manturzewski created a parallel, somewhat connected, but organizationally independent group called the "Neo-Pickwick Club." This club was later transformed into a large illegal grouping of young scholars, who, in 1953 (before Milovan Djilas elaborated his theory of the "new class"), formulated the concept of the "red class," a Party apparatus with a bourgeois ethos. That same year, the club was investigated by the secret police. As a consequence of this investigation, several of its members were harassed, and some were arrested.

After liberalization in 1956, some members became editors of the *Po Prostu* weekly, or joined the governing body of *Krzywe Koło*, the Crooked Circle club referred to earlier. Lipski remained president of *Krzywe Koło* until its demise in 1962. Shortly before the authorities closed *Krzywe Koło*, its offspring, the Center for Social Diagnosis, was created.[50] The dominant idea behind the center was the study of social and political processes that appeared under oppression and the attempt to "capitalize wisdom for us, not for the prosecutor" (Zbigniew Marek). After the activities of the *Krzywe Koło* ended, Lipski developed a new idea: the core members of the old group were to enter and take over the amorphous, atheist club *Towarzystwo Kultury Moralnej* (Association of Moral Culture), created by the government to promote secular ethics.

With the influx of new members, it became obvious that the same notion had been conceived by former high-ranking officers of the Home Army (the Polish army that existed during the war).[51] After some deliberation it was decided to leave the territory to the officers.[52] Lipski then suggested to me that I take over the Warsaw branch of the Polish Sociological Association. This branch, which contained half of the members of the Association, or approximately 1,000 people, cautiously began to serve as a forum for limited political debate. It also created two sections: Sociology of Law, whose function was to reveal and publicly analyze the negative by-products of Polish law, and Sociotechnics. Among other things, the Sociology of Law section initiated a successful attack on the official legal program against "social parasites" (a law which existed in the Soviet Union) and also successfully attacked the legal project on mental health (which would have resulted in a law that enabled officials to send those suspected of dissenting activities to psychiatric hospitals).

After the social unrest in 1970, the Sociotechnics section created a Sociotechnics Institute (camouflaged under the name "Institute of Social Prevention and Resocialization"). In 1972, the section prepared a comprehensive diagnostic study of around 250 pages that dealt with the entire country and was able to demonstrate the pathology of the Polish sociopolitical system through systematic empirical inquiry. As noted earlier, the Central Committee of the Party then interrupted activities, ordering the "reorganization" (destruction) of the institute in 1976. Although the institute was indeed dismantled in its original form, a few courageous scholars (among them Wanda Kaczynska, Andrzej Kojder, and Jerzy Kwaśniewski) tried to keep alive the idea of "a comprehensive social diagnosis and national reconstruction."

It is important to keep in mind that most political activities in the first *heroic* phase of the institute were undertaken by a single person, Jan Józef Lipski. He acted as a straight moral arrow. His stubborn obstinacy and his solitary fight against the mighty totalitarian structure of society and the institutional shrewdness of the secret police suggest that the decisive force of social revolution is located neither in the powerful inherent message of a new idea, nor in a new vision of social reality, nor an elaborated design prepared by experts; instead, it is an ethical, moral imperative.

Lipski was the real author of the famous "Letter of 34"—a letter signed in 1964 by thirty-four well-known intellectuals protesting against restrictions on paper distribution and the growing burden of censorship. (Lipski modestly attributes the authorship of this letter to Antoni Słonimski). He was the real author of Lipinski's famous letter (the latter lent his name to the letter, making a few cosmetic changes); he collected protest signatures in order to rid the Polish constitution of its links with the Soviet Union (through eternal friendship); he was the founder of the KOR (the idea for which was conceived in his home during a conversation with Jacek Kuroń, Jan Olszewski and Aniela Steinsber-gowa) as well as its treasurer, and the constructor of the KOR's ethos (although it was his idea that the KOR be dissolved, he was not the one who announced it, under Solidarity).[53] He was also the main strategist of the KOR but he was glad when others took over his ideas as their own; this was a guarantee of their active involvement.

He insisted that the KOR's ethos be fully respected, and he also undertook the task of codifying this ethos. According to him, it consisted of the following heterogeneous features: an authentic social-service attitude (helpful interest in a concrete person), an openness and trust towards others ("it was accepted that it was much more dangerous to create an atmosphere of suspicion than to overlook a few informers"; this particular rule was formulated by Kuroń), an attempt to take responsibility for everything and everyone, the attitude that funds belonging to the KOR were "sacred" (money was not to be taken for one's own activities), an intolerance for lies, a renunciation of violence, an acceptance of the Catholic moral ethos, an adoption of principles relating to the independence of Poland, and a tactical recommendation that during cross-examination by the secret service, one had to refuse to answer (Lipski 1983:57–70).

Once this perspective is considered, Ash's remarks on the KOR and Solidarity appear to be rather limited: "The first point about KOR was not that it was an initiative of the intelligentsia-based democratic opposition that set out specifically to support and work with workers and, subsequently, with other social groups. In any case, the most notable feature of Solidarity was not that it was a workers' movement. The most notable feature of Solidarity was that it was a movement in which workers and intellectuals worked together, at best, combining peaceful, dignified, mass mobilization and skillful, high-level negotiation to try to change their country" (Garton Ash 1991: 50).

Factors Conducive to the Rise of Solidarity

Ten distinct features characterized the rise of the Solidarity movement. They are as follows.

Social Warpedness

After continuous pressure from an alien Communist ideology and the heavy organizational structures based on this ideology, the social fabric of Polish society started to display an unusual set of phenomena. Social reactions to normal stimuli became unpredictable and chaotic. The usual links between cause and effect were broken, and a given social factor could produce a variety of erratic effects. Like one of Pavlov's dogs, which, after being conditioned by a series of contradictory commands, starts to react in an inconsistent manner, members of Polish society began to respond in a contradictory way. The social order of Polish society was broken, not because of a growth in the level of anomie (social norms were quite well known, and the declared attachment to respected norms and social bonds was relatively high), but because of a growing conviction that a state of social disorder was a passive strategy for survival. In such a situation, all orders from authority meet with an amorphous, indeterminate, and nebulous response. Under the rule of warpedness everything is turned upside down. To build order, and especially order of a procedural type, one has to start from scratch.

In 1972, I characterized social warpedness in the following way: "The state of social warpedness is the peculiar situation where the target of activity, due to its changeability, discordance, and cancellation of validity by norms directed against themselves, is transformed into a state of constant rejection of all possible rules" (Podgórecki 1972: 54). Stefan Nowak (1987: 653) described the situation of Polish society in a slightly different manner:

One additional consequence of this state of affairs is the danger of social disintegration. This was characteristic of Poland in the 1970s, at least at the middle level of our social system. This disintegration appeared between the level of national community and the level of small groups consisting of family and friendship circles. Later, the election of the Polish Pope, and the Solidarity period, filled several of these empty areas. Presently, research indicates that several social bonds have disintegrated again, and the meaning of intermediary organizations, located between the level of national community and the level of family and friendship groups has disappeared once more.

Walicki encapsulated Nowak's idea better than Nowak himself:

Thus, an average Pole does not belong to the large-scale institutionalized civil society; he belongs to different primary groups and, secondly, he belongs to his nation; not a nation as a system of political and economic institutions, but a nation as national tradition, national culture, the sphere of uniting symbols, of sublimated, lofty, patriotic feelings. (Walicki 1990: 33)

This situation, viewed by the leaders of "civil society" as a threat to national survival, contributed to the call for a rebuilding of social identity, thus preparing the ground for the Solidarity movement.

A New Generation of Skilled Workers

Several sociological studies have indicated that a new social stratum emerged in Poland after World War II. This was the category of skilled workers. On a scale of social prestige, this group was systematically placed on the second level, below the professions typical of the intelligentsia (professors, teachers, doctors), but above the white-collar workers (administrators and clerks). Skilled workers were relatively well educated—their brand of competence was required in various projects to build heavy industry in Poland. At a certain point, they began to recognize their own importance, so often proclaimed by the Communist government. They felt nevertheless that they were constantly exploited and that satisfaction of their own needs had been consistently deferred. They wanted only a consolidating idea around which to rally their accumulated frustration.

The KOR's Role in Forging an Alliance between the Intelligentsia and the Workers

The events of March 1968 have yet to be adequately described. It remains clear, however, that students found no support among workers for their dissident activities. Similarly, in the 1970s, the events in Gdansk and Gdynia convincingly revealed that workers alone were fighting against the government.

Once the historic importance of the KOR was established, a spontaneous yet calculated attempt was made to build a bridge between the workers and the intelligentsia. Indeed, the original idea behind the KOR (as expressed in its very name—*Komitet Obrony Robotnikow*: Committee to Defend Workers) was to find a practical form of protection for the workers against the oppressive state. The first task was to collect funds to pay court and lawyers' fees, support the families of arrested workers, and find (and pay) babysitters for workers' wives who wanted to go to court to see their husbands. Another task was to break down the mistrust between the intelligentsia and the workers. The situation was complicated because, while the intelligentsia and the workers both deplored the government, they did not trust each other (workers, especially, did not trust the intelligentsia).

Alain Touraine and his collaborators were thus totally wrong when they began their analysis of Solidarity with the following assumption: ''When intellectuals and young workers joined the Party, they were not simply bending to necessity and the desire to build a career, it was not simple hypocrisy. It was a willing, even an enthusiastic act, as well as being dictated by the fate of the nation'' (Touraine 1983:22). KOR was able not only to accomplish the task of authenticating an incipient understanding between workers and the intelligentsia but also to contribute to the development of the new ethos of Solidarity. It must be noted that, when this ethos was fully developed, its roots could be found deep in the history of the Polish nation. As Ash observed,

The nearest historical parallel to the state of Solidarity in its last months is the Polish Noble Democracy from the sixteenth to the eighteenth centuries. The regional conferences were Solidarity's *sejmiki* and the Congress its *sejm*. . . . Poland's Noble Democracy was unique in the Europe of its time. The right to resistance, the respect for individual liberty, the principles of government by consent, free speech and religious tolerance earned it the epithet of ''Golden Freedom,'' and prefigured liberal democracy which, in later centuries and more fortunate lands, would be extended to all citizens, not merely to nobility. Yet this ''Golden Freedom,'' this anarchic democracy, in keeping the central government weak, poor, and therefore inadequately armed, ensured its own eventual destruction. By 1800, it had been devoured by the hungry autocracies of its neighbours. It succumbed to what would now be called the ''geopolitical reality.'' Yet it left a rich legacy of ideas and memories; ideas which were cherished and cultivated, memories which seeped into the deep subsoil of the national conscience. (Garton Ash 1983: 220–21)

The Polish Pope

The election of a Pole as pope was an enormous boost to the morale of the Poles. This psychological boost was important not only because a virtually unknown Pole was placed alone, both ideologically and symbolically, against all the military divisions of the strongest armies in the world but also because the Poles were hungry for a positive, charismatic leader. In Polish history, charismatic leaders were practically nonexistent. Therefore, the election of a Polish pope had a spectacular psychological effect; the event was amplified by the pope's subsequent visit to Poland and his ability to mobilize amorphous masses. Enormous crowds showed an unusual degree of cooperation and, through their own devices, organized internal order and discipline, eliminating the state police from the scene. In effect, the masses had an opportunity to see their own power in unity, enhancing the belief that they could impose their own behavior, if not destiny. This spirit allowed Cardinal Glemp (who, a month later, became the Primate of Poland) to say in June 1981, "People who represent the Church and those who represent Solidarity are united in their opinions and ideas concerning the critical situation in the country, and they are concerned about the causes of this situation and ways to change the Republic . . . If the Church remains with Solidarity in partnership, this will not be a front of alien forces, but an alliance of fellowmen built on the community of mutual understanding and—I do not hesitate to say—on the community of brotherhood" (Holtzer 1984: 241).

Wałęsa's Charisma

Like Pope John Paul II, Lech Wałęsa is also a positive hero. According to Bendix, "Weber always used the term 'charisma' in the sense of an 'extraordinary quality' possessed by persons or objects, that is thought to give these persons or objects a unique, magical power" (Bendix 1977: 299). Certainly Wałęsa possessed this type of "supernatural" ability. It is difficult to understand how the son of a peasant could acquire such unusual political intuition, an intuition that enabled him to solve complicated political conundrums far more quickly, and far more efficiently, than the most sophisticated experts. How was it possible that he could change experts like gloves (himself being a sort of meta-expert) and, with the help of their contradictory advice, penetrate the problems at hand? Nonetheless, he had (and has) a unique ability to reach a proper political decision when a decision was (and is) required. The manifestation of this ability generated his charisma, which was subsequently reinforced by the sequence of his astonishing decisions. The personality of Wałęsa was therefore an independent factor contributing to the development of Solidarity's ideology and legend.

One can distinguish between micro- (or lowest level—that of a small group), mezzo- (or middle level—that of an industry, minority, province) and macro-sociotechnics. Macrosociotechnics deals with society as a whole. The tragic experiences of Marxist regimes strongly substantiated Karl Popper's idea that macrosocial engineering is utopian, politically motivated quackery. Wałęsa, however, as leader of the Solidarity movement, was able to abolish the Monolithic totalitarian regime through a peaceful and efficient revolution. Once again the question arises: how was it possible for a mechanic, the son of a rural country peasant, to guide the comprehensive social and political revolution in such an effective way? It would be fascinating to assess all the factors that provided Wałęsa with effective and just tools, and to discover how he used them. At present, one can only state that macrosociotechnics is possible.

The Revolution of Expectations

President Kennedy was once briefed by a prominent social-science professor. Asked later about the content of the briefing, he responded that he had heard a lot, but was able to assimilate only the term "revolution of expectations." Currently, indeed, this phenomenon is almost ubiquitous. This is partly due to the appeal of mass media, advertisements, and the commercial impact on the population of creating new, and strengthening existing, needs. One-quarter of the Polish population lives abroad, but retains rather tight links with families at home. These contacts provide Poles with a good (if not exaggerated) picture of living standards elsewhere. In effect, the Poles' accumulated expectations became fixed to frustrations created by everyday restrictions. The combination of expectations and frustrations prepared an explosive background for the political system of real socialism. These frustrations also supported criticisms of the existing system and the social and political movement that was determined to build a new, pluralistic (but not dogmatic and totalitarian) vision of a free society.

The sharp rise in suicides in Communist Poland supports this point of view. The revolution of expectations, which took place in Poland after 1989, accelerated public anticipation to a level much higher than any realistic evaluation should have allowed. According to the *Statistical Yearbook* (1991: 53), suicide rates surged after the Solidarity movement defeat in 1981 and were also high before 1989 (4,693 suicides in 1980; 4,517 in 1985), but decreased after the Fall of Nations in 1989 (3,657 in 1989; 3,841 in 1990), to rise again sharply in 1991 to the level of 5,500 (Ottawa *Citizen*, April 12, 1993, p. A7). An invisible and strongly perceived increase in social disillusionment and frustration, generated by unrealistic expectations, appeared to be the catalyst for these dramatic changes.

The Chameleon-like Ethos of Solidarity

Echoing the way individual Poles developed their own survival strategies, the largest justice-oriented social movement of the twentieth century adopted a chameleon-like facade to cope with the reality of a totalitarian regime. Although Solidarity was an authentic political movement, it operated in the guise of an "independent trade union." Although it was a revolutionary movement, it called itself a "self-limiting revolution." Although it was a movement oriented towards political independence, it operated under the cover of "consensus." It is interesting to ask to what extent these camouflaged strategies were consciously used by the Solidarity brain trust under the leadership of Wałęsa, and to what extent they were spontaneously generated as semiconscious tactics by civil society (which had an overabundance of experiences drawn from past political struggles). Although these questions are open, high-level political fights currently taking place in Poland make them difficult, if not impossible, to resolve. Mary Chambers distinguishes the ideology of Solidarity from its ethos: ideology is changeable and operates instrumentally under different circumstances, whereas ethos is stable. "Because the ideology was distinct from its ethos, and because of the nature of ethos, the ethos was able to continue to exist after the ideology had become anachronistic. The ethos of Solidarity still continues to exist" (Chambers 1992: 193).

The Soviet-like "Objectivization" of Society

It was noticed by several scholars, even some Marxists, that under a system of real socialism, official relations between authorities and workers (and also among workers) become reified. George Ritzer interprets George Lukacs's understanding of reification in the following way: "People come to believe that social structures have a life of their own, and as a result, they do come to have an objective character" (Ritzer 1988: 126).

With few exceptions, however, sociologists failed to notice that society as a whole could also be objectified, or reified. Ireneusz Krzemiński puts it thus; "How does one grasp in a succinct way the content of this negative social situation? 'Nothing can be done as it should be done' because 'they' have power. *'Man is negligible'*—he is only an axis organizing the whole complex of attitudes that creates the negative definition of the situation" (Krzemiński 1989: 47). The case of martial law in Poland, introduced to halt the development of Solidarity, clearly underscores this observation.

Before the installment of martial law, military units were sent to many parts of the country to "help" people, fraternize with them, intimidate them, and spy on them. Prescription lists, including names of those who should be arrested or detained, were prepared almost a year in advance. Artificial food shortages were created to direct people's frustrations against Solidarity. Tapes that recorded vulgar conversations of the Solidarity leader were faked and distributed. Rumors were spread that Solidarity, after its political takeover, intended to hang the family members of the security apparatus.

After the military takeover, society was generally organized according to a unified design suitable for manipulation. This tactic became more overt after the sudden introduction of martial law a few days before Christmas Eve. People's houses were brutally searched; there were tanks in the streets; each institution or factory had its own military commissar; and telephone calls were mechanically interrupted by a recorded voice saying, "Your conversation is under surveillance." Beatings of individuals or groups and strict curfews were the norm. These strategies were used by the regime to show that the government would not hesitate to use "dark social engineering" (with the eager help of some social-science specialists) to atomize society and, optimally, to reify it. Steven Lewarne (1984:37) puts it in this way: "The subjugation of such a large (9.5 million members) and socially diversified body could not have been achieved through random or blind measures. At the center of every sophisticated and (I use the term cautiously) political organization is some body or school of thought, explicitly or implicitly formed, to assimilate, cognate, and synthesize societal divisions and fluctuations with the ideological and value-oriented paradigms of the ruling élite." Indeed, macro "dark social engineering" is the best measure for reifying society as a whole. Some commentators have noticed that the totalitarian regime has introduced several dysfunctional elements into society. They were (a) its holistic, totalitarian character; (b) its nature as a vessel of anti-values; (c) the regime's use of the "game of illusions," hiding its true nature; (d) the perception of the regime as a "villainous and vicious monster" (only a metaphor can refer to its actual essence); and (e) the regime's situating itself outside of civil society and man, whom it abhors (Kowalski 1990: 28).

The Disintegration of Solidarity

Solidarity's initial fight kept its forces closely bonded together. When Solidarity was able to challenge the regime, to struggle with it peacefully, to neutralize its government, and eventually, to topple it, its integrity started to crumble and, subsequently, disintegrate. From its beginnings, Solidarity has had at least five different faces. The first was that of the trade unionist. This was its original function—to create an organization that would be able, through free elections, to serve as an authentic body representing the interests of "working people" (not just workers), Second, in its political guise, Solidarity claimed ideologically that the system could not be reformed; that all attempts to change it from inside were doomed (since one cannot improve something so profoundly bad); that all attempts to convince people that the situation could be improved were, from the start, a compromise of false consciousness. In cultural terms, the existing system, viewed in the spirit of the Solidarity, was in flagrant violation of basic human values, particularly those accumulated through the tradition of the Polish nation. In particular, this system contradicted the Christian ancestry of Polish society. Fourth, Solidarity's ideology rejected the idea of "class conflict," which was seen to spread animosity and "bad instincts," and accepted instead the notion of national solidarity as an adequate representation of Polish social and cultural traditions—this was not only a national solidarity but also a solidarity of all societies ruled by dictatorships. Finally, on the basis of all previous functions, the Solidarity movement articulated an autotelic, revolutionary "goal." It attempted to accomplish a revolution without violence. A mere idea confronted the power of deadly machinery and destructive, tightly organized oppressive social forces. As Wojciechowski succinctly puts it, "The cornerstone of the ideology of Solidarity may best be described as a *non-conflictual approach to social problems*" (Wojciechowski 1982: 12; original emphasis).

These traits bound divergent tendencies into a common front, cemented by a collective enemy. When this enemy began to disappear from the immediate vicinity, centrifugal tendencies began to run in different directions, preparing, at the same time, the foundations of political pluralism—a pluralism that was not an abstract ideology, but a set of real social institutions and organizations.

Solidarity led an *ignition* type of revolution. Its value was found not only in its own potential as a sociopolitical movement, not only in the political processes generated by its disintegration, but clearly in its legacy. Ash explains that, "in 1991, we can see Solidarity a little more clearly for what it was: a pioneering Polish form of social self-organisation, with the general objective of achieving, by means of peaceful popular pressure, combined with élite negotiation, the end of communism. In this, it succeeded" (Garton Ash 1991: 57).

6

Polish Post-Totalitarianism (1989–1992)

The main paradox of modern Poland is that her potential is now fabricated by those who did the same in previous periods. (Zygmunt Kałuzynski in *Polityka* 1992, no. 1860: 11)

INTRODUCTION

The father of totalitarian phraseology was Benito Mussolini (the term "totalitarian state" was used for the first time in a bill passed by the Italian parliament on December 24, 1925). His charismatic qualities, which many people found irresistible, lent original meaning to totalitarianism. This meaning was later completely transformed, and its sociopolitical applications led to its ultimate condemnation. Totalitarianism has also been censured on scientific grounds, thanks to Hannah Arendt's scholarly determination (Arendt 1962). Yet, both in its initial phase (the phase of glory), and in its later phase (of unanimous condemnation), its complete ideological dominance over political, social, and economic life was considered a constant factor.

Carl Friedrich and Zbigniew Brzeziński gave a fairly adequate definition of the concept. According to these authors, totalitarianism is "a 'syndrome' of interlinking factors . . . consisting of an ideology, one party, led, in principle, by one leader, a terrorist police force, monopolised mass media and armed forces, and a centrally controlled economy" (Friedrich, Brzeziński 1965: 9). Jan Józef Szczepański gets at the heart of totalitarianism when he writes:

Totalitarianism is frequently confused with other forms of authoritarian power—military dictatorship or primitive tyranny. The latter two are notorious for their naked and brutal violence but they lack the most dangerous element of totalitarianism, i.e., a monopolistic ideology. It is this ideology, irrespective of its specific orientation, which lies at the root of totalitarian coercion. It prohibits all opposition and discussion and puts all the power in the hands of one, usually minority, party. This party creates the fiction of the "will of the people" and monopolises public opinion by taking over the mass media. It provides the exclusive patterns of education, makes the decisions about the forms of culture and social relationships and everything that constitutes the domain of free and creative human will. And finally, it inevitably transforms into a power system led by the hierarchic and privileged party oligarchy which holds onto its power by means of a ramified bureaucracy and police. (Szczepański 1990: 7–8)

In his text on the post-totalitarian system, Jeffrey Goldfarb quotes several formerly left-wing and dissident Polish intellectuals (Barańczak, Michnik, Staniszkis) with a journalist's flair. However, the only original discussion of post-totalitarianism is to be found in the works of the Czech playwright and president Vaclav Havel:

Between the aims of the post-totalitarian system and the aims of life there is a yawning abyss: while life, in its essence, moves toward plurality, diversity, independent self-constitution and self-organization, in short, towards the fulfilment of its own freedom, the post-totalitarian system demands conformity, uniformity, and discipline. While life ever strives to create new and "improbable" structures, the post-totalitarian system contrives to force life into its most probable states. (Havel in Goldfarb 1989: 106–7)

Marxism, with its confusing analysis, pertinently suggested that liberal-capitalist societies, with their allegedly overpowering and oppressive nature (which is seemingly invisible, because it acts deceitfully), are even more totalitarian. Marxism thus avoided, at least for a while, any academic or public analysis of the problem. In the long run, Marxist criticism was, in some way, effective. As Andrzej Walicki noted,

[a] majority of scholars came to the conclusion that the concept of totalitarianism lost its cognitive power, became simplified and unsuitable for use as a diagnostic and prognostic tool. Several scholars went even further to treat the theory of totalitarianism as a result of the cold war, rejecting it altogether. As a result, American Sovietologists were in opposition to the "totalitarian model." This led to some extreme perceptions, such as the negation of historical continuity between Leninism and Stalinism (Stephen Cohen), the treatment of Stalinism as an accidental development (Robert Tucker), an exaggerated stress on the grass-roots support for Stalinist regimes (Sheila Fitzpatrick), or even a perception of the Brezhnev era as a "pluralistic system" (Jerry Hough). (Walicki 1991: 14)

The spectacular fall of Marxism in 1989, initiated by Polish Solidarity, brought the problem of totalitarianism dramatically to the fore once again. Yet, when Marxism collapsed, along with its pure totalitarian political creations, post-totalitarianism became a most interesting object of study.

The transition from Fascist totalitarianism to democracy has been quite well, if recently, elaborated. John Herz, in an invaluable and comprehensive edited volume, notes, "We have all of these, but one type we don't have: the overthrow of the regime by popular uprising" (Herz 1982: 277). Here he refers to the "revolution" in the traditional sense (the type of revolution that came into being from the great French Revolution onward, including the weak German revolution of 1918). According to Herz, except in Spain, all political transitions of this type occurred within the framework of international events. Indeed, this was the case in Germany, Austria (as part of "Greater Germany"), Japan, Italy (which, after ousting the dictator, had to reverse roles and join the Allies to defeat the Mussolini remnant), and Vichy France (which was defeated by another France that had fought alongside the Allies).

The situation of Greece and Portugal was similar, according to Herz, although more complicated in detail. He singled out several critical problems during the post-Fascist and post-Nazi periods. These are as follows: Does a new democracy interpret itself as legally identical to the antecedent regime? How are the "bearers" of the antecedent regime treated? How are antecedent totalitarian parties treated? (Were they outlawed?) What policies were adopted against the opponents of antecedent regimes? How were essential democratic institutions recreated? Was the principle of freedom granted to all parties (including post-totalitarian parties)? What were the rules for disindoctrination and "democratic indoctrination" (especially in the realm of public opinion and mass media)? How were *moral issues* treated? What were the fundamental principles behind the foreign relations of new democratic states? Interestingly enough these problems did not become central issues in the new post-Soviet democracies. They were decisively replaced by economic issues.

It should be noted that the situation during post-Soviet succession was different. The Polish Solidarity movement started the avalanche of freedom in a *peaceful* manner.

What is post-totalitarianism? To begin with, it is a socioeconomic system that, from the outside, gives the impression of political and cultural pluralism with liberal postulates. Organizationally and socially, however, it is still the cohesive outcome of a long-standing authoritarian regime. In other words, it is a system that, while free of the political forms of totalitarianism, is still affected by the social structures created by totalitarianism.

I propose that this thesis be tested. For the sake of clarity, I shall distinguish the following basic issues:

1. The continuous existence of "nomenklatura" (people appointed to executive posts on the basis of party membership), its "soft landing" (the safety-net mechanism of the nomenklatura), and the cohabitation of two opposing nomenklaturas.

2. An increased social frustration because specific categories of people have not been held responsible for their actions. Society demands that people be held responsible for their collaboration with the totalitarian system, not on the basis of personal complaints, but on the basis of previous participation in state affairs.

Society also demands that people who held higher posts in the party and state administration be banned from present state administration.

3. The perpetuation of a bureaucracy based on "expertise" that grew out of a systematic liquidation of the traditional "intelligentsia," and a parallel systematic creation and expansion of the technological-administrative group of "intelligentsia."

4. The continued and constant influence on social life of the official authoritarian legal system and its ensuing customs.

5. Continued state ownership of basic institutions and enterprises. The call for "privatization" does not change, by fiat, the existing state of affairs.

6. The perpetuation, as a result of inertia and their continued social "utility," of customs formed during the period of intensive "sovietization" of the country.

7. The unrestrained development of clerical and dogmatic-religious modes of thinking (which had previously functioned as a counterbalance to political totalitarianism).

8. Central planning based on once-prevalent, abstract principles of social, cultural, and economic processes that are systematically disappearing.

9. The low level of development of democratic institutions in Poland. Liberty must be learned. One must respect compromise, be aware of the limitations of polemic and of forcing one's own point of view. Various democratically established modes of social dialogue must be worked out. These include the selection of administration, principles underlying public discussion, promotion of "impersonality" in thinking about social issues and in social practice, liquidation of the effects of "false awareness," and elimination of various sham activities.

10. Continued enslavement of the "social mentality." One must become aware of the "muzzles" imposed on official and lay modes of thinking by the "Marxist training systems" that lasted almost half a century.

Exposition of the Ten Postulates

1. We know that the nomenklatura is a social stratum consisting of higher state and party officials, individually preselected and approved by the central committee of the political party currently in power. In countries where "real socialism" reigned, this stratum formed the executive apparatus of the Communist system. People were selected to the nomenklatura not on the basis of professional competence and practical experience, but on the basis of their predetermined political loyalty towards the central party organs and, at times, towards specific party leaders.

When real socialism collapsed, this stratum retained its power because (a) it knew how to locate itself in the entangled state organizations and institutions of its own making; (b) it manifested a considerable degree of conformity with the new administration; (c) it had learned over the years in office to cleverly justify or rationalize policies which were then convenient; and (d) it still had a monopoly over many "secrets" of administrative functioning. For these reasons, some people believe that keeping the nomenklatura in office is relatively innocuous, or even beneficial, in light of the other urgent economic and political priorities.

The nomenklatura made use of the initial period of uncertainty to further its fate, utilizing the potential to which it had direct practical access. When the call for privatization was launched, it immediately and noiselessly took hold of key posts in the new companies. Despite the fact that members of the ex-nomenklatura were now without political power, they were able, as a result of their instrumental abilities, to gain easy access to economic comfort. In this manner, they put into practice a deft soft-landing strategy. One example of such blatant safeguarding was the complete transformation of the Polish-German Gromada Tourist Company, which converted the tourist-class Farmers' Inn into a luxury hotel. The person in charge of the Berlin capital in Warsaw is General Straszewski (formerly with the Ministry of Internal Affairs), now the vice chairman of the Gromada-Tourist Company (Fredro-Boniecki 1990: 89). Referring to the Polish political scene of 1992, the then prime minister Jan Olszewski said, "There were three centers: the president and Belveder [his office], government and the so-called small coalition [a narrow front of political parties]. Somewhere on the margin there operated some forces which, although not actively involved in this game, constituted its very important backing—the former nomenklatura (Olszewski 1992: 79).

The old nomenklatura easily gave way to the new. Although there were loud protests against any insinuation that a new nomenklatura had formed, taking the place of or coexisting with the old one, observations of the selection process for executive posts, the existence of "drawing-rooms," and the tendency to select executives from among those brought up in these drawing-rooms suggest that personal factors—even cliquishness—not objective performance standards form the base for key promotions. Morally, of course, the new nomenklatura differs fundamentally from the old. The new one is determined, first and foremost, to undo all the wrongs previously implemented under the "dirty togetherness" principle.[54] The new nomenklatura firmly discarded the dirty-togetherness principle. Its activities were based on decency and accountability for one's actions.

Yet the old and new nomenklatura act in a specific symbiosis: the old one does not denounce the new (although it has access to old documents that it could make use of—every eighth citizen in the ex-GDR allegedly collaborated with the secret police) and the new one does not eliminate the old (the old nomenklatura works "reliably" for the new). This symbiosis, though conducive to the smooth functioning of the social system as a whole, is harmful enough to lead to internal stagnation. One might even predict that this alliance will only begin to work for the benefit of both when the new nomenklatura finds itself under threat. It can also be predicted that the new nomenklatura will then gain the absolute approval of the old one, because the only safeguard for the old nomenklatura is its new counterpart. History sometimes plays strange pranks. The hangman and the victim need each other: the hangman needs the victim in order to save his skin, the victim needs the hangman so as not to lose his newly gained privileges. Any way it is looked at, the coexistence of "opposing forces" that both fight against and support each other is clearly revealed.[55]

2. The new nomenklatura adopted a principle of not holding the old no-menklatura responsible for its actions. At a time when the country had to be reconstructed economically and politically and the new administration, still in-experienced ("one must learn politics as one learns to ride a bike"), faced the problem of sweeping away the bad interpersonal relations left by real socialism, and of exchanging the former evil with new, healthy, and rational (as demanded by the new middle class) or Christian relationships (as demanded by the majority of society and by the victorious church hierarchy)—at such a time, holding people responsible for their actions could prove to be a menace, sabotaging reconstruction on a global scale.

However, human frustration, accumulated over half a century, needs com-pensation. This task is within the sphere of social reality. How then does one discharge accumulated, justified frustration on the one hand, and still not hang the guilty (and, at times, also the suspect) forthwith from street lamps? A draft recommendation on political reform of the state, prepared in 1982 and dissem-inated in closed circles (the weekly *Tygodnik Powszechny* refused to publish it because the facts were out of date), proposed that:

the federation should forbid the holding of any state post by ex-members of the admin-istrative élite who held higher posts in the state administration. Those who led others to harm through their criminal activities can regain their right to speak in public when they actively work to annul the harm of their own doing. Persons who held *nomenklatura* positions should be brought before Desovietization Committees (equivalent to de-Nazification Committees) and should be treated in accordance with the decisions of these committees. (Podgórecki 1982: 10)

The basic idea was to treat the process of desovietization impersonally, and to avoid claims for compensation for personal wrongs. Instead, certain categories of people were to be punished for a given type of activity: that of implementing a regime with criminal outcomes. The object of punishment was to be an *objective category of people*, not individuals. Of course, the criminal behavior of specific people was to be treated individually. The administration of justice aimed at punishing not only those who were personally responsible for wrong-doing but also specific social categories of people that held official positions. This practice would both enable the discharge of frustration and avoid "witch hunting." It would also teach a lesson to those responsible for social wrongs, showing that wrongs could be "undone" with one's own hands. Again, opposing currents are found in this. On the one hand, there is the call for individual responsibility; on the other, there is the postulate that one must be responsible for one's par-ticipation in criminal organizations.

In connection with this issue, it is worth recalling the problem presented by Fuller in his important book *The Morality of Law* (1969: 244–53). He discusses there the question of what to do with "grudge informers," people who, under the vicious (fictitious) regime of the Purple Shirts, had denounced other citizens as enemies of the government. They used to do this to eliminate opponents of the regime, to harm their personal enemies. To solve the problem Fuller distinguishes five legal options. They are (1) to do nothing about so-called grudge informers: simply declaring the law of the previous regime invalid is exactly what this totalitarian regime did; (2) do nothing about the informers because one should not try by legal means to rectify problems created by a lawless war of all against all; (3) punish, in relation to the gravity of their crimes, those who represented or collaborated with the Purple Shirts and contributed to its successful functioning, though the whole regime functions outside the realm of law; (4) on the basis of relevant facts, draft a comprehensive law to provide appropriate penalties: and (5) allow people to handle matters generated by grudge informers in their own way, instead of calling the legal apparatus into play.

Of course, the problem of how to handle all matters arising out of the totalitarian legal and social system is much more extensive. Nonetheless, some similarities exist. Common and political crimes should be dealt with on the basis of the existing criminal code.

The problem of economic crimes, however, needs separate consideration. One may assume that the nomenklatura, as the especially privileged segment of the Party apparatus, did gain many economic advantages through direct and indirect exploitation during the totalitarian reign. To lessen the effects of this extortion, the members of the nomenklatura should return their gains. To do that, all members of the nomenklatura should declare how much they gained during their tenure and reimburse the Revenue Office with this amount. All benefits obtained during their period in office should be included: funds transferred abroad, goods delivered to others, money lost through various types of activities, chattels hidden in various places, values invested in jewellery, art, land, etc. Those who do not declare the totality of their benefits should face criminal prosecution, including prison sentences of, say, five years, and lose all of their possessions. This type of punishment would have the strongest deterrent effect, since, as Machiavelli observed, people would sooner condone patricide than the confiscation of their belongings.

3 and 4. One of the characteristics of totalitarianism, specific to Poland, was the systematic destruction of the traditional intelligentsia as a separate social stratum. Sovietization strove systematically to excise the ideology of the intelligentsia from the social conscience and replace it with the ideology of the "working intelligentsia," earlier described as a social stratum with higher technical or administrative (but not humanistic) education. The ideology of the new social category—working intelligentsia—was focused on providing the government in office with up-to-date reports on the state of society (Konrad, Szeleny 1979). That the "socialization" of this stratum had been effective became clear when members of the nomenklatura quietly crossed over to the victorious Solidarity. Thus, one of the unique features of totalitarianism was its ability to call

to life, in a relatively short period, a new social stratum that was completely lacking in ideals and ready to serve anyone in power who was willing to pay this new salariat (those whose existence is based on monthly salary).

A civil service and bureaucracy (in Weber's impersonal sense) of the kind familiar to the West did not emerge in Poland from the bourgeoisie, but from upwardly mobile peasants and small-town people. These people owed their own rise to power not so much to competence as to their loyalty to the new administration. However, since they were alienated from the customs of the traditional intelligentsia, they were at the disposal of current orders from the centers of power. Their readiness to obey orders provided the foundation for a new type of social loyalty—loyalty towards the Communist "co-fraternity."

The civil-servant and technocratic intelligentsia, formed during the period of Stalinist totalitarianism, rolled inertly into post-totalitarianism. Yet the expertise of this social category resembled the drunkard's lamp-post: it did not illuminate the surroundings, but merely served as something to lean on. Again, there is a clash of opposing currents: the ideology of the traditional intelligentsia demanded non-egocentric activity, whereas the new ideology of the "administrative and technological experts" was servile. It is this administrative "expert" stratum that is responsible for the current state of law in Poland. Law formulated by these types of "specialists" led to such absurdities that the Presidium of the Government settled the wages of charwomen, and the Ministry of Finance determined procedures for filleting and salting fish (Podgórecki 1957: 3).

Social life was dominated by the repressive, inquisitive nature of official law that penetrated by osmosis into civil law. The call for law and order was, in fact, the call for law to cover up reality, which in itself was anything but law-abiding. Intuitive law (that used by two trustworthy partners with a mutual reason for keeping up their trustworthiness) was eliminated by the bureaucratic degeneration of the system (Podgórecki et al. 1990). The post-totalitarian social and legal system placed before lawyers the extremely difficult and completely unrewarding (intellectually) task of weeding out the remnants of previous legal inflation, getting rid of the effects of the inconsistencies in hierarchies of legal acts, and finding a way to disentangle illogical and nonsensical normative constructions elaborated within theoretical Marxist "unruliness." Post-totalitarian lawyers also had to see to it that the new sensible legal acts be consistent with the old ones, which, though faulty, were still in force. Again, one sees the opposition of two currents.

5. In the post-totalitarian phase, the state still owned the basic economic spheres: railways, mining, chemical production, ship building, the military, "heavy," and textile industries, the banks (though new private banks are now beginning to open), science (including the universities, the Polish Academy of Sciences, and many research institutes), the core of the mass media, and the publishing houses—to name only the most important branches of life directly or indirectly related to the economy. All these branches were subordinate to public law formulated during the totalitarian period. Once again, there are op-

posing tendencies: on the one hand, there is a rigid structure of property based on the public law of the impersonal state, and on the other, there is a rapidly developing private market. True, this structure is crumbling here and there due to various trends towards privatization (introduced earlier in the form of joint-stock companies established by the "old" nomenklatura in the process of changing its skin).

6. Thanks to inertia, the customs elaborated in Poland during the period of systematic sovietization are still in force; they may even be blossoming, in the new atmosphere of freedom. In his recent book *Summer Meditations*, Vaclav Havel made some interesting remarks that stem, apparently, from his empathic insight as a writer and the controlling abilities of the acting president. He observes that "the authoritarian regime imposed a certain order—if that is the right expression for it—on these vices (and in doing so 'legitimized them,' in a sense). This order has now been shattered, but a new order that would limit rather than exploit these vices, an order based on freely accepted responsibility to and for the whole society, has not yet been built—nor could it have been, for such an order takes years to develop and cultivate. Thus we are witnesses to a bizarre state of affairs: society has freed itself, true, but in some ways it behaves worse than when it was in chains" (Havel 1992: 1–2). These vices appear in different areas of life and take on different forms: especially "dirty togetherness," the tendency to set up claims, and instrumentality.

Dirty togetherness was discussed earlier. Let me add only that it functions in society not only in the areas where it is directly established (what has been identified in Russia as the *Krugovaja poruka*—"circular assurance"). Existing dirty togetherness has the potential to seek additional connections with similar partnerships. Dirty togetherness uses the institution of "access." If a given case does not lie within the practical possibilities of a given partnership, it may, through its individual members, seek access to a different, similar partnership. This occurs because totalitarian society and to an even greater extent, post-totalitarian society operate on foundations built from a general matrix of different, interconnected partnerships. Just as the "second economy" supplements or "bites into" the state economy (Łoś 1990), dirty togetherness is a hidden reality that corrects or modifies all manifest social processes.

Another specific feature of dirty togetherness is that it makes use of all formal and official structures in order to take them over for private goals, taking advantage of their administrative potential and formal power. Things that cannot be arranged legally and officially are arranged through dirty togetherness by a chain of connections: private—official—private. Of course, the pool of official positive decisions is limited, so the dirty partnership uses its private connections to take over part of this pool for itself. Hence, less is left for official procedures. Sometimes dirty togetherness takes over the entire pool.

Another side-effect of the sovietization of Polish society was the widespread tendency to set up claims. Whether or not they possessed legal justification, people demanded from other people, institutions, organizations, and the state that they be given what they claimed was theirs. These claims may have been related to their most basic needs, but they may also at times have been quite esoteric. They were usually excessive. In making such claims, people tried to be as visible as possible. When contending with each other over justified demands, it was important to be dynamic and aggressive in the process. People believed that, if they demanded a lot, they would receive at least part of what they wanted.

This general atmosphere of claims was obvious within the country. Everyone was claiming something, so there was little variation in styles of behavior. However, differences became striking as soon as one left the country. Polish emigrants, who appear on various European and non-European scenes (especially Canada and Australia) differ in terms of the intensity of their claims, but they are always rapacious. The following generalization may nonetheless be suggested. The later that someone left the country (the longer the influence of sovietization), the more intense the claims.

Instrumentality was the most general product of sovietization. Since survival itself became a problem, not to mention subsistence survival, one had to grasp all possible means to guarantee survival, according to the canons of social experience. All means leading to the goal were acceptable. Hence, for example, the imperative that the traditional intelligentsia serve its own society became almost ridiculous. Such concepts as patriotism, Fatherland, and social service (additionally ridiculed and devalued by the Stalinist demand for ''social action'') very rapidly became empty words. ''One's own business'' became important; this was frequently understood as the welfare of one's children, though it is, then, actually one's own business too. When people guarantee that their children have comforts that they did not have, they are compensating for their own deprivations. Totalitarian VIPs and various ''official'' patriots sent their grown children abroad. This, of course, required careful, instrumental preparation.

These various customs, born under the pressure of an enforced alien totalitarian ideology, were completely functional when they served in self-defence. In the post-totalitarian period, they still retained considerable utilitarian potential. They still live on (autotelically) and almost function autonomously, even though political oppression no longer exists.

There are undoubtedly several reasons why this is so. Two seem predominant. First of all, instrumentalism is a universal trend nowadays. It is particularly conspicuous in American, German, and Japanese youth, as well as in the young Jews who underwent many years of communization in Soviet Russia. We also find it in the young Chinese. Second, the ideology of the traditional Polish intelligentsia was undoubtedly a great burden. Once discarded, it gave way to a feeling of considerable personal ''freedom.'' In the absence of clear ideals and values that could lend cohesion to society as a whole (with the exception of negative ideals such as opposition to communism), the strategy of survival on one's own terms seems more attractive.

Leon Petrażycki spoke of ''social venoms.'' These were particularly ripe under the totalitarian regime. Suspiciousness of neighbors, family, or sometimes even one's own children; instrumental and "altruistic" denunciations; corrosion of friendships; administrative corruption; dirty togetherness; the systematic transformation of traditionally respected linguistic symbols into negative slogans (democracy); generalized fear; reluctance to speak the truth; constant self-censorship—these are some of the venoms. They cannot be wiped out within a few days. In the post-totalitarian era they have become automatized and continue to live on as an internal negative automatic force.

It can be assumed that the mental heritage of the totalitarian era acts as a miasmatic overhang, lying in wait, ready to collapse at any moment, forcing society through the process of psychic rebirth.

7. One reason for the breakdown of totalitarianism was that traditional Polish Catholicism opposed it. Catholicism was connected to various patriotic attitudes that were not always sufficiently clarified, and it proved to be a persistent adversary, having gained experience through a centuries-old quest for survival. A side-effect of the overthrow of totalitarianism and the victory of religiousness was unexpected widespread clericalism (the increased feeling of power among church authorities, which has led to pride in overthrowing totalitarianism, the martyrdom of several Polish priests, and the charisma of the Polish pope, has spread to all representatives of the Church).

The sudden boost in clerical self-esteem has not been accompanied by an intellectual deepening of the Christian doctrine (nothing new has appeared here except for the reception of French personalism and isolated phenomenological discussions). Catholic dogma has tended to become more rigid in both ideological and practical terms. The complete intimidation of the Senate when voting on the anti-abortion bill was a conspicuous example. The mere receding of totalitarianism does not guarantee the parallel systematic development of tolerance or the cultivation of a pluralistic outlook, but is connected, paradoxically, to the reinforcement of a different totalitarian outlook.

Perhaps it sounds blasphemous to compare Fascist or Communist totalitarianism with Catholic totalitarianism. Yet this comparison does not focus on the criminal practices of fascism or the patriotic pro-social outcomes of communism, but rather on their similar mentality: everything is subordinated to an all-encompassing ideology. Again, the opposing currents are revealed: after almost complete incapacitation by criminal totalitarianism, society faces a trap—the cul-de-sac of gratitude for the savior, and the coercion of another form of totalitarianism.

It is worth noting that the nomenklatura has not completely withdrawn into a defensive position. There are some persistent, although not easily verifiable, indications of a well planned and executed anti-Church movement. In morally and politically controversial areas, there are clear signs of a disinformation campaign. For instance, highly repressive opinions regarding abortion and related matters (such as the planned family) have been attributed to the Church, which even now is not willing to denounce these principles. A careful reading of official church pronouncements shows that the Polish church leaders' stand on controversial matters has been quite reasonable and restrained. Contrary to general belief, they have not lent their support to the highly punitive anti-abortion bill that preoccupied the attention of the Polish parliament (the Diet) in 1991. The image of the Church appears to have been manipulated, and there are signs that a semialliance of former security forces, ex-Communist party activists, and anti-Church leftist circles has been responsible for it.

8. Macrosocial categorization falls to pieces in the era of post-totalitarianism. Yet no new political doctrine automatically takes its place. People are unwilling to acknowledge that there is no single, synthetic, true philosophy of thought and action. They yearn for a general truth. Since none appears immediately, attitudes backfire, and people begin to turn once again to the Party "gods" of the previous era, who have meanwhile changed to Western clothing. Hence, Zygmunt Bauman or Leszek Kołakowski have had a come-back (what is more, the latter, previously an outspoken enemy of Catholicism, now gives a hermeneutic lesson on understanding Christianity to the chief editor of the Catholic weekly *Tygodnik Powszechny*). Thus, in post-totalitarianism freedom and truth can appear alternately as mulch for the still-totalitarian garden.

9. The Poles must learn to be free. Recently, a series of lectures was held in one of the capitals of a Western European country, given by leading Polish intellectuals. After one such prestigious lecture, the speaker was asked which Western institutions he thought could be transferred to Poland. The transfer was meant to help Poland in its democratic reconstruction. The speaker flushed with joy. He said, "I've thought a lot about this. I always repeat the same thing in such cases. We must apply a three-in-one-system. The first element is cognition. Then we must add a second element—the development of adequate abilities. Cognition and abilities must be supplemented with attitude modelling. Then the three-in-one system will begin to function. And it can be fully utilized for democracy." All-encompassing, abstract, Marxist rubbish gives birth, through its persistently cultivated implementation, to another type of bastard. The sense of every utterance is differently verified at various levels of generalization. If freedom is to consist of feeding the hungry with abstract gibberish, this may lead people to yearn for the Stalinist whip. That, at least, gives a straightforward answer.

In Poland, there is no orderly and systematic process for the selection of people for specific posts. It would be difficult to believe that "the last human response on the road to Heaven—log-rolling" could immediately be eliminated. This procedure could, however, be limited quite drastically by the widespread introduction of competition. Even the simple mechanism of democratic discussion, seconding, is unknown in Poland. There is not even an appropriate term in Polish for this practice.

It is essential to hammer home a sense of "impersonal" procedures in a society polluted with dirty togetherness and favoritism. It is also important to clarify the various concepts of Marxist "false awareness," to excavate with archaeological precision the true values and meanings of concepts, ruthlessly eliminating myths—myths that pertain to both scientific and pseudo-scientific conceptions, and that widely disseminate legends about particular people. It is noteworthy that in the era of totalitarianism, when censorship enforced silence, the same names were heard again and again. These names were imprinted in public consciousness by Party propaganda. Why, in post-totalitarianism, do we still persistently hear the voices of those who bear these names, although they now declare ideas that contradict their previous opinions? Have they made an effort to compensate for the now obvious harm they have done? Where are those who carried the burden of keeping alive the values of a "civil society"? Are they all gone? Who notices that those whose names were not made public by the negative propaganda of Stalinist totalitarianism are banished to the state of "civic nonexistence"? Not everyone joined the disciplined lines of the fighting Solidarity.

Totalitarianism encouraged people to take up sham activities, defending themselves against its consequences at the same time. The post-totalitarian period is also full of sham activities (maniacal rummaging through personal data and empty disputes, avoiding any declaration of political programs, covering up ignorance of economic matters on a broad scale, celebrating various religious feast days and patriotic anniversaries, waiting for help from the West), though content and goals are different. Post-totalitarianism tends to inhibit spontaneity in order to counteract sham activity, but at the same time, it shuts off the possibility of a real search for new ways. Hence, a new network of "opposing currents" surfaces: sham activities close the door on authentic activity in the totalitarian system, whereas in post-totalitarianism, authentic activity is inhibited in order to counteract sham activities.

10. Post-totalitarianism has the prerequisites to discard the thought muzzles of totalitarianism. However, the existential experience of the threefold loss of independence and the fourfold changes in the sociopolitical system were unable to stimulate the literary and scientific description of these mutations, which were unique in the history of humankind. In such a case, is it not deplorable to expect inspiration from the West or to copy its fads? During the war, life proceeded in a make-believe fashion. Does it not proceed sluggishly nowadays? Aleksander Matejko makes a similar point. "Poland is a country which *moves* from state socialism to democracy and a free market economy, but in reality, still remains consumed by a structural maladaptation to the new status quo: the dominant public sector is difficult to reform, political culture is highly incompatible with the new arrangements, attractiveness for foreign goods is limited, the expectations of the populations are quite unrealistic, the internal equilibrium is far from being achieved" (Matejko forthcoming).

CONCLUSIONS

In a totalitarian system, the economy is subordinate to politics. Yet this political preponderance refers to a relatively short period of time. The material status of the people is the decisive factor in the long run—not the status determined by ownership (real or ostensible) or the ownership of the means of production. What counts is having at one's disposal material resources that allow for the gratification of basic needs, including those dictated by a worldwide "revolution of demands."

Totalitarianism creates not only rigid, centrally controlled economic mutations but also a redundancy of "legal" regulations. It also establishes centers of social control that block the uncontrolled proliferation of sociocultural activity. Additionally, the social structures created by the system continue to exist when the political and ideological monolith of totalitarian power has ceased to exist.

The most enduring remnant of the totalitarian system is not only an efficient "old nomenklatura" transformed into a conformist quasi-private stratum but also thought habits and "psychic venoms" which, though externally intangible, penetrate everything.

The most characteristic feature of the post-totalitarian system is the dual current of social life. On the one hand, there are open pluralistic political reforms, open public discussions, liquidation of state censorship; on the other hand, we find the internal censorship of the new, anti-totalitarian totalitarianism, the lack of means or efficient "transmitters" that pass the outcomes of public discussions to the centers that have real influence on social life, and, most importantly, the systematic perpetuation of the social heritage of the totalitarian system.[56]

The development of post-totalitarianism leads to new paradoxes. Although it may seem that thoughts are the most volatile, intangible, and mobile of things, many thought relics of totalitarianism have become so deeply imbedded in human minds that it is impossible to get rid of them or to formulate new ideas. One would think that now, at last, when totalitarianism has fallen, uprightness can become a widely respected virtue, and yet it is quite the opposite. Upright people are a challenge for others. It is better to keep them at bay, since everyone has something on their conscience. Since in the era of totalitarianism many things were settled once and for all, and in post-totalitarianism many problems require creative and often tedious reflection, many people reveal a nostalgia for the previous repressive order. Ultimately, the victims of totalitarianism must abdicate justified compensation because the inherited system is economically inefficient.

This discussion shows that social change in a post-totalitarian system is not directly contingent upon economic factors. These can play a significant part in the immediate claim for improvement in standards of living through strikes, riots, peasant demonstrations, or channelled claims (demand for improved conditions of work, slogans modelled after the "revolution of demands"). In a totalitarian system, the "means of production" were formally owned by the working class on the basis of political proclamation and constitutional law. In reality, however, they were owned by the nomenklatura, popularly known as the "owners of the Polish People's Republic." This ownership was based on the imposition of norms contrary to intuitive law.

Intuitive law is usually popularly accepted even though it is inconsistent with official law. In this case, however, it was not accepted. The schizophrenic split of law and doctrine was well recognized by society. This also led to the rejection of any legitimation of the socialist system. Under totalitarianism, the "ownership of the means of production" had the economic consequences mentioned above. Under post-totalitarianism, it took on a new meaning—it enabled privatization, and the reification of previously wielded power.

Under post-totalitarianism, the old political forces, now powerless and always without legitimation, are quite insignificant (although they have their plugs in certain branches of the social-control system), and they meet with explicit social condemnation. The new authorities have, at the highest level, widespread social approval. However, they are inefficient in recruiting higher-level administration because the executive authorities (a) are still partly on the side of the old apparatus, (b) have a shattered morale, (c) are cynical to a considerable degree, (d) are impersonal, and (e) frequently obey orders merely to conform. Unconditional acceptance of the highest authorities springs from the negation of the old regime, and not from an acceptance of their program. These authorities do not have sufficient support and understanding at the lower levels of the administrative apparatus. Post-totalitarianism not only brings with it an ebullient state of social warpedness (uncertainty whether people, constantly dissociated, are responding predictably to typical social motivations, appeals, and incentives, or whether they are reacting haphazardly and unpredictably). In post-totalitarianism, a crooked middle-level administration formed under the totalitarian system is observable. We can also see that the new administration, based on the idea of "acceleration," will have to reckon not only with the remnants of totalitarianism and post-totalitarianism but also with several elements of the new nomenklatura, which, having only just gotten a taste of power, will be reluctant to lose it.

Old monolithic outlooks will have a limited role in post-totalitarianism. The "derivative-ideological" role of the Communist doctrine is well recognized. Catholicism, in turn, is beginning to limit its scope to celebrating rituals or returning to its proper role of "timeless" consolidation of the covenant with the suprahuman. The strength of the new, incipient programs lies mainly in their destruction of previous outlooks.

"Social structures," as they are popularly (and intuitively) called, are decisive in the present *multidimensional* kaleidoscope of factors. These structures, according to our earlier discussion, should be interpreted as consolidated social meta-attitudes. These attitudes, though invisible, are central among historically determined collective motivations, functioning with specific force and camouflaged inertia.

The term meta-attitudes is understood to mean social sets that combine "ordinary" or "mundane" attitudes into a consistent whole. The following configuration of meta-attitudes can be regarded as typical for Polish society: instrumentalism, survival, spectacular adherence to principles, and "all thumbs" or pudginess (the confusion of authenticity and unintended pretense). Although these meta-attitudes appear in different historical-political and socioeconomic settings with various force, they are the product of mutations characteristic of this society as a whole (Podgórecki 1976: 1987).

In sum, the uniqueness of the post-totalitarian social system, as manifested in Poland, can be summarized in the following way: the comprehensive and unequivocal populist rejection of totalitarianism that culminated in 1989–1990 pushed social forces, movements, and ideologies (new to public life) in a direction opposite to that of the former Communist thrust. Since the opposite pole of officially accepted options was still "occupied" by the "social void" (Podgórecki 1976; Nowak 1979), these emerging post-totalitarian forces, movements, and ideologies tended towards those tangible remainders that were still discernible. The overwhelming rejection of totalitarianism (with the exception of a small but relatively influential "nomenklatura") as a sociopolitical system did not necessarily mean the rejection of those cognitive categories, behaviors, structural informal arrangements, and institutional and organizational schemes that were created during the prolonged rule of a totalitarian regime. These patterns, although criticized for their emptiness, persisted as the main schemes available for public interaction.

Thus, the main current of the newly generated official life was channelled through once-void patterns, eventually entering into the territory of an entirely different authenticity. It belonged to the double-structured entity of a disparate epistemological order. From one point of view, this entity was (and is) concerned with "eternal" phenomena, but from another, it was (and is) engaged in guiding present sociopolitical processes *hic et nunc*. This body, traditionally rooted in national and social life, recently gained considerable sympathy when it was engaged, despite its "destiny of a higher order," in an open war against the vicious, frontal, manipulative assaults of totalitarianism. Clearly, it was a war impossible to win.

Under persistent battles, fiscal pressures, administrative measures, and physical terror, repetitive persuasion has been defenceless against normative solicitations and appeals. This institution, was, of course, represented by the Polish Catholic church. Although the Church could not win the ongoing war in any of its phases, its latent, well-recognized function was to counter-balance constant totalitarian pressures, and to remind the overwhelming majority of the population that zero hour will inevitably arrive. Under the regime of totalitarianism, nobody expected that it would come so soon, and that the Church, surprisingly, would become the monopolistic beneficiary of totalitarianism.

It may be useful to remember that totalitarianism appeared in the twentieth century as a result of the activities of fanatic and militant teams led by ruthless leaders, in combination with the resentments of the lower echelons of the middle class. In Poland, it is currently expected that the new middle class will emerge as the beneficiary. It is also expected that the Church may help to consolidate this new middle class, which in turn is expected to reject all elements of post-totalitarian decay and play a decisive role as the herald of rationally oriented processes, triggered and monitored by the market economy.

It is clear that the study of totalitarian and post-totalitarian law and the inquiry into effects of its prolonged existence does add some important insights to the understanding of these puzzling phenomena. Therefore it might be useful to extend the examination of these types of law in general. Anticipating further considerations, one may hypothesize that if law (in its official and intuitive constructs) embodies power, then it may be regarded as an oppression in its "frozen" form. Thus power and oppression would be two faces of the same Janus.

Four generalizations can be built on the basis of the foregoing considerations:

1. Intuitive law is supported only by mutual or negotiated duties and claims. Official law, with its octopus-like, all-embracing potential, once backed by the established power, has a tendency to subjugate everybody and everything. The normative potential of totalitarian law "waits" for appropriate sociopolitical conditions to surface and blossom. It has, as well, considerable potential for *inertia*. If the concept of "autopoesis" has any sense at all, it should be understood to mean that the aggressive potential of the official law is constantly looking for a suitable prey.

2. Each norm of official law, under totalitarian conditions, is valid only if the corresponding "shadowy" power-related norm approves of the official one. This conditionality, more or less socially visible, creates a situation where the legal order becomes *whimsical*. This whimsicality spreads a generally discernible and high level of insecurity among the population.

3. *Totalitarianism effectively renders "middle-level social norms" inoperative.* Yet totalitarianism cannot entirely eradicate "grassroots" intuitive laws. These laws function vitally in the body of the "living" society, monitor closely its essential, private processes, and have a certain degree of independence. Totalitarianism is also unable to liquidate general ideas that belong to the heritage of humankind; these ideas exist, on an abstract level, in a dormant state. Yet totalitarianism was, and is, successful in destroying all patterns and habits controlled by middle-level norms regulating the bulk of social life. The current experience in Eastern Europe makes it clear that rebuilding this type of infrastructure presents the most difficult task, not only for the social but also for the economic and political strategies of reconstruction.

4. Law, especially official law, emerges as the main instrument of this reconstruction. Planned social change is the crucial phase of the transition process from totalitarianism to democracy. Contrary to general opinion, it is not so much the economy that directly restores democracy: the law must first establish suitable conditions for free-market development. As a consequence, it is law that lays solid grounds for the development of democracy. This point stresses again the importance of the "de-totalization" of law.

7

Transitory Societies

THE CONCEPT

The concepts of developed and underdeveloped societies are well established in political science, sociology, and history, although they are not always precisely defined. The criterion employed to classify a particular society on the development scale is currently determined by the society's degree of civilizational progress, which is measured by technological advancement. The concept of transition is vaguely defined, if it is defined at all. For example: "By *transition* I mean, in a strict sense, the ambiguous, intermediate period when the previous regime has abandoned some of its nondemocratic structures without having acquired all the structures of the soon-to-emerge regime. This is a period of institutional flux and uncertainty during which the actors involved confront each other with different interests, projects, and political strategies" (Morlino 1987: 53–54).

Since the 1989 victory of Solidarity and the subsequent decomposition of the Soviet Union, several new macrosocial bodies have come into existence and they cannot be categorized under the old criteria; the "Fall of Nations" has created a new situation wherein these societies must be classified in an entirely different way.

Several twentieth-century societies made a detour towards the Communist track, mainly under pressure from the former Soviet Union. After almost half a century, the widely recognized failure of this pathological model has precipitated a need for recovery. Since almost all former Communist societies abandoned political structures based on Marxist principles and took an unprecedented step towards the family of societies based on "free market" principles, a problem in recognizing the specificity of these societies emerged.

Especially revealing are political institutions of the transition period. Concluding an empirical and collective study on transformation of the Polish contracted parliament (based thirty-five percent on democratic elections and sixty percent on Communist nominations) elected in 1989, Jacek Wasilewski comes to the following conclusion: "Processes seen in the contracted parliament and those in society at large did not lead after 1990 to the establishment of a pluralistic élite, but on the contrary, to the disintegration of a spurious consensus" (Wasilewski 1992: 304).

It is reasonable to label them "societies *in transition.*" Neither the criterion of cultural affiliation (native, Christian, Oriental, Jewish) constituted by the incompatible basic existential values, nor the criterion of civilizational development (as this was applied to some African nations) is suitable for classification. Instead, the existence of a collective will to return to the previous status quo becomes decisive. The fact that these societies, attempting to throw off the ballast of Communist heritage, strive to achieve a social structure founded on the combination of pluralistic political orientations, social democracy, and the "free market" places them in this new category.

PRECIPITATING FACTORS

Polish society was the first society in transition to be established after the Fall of Nations in 1989. As such it furnishes the most striking example of this new societal category. It is thus of theoretical interest to investigate the basic features of Polish society.

It is important to remember that Polish society underwent a prolonged period of underground civil activity from the eighteenth to the twentieth century. These activities were most pronounced under the loss of independence (1795–1918), the German occupation (1939–1945), and the extended Stalinist period (1945–1955). The activities that flourished during these periods were not only attempts at economic and personal survival; they were also oriented towards cultural survival. Much of the experience amassed during these periods was subsequently employed under the period of martial law (1981–82). This is particularly true of "second economy" activities that were characteristic during the occupation in the Second World War.

Underground literature (books as well as daily newspapers and magazines) was published by independent institutions. The "Flying University" was reactivated. Its lectures, held at locations that were constantly changed for security reasons, dealt with recent Polish history and sociopolitical relations. Forms of mutual help were also rekindled. Many new types of resistance activity were invented; for example, after the imposition of martial law, almost all artists and actors refused to cooperate with government-owned and directed radio and TV. Many in these professions lost both their positions and their salaries. As a result, their families were often brought to the brink of starvation.

Under martial law, the Polish people, although engaged in resistance activities, did not adopt violence as a means to solve political conflict. In keeping with the generally accepted national ethos, public resistance was to be non-violent. Some writers have argued that this new "Ghandi-like" form of peaceful resistance on a mass scale was reinforced additionally by the spirit of Solidarity.

Other social scientists are more skeptical. They claim that this type of resistance was a political necessity that had been elevated to the status of virtue (Kowalski 1990: 67). According to Sergiusz Kowalski, violent behavior might have provoked the Polish regime to adopt a militarized form of retaliation. This perspective asserts that, according to widespread popular feelings, violence was not a reasonable alternative to the reality of internal pacification, or, even worse, to the possibility of bloody intervention from outside.

Independent of its origin, a massive trend was subsequently established: non-violent anti-oppressionism. Isaiah Berlin's statement that "the two great liberating political movements of the nineteenth century were, as every history book informs us, humanitarian individualism and romantic nationalism" (Berlin 1969: 5) was enriched by the nonviolent anti-oppression movement against authoritarian social subjugation.

The martial-law period exacerbated erstwhile Polish attitudes towards the Communist regime. These attitudes, as everybody knew in Poland, sharply distinguished two dimensions: "we" and "they." "We" encompasses those who belong to our social group; those who are accepted by us and whom we can trust; those with whom we interact. "They" comprises those who are alien to us and whose values contaminate our own ethos. "We" do not belong to "their" social circles. "We" try to avoid any social interactions with "them" (professional contact, on the other hand, was necessary to survive). "They," as a whole, could "freeze" themselves into a separate epistemological entity. They could freeze themselves into a "system."

Kowalski gives a persuasive description of widespread systemic understanding. The "system" is composed of five elements: (a) it has a total character; (b) it is a "vessel of anti-values"; (c) it tries to hide its real nature, disclosing only the "play of pretences" (the widespread use of spurious activities); (d) it resembles a hostile being—a "vile and vicious" monster; and (e) it is an agency that has the power to "give and take away" (Kowalski 1990: 28).

Solidarity gained momentum upon achieving a spectacular victory over the system. This movement was registered at the Supreme Court (by Professor Wiesław Chrzanowski) as an officially recognized *independent* trade union. After its turbulent development, Solidarity was suddenly defeated by the imposition of martial law in December 1981. It is important to note that it was defeated as a formal organization, not as a social movement.

After eight years, Solidarity regained its momentum when the "system" (the establishment), in response to the escalating economic crisis and increasing pressure from grassroots organizations, was compelled to enter into negotiations with the underground Solidarity in 1989. Paradoxically enough, the very fact that Solidarity, employing the "good services" of the Church, agreed to undertake *formal* discussions with the government gave the state apparatus its first legitimacy since 1945. These talks ended in an agreement to hold partially free elections to the Sejm, or lower body of Parliament (free elections were restricted to only thirty-five percent of the Sejm's seats and all of the Senat). These talks marked a turning point since they triggered the beginning of Solidarity's unexpected decomposition.

Since its inception, Solidarity had been struggling with inconsistency in its own functions. As discussed earlier, Solidarity was at once a trade union, political party, cultural agency, and "self-limiting" revolution.

The trade-union duties of Solidarity comprised its original, but not necessarily primary, function. In typical trade union fashion, Solidarity was fighting for better working conditions, higher wages, the right to strike, and the professional and material well-being of its workers. Solidarity was not eager to disclose its real political orientation, which was based on an overwhelmingly negative attitude towards the "system." This was quite a shrewd strategy on its part. Indeed, for as long as Solidarity did not possess sufficient national support and a well-elaborated network of organizational connections, it was well advised to hide behind the relatively safe trade-union facade. Lech Wałęsa's political instinct dictated this tactic when he was consulted on this matter.

During the period of martial law, Solidarity, in concert with several Church agencies, cosponsored various types of cultural activities. Solidarity was able to organize university activities under the protection of the Church. University professors used to travel to small towns and villages to deliver lectures and seminars in civil law and administrative or agricultural law. Peasants treated education very seriously. The Church also donated space for theatrical performances and concerts. Solidarity monitored the pace and volume of its own development so as not to cross the invisible line that stood between it and state retaliation. Thus, as a revolutionary movement, Solidarity was determined to protect the system in order to have the chance to abolish it later. The heterogeneous functions of the Solidarity movement contained the potential germs of its own decomposition.

Decomposition was further reinforced by several political and social by-products of Solidarity's own activities. Firstly, Solidarity established a nationwide network of Citizens' Committees whose task was to organize and monitor the supervision of national elections. Although the elections ended in Solidarity's victory, the Citizens' Committees continued to exist for a relatively short period as an independent organizational entity. They were eventually dismantled on the personal order of Wałęsa, who may have wanted to retain undivided authority over the entire movement.

Secondly, following the astounding parliamentary victory, a Civic Parliamentary Club was established to pursue policy in opposition to that of the Communists (Thirty-five percent of the Sejm consisted of non-Communists, and ninety-nine percent of the Senat). Although the club began as a Solidarity initiative, it quickly gained independent political momentum.

Thirdly, Tadeusz Mazowiecki, who became the first prime minister of a semi-independent government, acquired this position (and his former position as one of Wałęsa's advisers) on the coat-tails of Wałęsa's charisma. Thus, he assumed the position of prime minister on *borrowed*, or "mirrored," charisma. Mazowiecki's charisma was reinforced by the fact that he was the *first* prime minister to be independent from Communist dictates. For this reason Mazowiecki became even more popular than Wałęsa himself, according to various public-opinion polls. A developing tension began to spoil the political climate between the prime minister's office and the Solidarity leadership, as represented by Wałęsa. This strain developed precisely when a climate of cooperation was needed to counteract the shrewd behavior of the former nomenklatura. It also added new elements to the tensions that had already begun to disrupt Solidarity.

It is important to note that the Communist system was able to plant destructive seeds into the psyche of Polish society. The suspicion, mistrust, and apprehension that were trademarks of the Communist party succeeded to some extent in contaminating the society to such an extent that a psychological poison began to disrupt the cooperation of former allies.

The derivation-rationalization intentions, to use Pareto's language, that Mazowiecki wanted to "create" and develop between his role as prime minister and Wałęsa's position as leader of Solidarity were not without merit. He wanted to institutionalize an executive power that was independent of political pressure. Such pressure had dominated the period of Communist rule. Mazowiecki's idea (if it was not a product of his hunger for power, as some factors indicate it might have been), although sensible, was premature. At that moment, the country needed a strong and united power center that would be able to counteract the "invisible" accumulation of certain elements of economic power in the hands of the shrewd, conforming "red nomenklatura." As a direct result of these tensions, the competition between Mazowiecki (and his burgeoning "white nomenklatura," a journalistic concept that needs careful sociological analysis) and Wałęsa shook the internal integrity of the Solidarity movement.

BASIC CHARACTERISTICS OF THE "SOCIETY IN TRANSITION"

Since Polish society can be treated as a classic model of a society in transition, it might be possible to examine the main features of such a society through the Polish example.

The characteristic features of a transitional society are as follows:

1. Internal rejection of the Communist system. An overwhelming majority of the population regards this system as unjust, economically inefficient, and standing in violation of the basic principles of human dignity.

2. Rejection of communism as an ideology employed to camouflage an imperialist regime with a single power center that subjugates several societies and

deprives them of their state's sovereignty and economic, social, and cultural independence.

3. A hidden and well-elaborated mass of "leftovers" (high pensions prescribed by state orders, luxurious apartments, children studying in Western countries, Swiss bank accounts, old-boy networks) accumulated by the previously powerful nomenklatura.

4. A myriad of highly developed small-group affiliations (treated on the one hand as authentic centers of belonging, or as instruments for survival, and, on the other, as a dedication to abstract, historical ideas of democracy, pluralism, and tolerance).

5. A highly developed rhetoric that enables individuals to get something for nothing, although they are unable to act in a coordinated manner to effect economic change since the rhetoric supplies them only with techniques and overdeveloped skills for achieving spurious goals.

6. Highly underdeveloped skills in administration and organizations where institutions should seek common benefit in a rational and impersonal way. The "personalized" bureaucracy is corrupted not only at the periphery but also at the center. This society inherited a system of law that was uniquely functional for a totalitarian society (Podgórecki 1991: 163–94). Frantic parliamentary and governmental efforts were launched to find socially reliable and efficient ways to prepare, test, legislate, and pass new types of laws.

7. The existence of various social mechanisms that defend the transitional society against prevalent forms of oppression, but deprived it of mechanisms for designing institutions and procedures that are conducive to common advantage. Consequently, the society generates dispersed political orientations, based not on real differences in political programs, but on personal differences (if not animosities).

8. An unpreparedness for entering into economic competition with advanced societies from the West. The transitional society is thus exposed to danger by those who advocate an economic and public "security" (or sui generis conservatism) based on previously established and "tested" norms of behavior. These habits or norms were inculcated into Polish society through the prolonged and obstinate process of Communist "socialization."

9. A huge pool of burdensome post-Communist enterprises, originally designed to support the economy of the Soviet bloc. Since the collapse of the bloc, these enterprises have become completely dysfunctional in the new society in which they operate. Nevertheless, they still employ an army of workers who would otherwise add to the growing mass of the unemployed. In addition to the workers, there exists an army of entrepreneurs. These operators engage in a myriad of relatively small, experimental economic activities that are oriented towards quick economic gain.

10. An inherited and sizeable segment of nihilistically oriented people who despise their leaders, detest social discipline, and rally against all attempts to implement organized cooperation.

Exposition of the Basic Characteristics

The foregoing statements require exposition, if they are not to be taken as trivial.

1. The Polish Communist system did not enjoy social acceptance, nor was it ever legitimized, for the following reasons: (a) it was imposed by the traditional Polish enemy and oppressor, the Soviet Union; (b) it violated traditional Polish values of patriotism and Christianity; (c) in social practice, it revealed itself as an inefficient, externally imposed administrative machine, contradicting the basic principles of a socially accepted cooperative infrastructure; (d) it gained the support of a peculiar social coalition that comprised "young cavaliers," landless peasantry, envious petty-bourgeois drop-outs, and "string" intelligentsia up-starts. In sum, this system had the support of a heterogeneous social stratum that was regarded as a source of social pathology by the "old" intelligentsia (the traditional generator of the Polish ethos); and (e) it was ruled by Soviet-produced ideologies or pseudo-ideologists who were never able to gain authentic support from the Polish population.

2. The forcible inclusion of Polish society into the Soviet imperium violated Poland's expectation that it would regain independence after the sacrifices of World War II (during which, as noted earlier, Poland lost six million of her citizens, including three million Jews). Additionally, this subsumption antago-nized the legal Polish government, which remained in London during the Second World War. This government was recognized as legitimate by the Allies and enjoyed a high level of popularity among the Polish émigrés scattered around the globe (comprising approximately one-quarter of the entire Polish population).

3. The number of those who belonged to the Party nomenklatura is virtually unknown. Before Solidarity's success, approximately three million Party mem-bers operated in Poland. The emergence and development of Solidarity reduced this figure to approximately two million. Of thirty-seven million Poles, young people who were not eligible for Party membership comprised the majority. It is estimated that one-fifth of the Polish adult population belonged to the Party before Solidarity. Since affiliation with the Party possessed an instrumental and pragmatic character (it was a miracle to find a "Communist believer"), nothing except the tight, interpersonal network of mutual arrangements built under the Party umbrella attracted people to the Party.

This network accelerated the development of the "dirty togetherness" phe-nomenon. Dirty togetherness (at a "meta" level), based on a dispersed Party togetherness, provided the basis for the nomenklatura's success in the Fall of Nations in 1989. Indeed, the influence of this metatogetherness was quite sub-stantive since the nomenklatura was able to invoke about twelve percent of the total vote in the first free elections of 1990. Metatogetherness was in part re-sponsible for the "velvet" revolution, a term coined in Czechoslovakia to in-dicate nonviolent abolishment of the existing establishment; a revolution that was paradoxically gainful for those who represented the abolished power. When the "war in the sky" (a term used by Wałęsa designating the power struggle going on above the heads of average people) took place between Wałęsa and Mazowiecki and their respective followers, the metanomenklatura, by manipulating its former power, was able to start the subtle process of intercepting public property in the form of large enterprises, which it transformed into private companies. Of course, members of the nomenklatura placed themselves in lucrative positions.

This operation, which was well-correlated but without central coordination, was accompanied by a disorganized parallel process among the public. After a relatively short period of shock and a subsequent phase of oversleeping, disparate and inexperienced elements of the population tried to establish various forms of private enterprise. These included travel agencies (with trips to Hong Kong), publishing houses, rabbit "plantations," and even a disco-saloon in Hitler's former headquarters. The problem with these initiatives was (and is) that they were undertaken by people who had no practice in this type of entrepreneurship. They were only interested in fast gain, often acting without thought to the firm's image.

4. As various research studies indicate, Polish society presents a peculiar mixture of elements. At the bottom are many small, tightly knit groups (nuclear as well as extended families, groups of friends, cliques, units created by "dirty togetherness"). These groups may sometimes appear as individual solitudes. A relatively young intellectual who perceives himself not only as a count but as a "square" count, asserts that "our generation has had three different affairs: with the Communist party, with 'Solidarity' and with the Church. All these affairs deserted us. The romance with 'Solidarity' was perhaps the most decent, most honest. . . . The pendulum swung in an opposite direction and the solitude remained" (Król 1992: 3). These bottom groups or solitudes have created opposing but compact and consolidated fronts, political loyalties or mutual business obligations. At the top of society's pyramid, one finds patriotic ideas, lofty concepts of social freedom, democracy, and tolerance, towering demands to follow the rules of the knightly ethos of the past Polish nobility, and respect for a plurality of world views. Stefan Nowak effectively popularized the idea that, between these two layers, in the center, there was a void (Nowak 1989, 1991). Under "real socialism," the official social structure was completely rejected by the populace. Yet because the common people felt alienated from administrative and state-affiliated bodies, they acquired the knowledge to communicate in a form of double-speak, skillfully presenting their facade selves as conformist and obedient citizens. Although, this man-made void appears to be empty from one perspective, it appears from another to be an enormously dense mass of spuriously cultivated activities. This void-mass phenomenon is also the result of spurious types of behavior.

5. Various observations were made earlier about spurious activities and the highly developed rhetoric of demands, whose genesis was determined not only by the fact that under "real socialism," one had to shout louder than others to

be noticed but also by the assimilation of official propaganda. Charges triggered by this process (which also generated conflict over allegedly accessible goods and services) were detrimental to the development of an impersonal, pragmatic, and reliable school of legal-rational (in the Weberian sense) behavior. When, in everyday behavior, the bulk of people's activities is contaminated by demands, emotions, and a plethora of tricks, the void-mass of spurious activities is likely to continue growing.

Polish post-totalitarian society faces an enormous task in filling this vacuum with the space for normalized patterns of socially accepted behaviors, applicable in various social contexts, and ruled by objectively structured and prescribed procedures. Thus, the development of a new middle-ranking class capable of impersonal interaction and strategies comprises one of the main tasks for social reconstruction. In order to rebuild its economy and consolidate democracy, a society in transition must establish an infrastructure of formalized social relations.

6. Post-totalitarian law is dysfunctional in the current post-Communist society. As a consequence, a new body of law must be created. The transition from one social system to another depends not only on material (economic) readiness for change but also on procedural preparedness. Law becomes an important independent variable in determining the process of change.

If Polish society, in its recent transformation, can be treated as a macrosocial laboratory, it must be acknowledged that legal factors are elements of primary importance. The nonviolent post-Communist revolution of 1989–1991 was evidently hampered by the inability of Parliament (the Sejm and the Senat) to successfully enact laws. Members of the Senat were often aware that the laws at hand were not good enough to legislate, yet they passed them anyway. They knew that their objections would send the proposed bill back to the Sejm for further elaboration, leaving space to ''reactivate'' totalitarian law; hence their refusal to change the bills was to some extent legitimized, at least for the time being.

This natural macroexperiment in law making supports Leon Petrazycki's and Roscoe Pound's assertions, well known in Polish jurisprudence, about the role of law in the process of social change. It also shows that the validation of legal policy is the crucial point in jurisprudence and the sociology of law (Podgórecki 1962; Podgórecki 1991: 195–234).

Recently, the Legislative Council received a recommendation from the prime minister, Jan Olszewski, to review the Polish system of law. After three months, the Task Force Committee submitted its report, stressing the primary role of law (*Przegląd Rządowy*, 1992, nos. 13–14: 5–115). According to this report, the legal system created from 1989 to 1992, although marked with several advantages, is also marked with several mistakes, including inconsistencies in several axiological assumptions; functional inconsistencies in some normative acts; excessive dispersion of legal regulation; removal of basic executive recommendations to separate normative acts; lack of stability of legal acts, loopholes in legal acts; excessive, sometimes casuistic, legal regulation, and lack of respect for the proper legislative technique (*Przegląd Rządowy* 1992: 57). I presented a similar list of faults in 1957 (Podgórecki 1957: 13–40).

The Task Force Report also suggested that the status of the Legislative Council be raised. The council should be "situated in the office of the Prime Minister as a purely professional body, not associated with any political parties. It should be staffed with a few highly competent specialists, permanently employed and headed by the Deputy Prime Minister. Its main task should be the assessment of assumptions and respective projects of normative acts, and its task should also include the *ex post* control of the normative activities of various governmental bodies" (*Przegląd Rządowy* 1992, no. 13–14: 61).

It isn't just the laws on the books that are important. Of greater significance are socially operational and accepted impersonal mechanisms for dealing with socioeconomic matters. From one side, all rules that are socially beneficial and have social support should be cultivated. From the other, all possible mechanisms should be used to embed "laws on the books" into the current social infra-structure. Thus, grassroots rules of self-government, cooperative entrepreneur-ship, mechanisms for voluntary association, socially sponsored monitoring activities, community-sustained social-control apparatuses, collective, formal self-determination, vigilance communities, and all other extralegal groups that currently assume authority to maintain the integrity of social order and actions by condemning crimes should be studied and, if possible, transplanted to other social settings. A system of rewards for developing these middle-range legal systems should be presented to the public.

7. The post-1989 explosion of political freedom was, by and large, a positive opening. It also generated several negative by-products. A lack of constitutional restrictions on the number of political parties led to a drastic increase in their number. At present, there are more than 150 political parties in Poland. It is interesting to note that none of these parties prepared advance political programs for the "zero hour." They did not discuss the differences in their respective political visions. They did not discuss their visions with their constituencies. These parties have mainly been preoccupied by the game of musical chairs played by those who have been able to attain, by various means, nationwide political visibility.

It is a striking fact that these political figures, with very few exceptions (one exemplary exception being Jan Józef Lipski), are *instrumentalists*, in terms of their personality structure. This type of personality plays a significant role in the disciplines of social science and politics. Instrumentalists always seem to take the upper hand. While instrumentalism in politics appears to be "normal" in countries that are just beginning to develop (instrumentalists have more man-oeuvrability and are more apt to manipulate those who might be immune to outside manipulations), it can be dangerous in the early stages of rational political life. In the politics of developed nations, instrumentalists can play a positive role in the implementation process if basic social values have been clarified. In situations where political values are *in statu nascendi,* the intervention of flexible instrumentalists does not assist in the clarification of values, but adds instead to their obscurity. When instrumentalists deal with means, they can be useful; when they tackle goals, they are dangerous.

Usually, the public evaluates the functioning of its government through an assessment of the actual economic situation. In the current Polish situation, however, a public perception of politicians as manipulators is likely to influence even the most "objective" perception of social reality.

Research pertaining to the perspectives of material improvement, after positive evaluations in the first quarter of 1991, is constantly pessimistic. . . . Research covering 1991 shows that the improved situation of households was accompanied by constantly deteriorating evaluations concerning one's own situation, as well as pessimistic perspectives on the situation in the future. One may assume that these evaluations were affected not only by the general economic situation of the country but, as well, by the assessment of its current political situation." (*Przegląd Rządowy*, 1992, no. 15: 95)

8. The potential for a return of Communist forces is still a viable threat. "Files" activities (actions to reveal the files of those who were actively implicated in security activities) have thus been necessary. Although these activities carry some dangers (they may reveal files purposely fabricated by the former security apparatus; they may mistakenly implicate the names of the innocent; they may put innocent people in awkward positions, if the evidence of their innocence has been destroyed; they may unconsciously utilize undisclosed tricks of the former security apparatus), on the whole, from the perspective of *social catharsis*, pursuing them is a reasonable policy. The residua of Party loyalty seem potentially solid. One well-known Polish sociologist says, "I am glad to hear this defence [Walicki's defence of party members]; I have over thirty years of Party affiliation myself, and differently than A. Walicki, and I do not have reason to say anything particularly bad about my former Party comrades. I honor many of them" (Szacki 1991: 109).

One of the more serious mistakes made under Mazowiecki's prime ministership was the drawing of a line between past and present—the idea (and its adoption as policy) that an investigation into the moral and political past should not be given priority, or that the past should be, in a Christian way, forgiven and forgotten by all, since the country faced a serious socioeconomic crisis. This was a timely political gift to former security members who were able to destroy, send away, or remove material that implicated the guilty.

The Western reader may have difficulties in understanding that Poles as a rule have a tendency to evaluate an individual as a whole. Thus a "hiatus in biography" (migration from one country to another; move from one city to another; change of name, political alliance, religion) does not necessarily influence the total evaluation of a given person. Personal continuity is not disrupted by a change in residence or ideology. Moral continuity in a person is based on someone's behavior in his or her life span. Quite often this continuity is assessed from a generational perspective. Therefore a supposedly "keen" observation of an American writer may amount to nothing other than his ethnocentrically limited ignorance in perceiving other people's existential memory. Kinzer (*New York Times*, May 16, 1993: 5) notes,

One evening recently, the nightly television newscast carried a graphic report that Croatian forces in Bosnia had attacked a Serbian village and systematically killed every man, woman and child there, using not firearms but implements of torture. Inquiries revealed that the report was substantially true, but that the reporter had omitted one detail. The massacre took place more than 50 years ago, during World War II.

The advisers and decision makers of the initial post-Communist period were ignorant of certain lessons coming from the "de-fascization" of rightist post-totalitarian systems. Psomiades (1982: 263–64) describes the technique that might, mutatis mutandis, be applied also to post-Communist societies:

The policy of a limited purge of junta principals conducted under regular legal procedures and after public passion had subsided also relieved much of the anxiety of the officer corps. Moreover, the trials, which received widespread radio, television, and press coverage, served to demystify the dictatorship. The trials made possible the exposure of seven years of maladministration, repression, scandals, corruption, and conspiracies and depicted a regime much worse than even the military had imagined. . . . The statements and the demeanor of the accused revealed to many their pettiness and their incompetence and destroyed within seconds the military image of the strong man.

The Communist comeback in the 1992 elections in Rumania and Latvia indicate that Communist resurgence is not merely a theoretical possibility. Recent political events in Vilnius provide an excellent example. "Surprise, surprise. The story of the Lithuanian elections. Vytautas Landsbergis, Prime Minister and leader of the Sajudis independence movement, suffered a humiliating defeat at the hands of his old rival, Algrirdas Brazauskas, former leader of the Lithuanian Communist Party. Is the clock really being wound back?" (*Manchester Guardian Weekly* 1992: 12). Less economically developed societies are more acutely exposed to this danger. If economic reform, painful and technically difficult as it is, encounters serious obstacles (whether spontaneous or imposed by the Communist residua), and if the government does not possess adequate stamina to face social resistance, large segments of the population may turn to those advocating a return to the old, well-known patterns of behavior. Old behaviors, although bad, are perceived as easier to handle.

9. After the political changes in 1989–1990, Polish society faced several problems. The process of privatization, once begun, was not slow. In 1991, twelve percent of all state enterprises went to private owners (*Przegląd Rządowy*, 1992, no. 9: 68). The liquidation of some state enterprises contributed to the emergence of unemployment. This phenomenon began to grow in 1990. At the end of 1991, 2,156,000 persons were registered as unemployed—the fourth

highest level in Europe (*Przegląd Rządowy*, 1992, no. 15: 92–93). Youth appeared to be affected more by this phenomenon, especially younger women (*Przegląd Rządowy*, 1992, no. 13–14: 143).

Privatization was not without problems itself. New types of crimes emerged: material taken from state enterprises was assessed at less than its real value; those with "connections" had priority when buying state enterprises; several such enterprises were brought to bankruptcy so that they could be sold for less. All these crimes appeared under reprivatization.

Unexpectedly, exports went up in the first half of 1992. They were twelve and a half times higher than in the first half of 1991 (*Przegląd Rządowy*, 1992, no. 15: 137). The deficit, however, is expected to rise to twenty-five billion zloty (roughly $67 billion U.S.) in 1992 (*Przegląd Rządowy*, 1992, no. 15: 62). According to reliable extrapolations, approximately fifty percent of the gross national product will be produced by private enterprise by the end of 1994 (*Przegląd Rządowy*, 1992, no. 15: 6).

One can hypothesize on this basis that the public, suspicious as it was during the former period, might perceive these new problems as the creations of politicians trying to make themselves indispensable. Data from other sources indirectly supports this observation.

According to several surveys conducted by the Universities of Warsaw and Poznan, and other institutions in 1975, positive attitudes towards one's own country were shown by 93 percent of the adult population in Poland, whereas in 1985, these attitudes were down to a mere 73 percent (for the young generation, it was even as low as 60 percent). The approval rate of one's own country has been in a constant decline for the past twenty years. In 1989 and 1990, when asked to provide the main distinguishing characteristics of the Polish population, the majority of young Poles listed such traits as drunkenness, laziness and hospitality [traditional Polish hospitality]. On the basis of 1991 studies, this negative evaluation of one's own country is associated with an uncritical attitude towards Europe, which, as a point of reference rather than the U.S. leads to the Polish attitude of inferiority. (Skotnicka-Illasiewicz 1992: 123)

10. The clash of opposite tendencies in socialization and education (both traditional and imposed by the binding ideology of communism, as well as Christianity, patriotism, and internationalism) led to a widespread "Pavlov effect" under the prolonged Communist regime. This results in a situation of social warpedness. In this situation, when various arguments contradict each other and members of society (particularly the young) are bombarded with constant argumentation, but are neither ready nor well prepared to absorb and weigh the relevant issues, all authority, whether directly challenged or not, is in jeopardy. A nihilistic attitude prevails. This invisible attitude is one of the most dangerous enemies for a society in transition, since all new, reasonable, logically based or pragmatic arguments tend to be treated according to the patterns of the warped perspective: they are rejected or accepted without rational pattern.

CONCLUSIONS

Societies in transition have emerged as new sociological entities. The consolation that may be articulated when their harshness is revealed, that these societies have only a historical significance, is ironic for those who have to live under and through the conversion period. Societies in transition were first generated by a widespread rejection of communism; secondly, by the difficulties of entering the community of other developed societies, amplified by the gap created under Communist dominance; and thirdly, by the problem of eradicating the devastation produced by Communist rule, not only in individual Communist countries but also in the artificially created Communist bloc.

Paradoxically, it is much easier to change the state structure, its formal design and institutional arrangements (including the constitution and criminal or civil codes) than it is to transform the residua generated by a persistent governance of the social system.

The case of Polish transitional society shows that, in a time of social change, the introduction of new attitudinal transformations may be more essential (and difficult) than the transfiguration of the "objective" constitution and economic conditions. An additional general conclusion is that middle-range legal factors (laws dealing with trade, property, organizations, political institutions, and so on), which as a rule play a dependent role (since they are shaped by economic and political factors), gain importance as necessary preconditions for the subsequent economic changes in societies in transition. It would thus be wise to make the emerging discipline of legal policy the center of study and attention in social science.

The general economic inefficiency and illegitimacy of "real socialism" were so evident that they created a widespread social belief that the abolishment of communism would immediately remove the main cause of all socioeconomic evils. In consequence, the demise of communism gave birth to an acute crisis of expectations. Public opinion did not appreciate that in order to remove communism, it was not enough to remove slogans and a variety of power symbols: it was necessary to break with the whole Communist heritage. Thus, the political demise of communism generated false expectations. That these expectations were left unfulfilled became an additional, independent source of popular dissatisfaction. This dissatisfaction, added to the aversion to communism, created a dangerous "critical mass" that could push transitional societies to an unprecedented level of crisis.

Two final observations might be made, one general and one specific.

The more privacy an individual gains in a post-totalitarian society, the more that society shifts away from the post-totalitarian model, and the more civil society gains grounds there, the further this transforming society moves away from the "pure" totalitarian paradigm.

There are several crucial destabilizing features in the new socioeconomic situation in Poland. The most important are as follows.

1. The new social reality did not have enough time to establish itself, or to do the spadework indicating clear avenues to attractive profits for the general population. At the same time, it was successful in demolishing the former well-known rules (and anti-rules) of the "game" of real socialism. This generated tensions that deepened the generalized feeling of insecurity, especially among older people, workers without resources, and less well qualified white-collar workers.

2. Post-totalitarian heavy industry is not competitive with Western industrial capacities. In addition, it has been ousted from the near-defunct network of contracts with former socialist countries. Due to legal problems, this heavy industry cannot easily be transformed into dispersed centers of light industry. Finally, the centers of heavy industry are used as working places for an army of demoralized workers. These factors combined ensure that this outdated heavy industry has become an immovable institutionalized burden.

3. The Polish populace, hungry to be compensated for the protracted punishments of the period of real socialism, wants to achieve fast gains even though it stands no chance of obtaining speedy investments and lacks both managerial competence and sufficient skills to build grassroots, privately owned light industry. When these gains do not materialize, a skepticism emerges towards the so-called new political class. Also, paradoxically, a political nihilism reappears, if not actual nostalgia for the previous, hated social "order."

8

Conclusion: A Wasted Theoretical Chance? The Polish Case (1945–1992)

THE UNIQUENESS OF POLISH SOCIETY

Are there universal truths to be learned from Polish sociology?[57] At the beginning of the twentieth century Polish society remained, for the most part, under the influence of the intelligentsia's ethos. After World War II, it was exposed to the influence of an alien, economic, political, social, and cultural "super-system." This prolonged exposure resulted in "sovietization" (the violation of basic social values, or negative socialization). Determinants, processes, counter-processes, and more or less conscious defence mechanisms that were triggered by this kind of socialization constructed, over almost fifty years, a complicated, psychosocial structure in Poland.

By the end of 1970s, skilled workers (with their instrumental, goal-oriented attitudes) and their Solidarity union (the first de jure and de facto common front of workers and intelligentsia in Polish history) mobilized, paradoxically, against the "workers' state." This common front relied heavily on the traditional drive of the Polish intelligentsia to work for others. It was also reinforced by the encouraging, mediating, and sometimes actively sheltering role of the Polish church, further reinforced by the "superstar" performance of the Polish Pope. Unable to fight their arrogant and shrewd neighboring superpower, the Polish people manifested their ingenious survival strategy through a persistent Gandhi-like attitude of nonviolence.

The predominantly youthful character of the Solidarity movement, coupled with the newly acquired pragmatism of an experienced older generation, placed high values on pluralistic and horizontal perspectives in order to break the monolith of communism. Pluralism (respect for different ways of life and political philosophies) and a horizontal perspective (abhorrence of the idea of central democratization, and respect for efficiency) were favorable to the democratic renewal of civil society. They also strengthened a nationwide (in declaration only) respect for the "good work" attitude and watchword (this was developed into a scientific approach, called praxeology).

Paradoxically, through osmosis, these perspectives influenced the accelerating decomposition of Communist party discipline and ideology. The instrumental and pluralist perspectives, in a boomerang effect, diminished membership inside the Communist ranks. When martial law was declared in 1981, the ingenious survival strategy of the Poles did not, as one might have thought it would because of the "belligerent" nature of Polish spectacular principledness, opt for open war with the Polish puppet army or with the Soviet forces stationed inside Poland. Rather, it unexpectedly left the door open to an "all thumbs" attitude (social gawkishness). This seemingly ambiguous attitude transformed emotions, which were boiling on the inside, into an outwardly cool and conspiratorial lifestyle, a phenomenon that had been well developed during World War II.

The underground life, with its rapidly devised legends, newly created martyrs, and instant subculture, crystallized, preserved, and reinforced the spectacular principledness (principled heroics) of past generations. Hence the development of the Solidarity movement should be understood not simply as a dramatic, pluralistic, and nonviolent protest against the overgrowth of an "inner society of dirty togetherness." It should also be understood as an ongoing process aimed at preserving "sacred" traditional values contained in an underground "counter-culture."

THE UNIQUENESS OF THE POLISH ETHOS

There are many connections between the various types of Polish ethos and the society's social structure. Instrumentalism in individual and social life, and especially an instrumental attitude towards the law, is obviously not the only manifestation of the Polish defiance towards foreign dominance and occupation, particularly towards those powers that occupied Poland over the last two centuries. Instrumentality is also a result of the acceleration of sociopolitical mobility (vertical, as well as horizontal) that began in the twentieth century after World War II. During this period, authorities representing the ruling social strata, having lost official legitimacy, and having been forcibly replaced by unaccepted power centers, contributed unwillingly (as a result of ongoing value struggles) to the process of growing social skepticism. From these normative battles (fights between various sociopolitical and legal authorities and attacks on one another's prestige), an attitude of public instrumentality, if not nihilism, was generated.

Spectacular principledness has linked together many features of Polish mass behavior throughout the centuries. A grandiose (sometimes farcical) medieval heritage as one of the most powerful and peaceful European states established in the tenth century was linked with a powerful nobility. In the sixteenth century, the nobility constituted eight percent of the entire Polish population and had the right to elect its kings democratically. The highly treasured ethos of the nobility (the earliest interclass democracy in Europe) is linked with a heroic national resistance to any type of external oppression.

Later, when Poland was bordered by two powerful and aggressive neighbors, the Polish people developed supplementary tactics to enhance a survival strategy that contributed to the preservation of national values. Some tactics were of a social, showy, or "potlatch" (based on a gesture) character. They emerged especially during the homicidal period of German occupation during the Second World War and the prolonged, puppet-like Soviet occupation after the war.

It is interesting to note that these attitudes are responsible for a relatively widespread distribution of "alternative life styles." A thorough study dealing with alternative lifestyles concluded that there existed "strong pressure from needs and duties, aspirations to 'affluence' (without any real possibility of its general fulfillment), insufficient motivational power in many individuals and families, conflict-bearing economic conditions, disharmony between private and public life. An early indication of social and political conflicts was the rise of 'alternative styles' " (Siciński 1988: 388).

The ability to change lifestyles—to jump from a respectable, "normal" life-style to an alternative version—is one of the virtues of the all-thumbs attitude. This attitude, strongly connected to the amateurish ethos of the Polish nobility and its heir, the intelligentsia, manifested itself through an inherent inability to achieve something tangible and apply it to a task-oriented pattern of social behavior. It also manifested itself through a consistent and continuous domination of the weak ethos of the Polish bourgeoisie (since the task-oriented Jewish middle class was, to a large extent, alienated from Polish society), as well as through a subjugation of the weak Polish working class. Under its influence, the Polish working class was inclined to regard national independence as more important than the problem of "class revolution." Self-irony, typical of the all-thumbs attitude, attempted to hide behind the theatrics of mockery, both individual and societal.

After World War II, Polish society's main achievement was the establishment of a forged union and strong alliance between the intelligentsia and highly skilled workers, even after the decomposition of Solidarity in 1989–1992. Some sociologists claim (and hope, at a political level) that this alliance will generate a "new middle class." This expectation is not without ground, since the alliance between the intelligentsia and skilled workers linked the lower echelons of the "working intelligentsia" (administrators and technical personnel) with workers captured by the "revolution of expectations."

Few analysts of Polish society seem to be aware that the period of post-totalitarianism and the decomposition of the Solidarity movement contributed to the emergence of an entirely new sociopolitical entity on the Polish scene, as well as in Eastern Europe. An ethos emerged, based on the "caddishness" of the former nomenklatura (and some disillusioned members of the lower Party apparatus) and the nihilism of discredited elements of the half-intelligentsia. The complete instrumentality and nihilism of the "disillusioned" Party members, their vested interests in claiming that the Communist period was not so bad after all, and their vicious resentment of those who acted inefficiently but honestly linked them closely with the "drop-outs" produced by the intelligentsia's excessive social demands.

The drop-out category, stigmatized by an inherent inability to fulfill the intelligentsia's standards of snobbery in the post-totalitarian period, represented the defeated needs of the new clerk apparatus (new Communist administration), which wanted to have everything, and have it immediately. This apparatus was potentially ready to agree to any power exchange for profit or perks. This string-intelligentsia (people of a lower class who pretended to belong to the intelligentsia) was prepared to use any ideology, including that associated with "dirty togetherness," to divert attention from previous damage, real or illusory. In consequence, the amalgamation of political instrumentalism and nihilism linked the interests of post-totalitarian drop-outs with those of the new wave of pseudo-intelligentsia upstarts.

These internal transformations opposed the traditional spirit of the Polish intelligentsia. An intelligentsia traditionally directed towards ensuring the benefit of others suddenly realized that it did not exist in any politically uncompromised form, beyond its own boundaries. This realization pushed the remaining traditional intelligentsia into a corner. As a result, the most valued traditional goals of the intelligentsia, such as its commitment to bring education voluntarily to those who needed it, fight for national independence (and independence for other subjugated nations), and struggle for social justice, vanished rapidly. In the post-totalitarian period, a vacuum was created, leading to an almost instinctive desire to grasp whatever was available, especially power.

From my childhood, I remember a song that my father, among others, used to hum while shaving:
"Water splashes
in a deep well,
it is easy to be a minister
but difficult to rule."
Apparently, I asked him about the meaning of this chant, since I was later convinced that I had comprehended its sense. But it also transpired that the real difference between the position of a minister and an ability to rule is exactly like the erotic dream of a boy facing a mature, alive woman. (Kuroń 1991: 21)

Indeed, Jacek Kuroń did not have any doubts that his heroic political courage (which had been well tested—he spent approximately seven years in prison for dissident activities) equipped him with the requisite skills for an executive governmental position. While demanding a high political position, he was curiously silent about his earlier experience with the government. He did not try to find out whether there were others who could govern the country more competently.

The pursuit of power was symptomatic of the dramatic change in the new intelligentsia's attitude. The post-Solidarity intelligentsia did not want to be perceived as a "missionary angel"; it wanted to rule. There are at least two possible explanations for this transition. First, during the Communist regime, the intelligentsia underwent a profound transformation. This social stratum was fundamentally different from the intelligentsia of the late nineteenth and early twentieth centuries. It was a "working" type of intelligentsia. Second, the new intelligentsia would never lower itself to undertake the task of "cleaning stables."

One day after the acceptance of a position in Mazowiecki's government, the former head of the Organizational Department of the Central Committee of the Party came to me. His name was Andrzej Gdula. He was unusually happy. He said, "A few moments ago, French journalists asked me why I am so pleased, now, when we have just lost power. My answer was," continued Gdula, "because I know the order in which we leave them the whole business." (Kuroń 1991: 9–10)

Only the future will reveal the social effects resulting from this inherent transformation of the intelligentsia. It would appear at present that they are certainly dysfunctional. Members of the emerging intelligentsia were not socialized to handle task-oriented endeavors and, like the Communists before them, did not seem prepared to accept personal responsibility for their conceptual mistakes or mistaken "expertise."

This pragmatic attitude towards power, coupled with the ominous alliance between the half-intelligentsia and the "caddish" ex-Party elements, may greatly influence the future development of Polish society. It may even deprive Poland of its traditional and unique post-nobility ethos, as it pushes to cooperate with its traditional adversary—Germany, the central state of a United Europe. This cooperation, if indeed it takes place, may be sugar-coated with the idea that the drive towards innovation (enthusiastic, stubborn, and often brilliant, though unstable), coupled with German orderliness, systematic dullness, and rigorousness in enforced teamwork, may help Polish society to achieve great success in material, and possibly even cultural, terms.

The legacy of "real socialism" placed a heavy burden and a visible mark on the Polish ethos. It tended to develop a well-guarded body of privileges. If, under socialism, an individual acquired a position that allowed him to pretend that he was doing something, he immediately looked for rewards. If he acquired a position of power, his first official act was to release himself from the performance of any real duties. Then, of course, he could not be held responsible for his performance. If someone pretended that he was doing something and had the power to impose on others the belief that his activities were *real*, he could then indeed claim privilege after privilege. He would receive a better apartment (if not a house), a car, possibly with a driver, vacations abroad (in other socialist countries), special health services for himself and his family, high rent and retirement privileges and access to shops "behind curtains" (shops open only to those in privileged positions).

The leap from a job involving spurious activities to the opulent world of privilege was not so great, since all political activities in real socialist countries were structured on a false foundation. The privileges rendered by spurious activities have been given posthumous (post-totalitarian) validity. Discredited people like Edward Gierek, Piotr Jaroszyński, Wojciech Jaruzelski (whose book was originally published in France with an introduction by Adam Michnik, who himself spent seven years in prison under the Jaruzelski regime—something that would never have occurred under the previous Polish intelligentsia), Mieczysław Rakowski, Franciszek Szlachcic, Jerzy Tejchma, and Adam Schaff gave interminable interviews to ex-Communist journalists and, without writing them, produced books that became lucrative best-sellers.

Thus, fictitious descriptions and rationalizations of phoney, if not outright criminal, activities created "real social facts." In addition, debased former Communist officials, using their privileged positions, were able to benefit from the fabrication or falsification of history. Instead of facing the courts, they reaped further profits. They even gained, by employing journalists trained in justification and the stupefaction of more naive readers, positions of belated prominence. Even worse, this pattern was followed by decent post-Communist politicians like Andrzej Celinski (a dissident hero) or Ewa Łętowska (an apparently competent lawyer but a "leftist"), or ex-Communists like Bronisław Gieremek and Jacek Kuroń, who began, evidently by osmosis, to behave in exactly the same manner.

In conclusion, it is clear that for some individuals in totalitarian and post-totalitarian systems, the magic wand bestows lavishly. Spurious, empty activities, performed at a certain level of power or after a disgraceful relinquishing of power, are easily transformed into flourishing privileges. Although some maintain that the upper reaches of bureaucracy in various countries display the same traits, which are then taken to be universal, it is the accumulation, density, and frequency of these features that make the Polish case unique.

THE UNIQUENESS OF POLISH SOCIOLOGY

The analysis of Polish society does contribute some new concepts to general sociology. It is necessary to state that this is not the kind of sociology that is usually developed. It is not concerned with various segments of society, with interrelations between different divisions in the society, with models of abstract social concepts; rather, it deals with concrete society taken *as a whole*. This is not so much an entirely new or innovative approach. Instead, it is based on the conviction that, in order to understand one separate element of society in the world as it exists, one has to see it from a holistic perspective. Therefore, to comprehend Polish society adequately, it is necessary to introduce several new theoretical notions.

These new theoretical notions have the following objectives. First, they seek to describe different types of social order comprehensively and to find an appropriate place for totalitarian order among them. Such a description must be made in objective terms, without introducing politico-normative ingredients into the picture. Second, they attempt to develop the concept of "spurious" (shameful, bogus, fake) activities as types of behavior that culminate in societies of a totalitarian character. Third, they try to present strategies for planned social action that can change the society as a whole. In other words, they present the basic features of sociotechnics in order to establish which features are most specific to a totalitarian regime. Fourth, they aim to discuss, at least in the Polish case, the most decisive element of social change: was it the role of "objective" material forces, or was it the ethos that arose from the coalition between intelligentsia and workers? Fifth, they endeavor to explain the phenomenon of the intelligentsia and the development of the "ignition" type of revolutionary movement represented by Solidarity. Sixth, they strive to explain the role of meta-attitudes in the process of shaping basic social interactions in a given society. Seventh, they pursue the emergence of a new sociological branch in Polish social science: the sociology of morals. This is a subsociological discipline that describes and explains moral phenomena in society.

Types of Social Order

Ossowski elaborated an original typology that is applicable across different societies. He distinguished three basic types of interactions that appear in social settings (Ossowski 1967, vol. 4: 173): (1) the kind where members of a community act in a way that is consistent with the patterns and norms consolidated in the psychological disposition of individuals; (2) that in which common behavior is a result of the mutual interaction of individuals or of group decisions, so that members of the community are guided by individual motivation or by the motivation of small groups that operate within the larger community; (3) the kind whereby behavior of members of a community is determined by one decision-making center. This simple classification presents a clear point of departure from which it is possible to locate totalitarian social systems as well. Traditional social communities and closed social systems belong to category (1), where individuals have been encoded in social norms and patterns generated by the accumulated processes of social development.

Liberal or pluralist social systems, category (2), depend on built-in mechanisms to monitor and correct the power balance of opposing interest groups. These systems include also *Gemeinschaft* (based on community) and *Gessellschaft* (based on formal institutions and organizations) types of societies.

In category (3), totalitarian social systems,—which include such historically distant political bodies as the Egyptian, Persian, and Mongol systems in addition to modern military or police states—impose one ideological system on the entire society, regulating the life of that society according to a predesigned, all-encompassing pattern.

It was shown that the Marxist totalitarian order typically evolved in several stages (Łoś 1990). Maria Łoś has revealed the existence of at least four stages in the development and decomposition in the Communist state. The first stage is "distinguished by a high level of national mobilisation, attempts at a 'crash' industrialisation or radical reconstruction of the economy, intensive class struggle, vigilantism, likely mass movements of the population." The second stage is characterized by "the growing monopolistic tendencies of the party-state to create very large economic conglomerates, and either a further reduction of the private sector or its greater regulation and co-ordination with the planned economy." The third stage is described in the following way:

When the period of industrial mobilisation and reconstruction is over, the question of low productivity and its organisational causes comes to the fore. The party leadership's realisation of the intrinsic limitations of the centralised economy is likely to prompt two types of reform that attempt to introduce certain elements of market: (1) internal reforms of the state economy and/or (2) partial legitimisation of the second economy. . . . [In the final stage] a forced marriage of the state- and market-economies not only heightens their respective intrinsic contradictions, but also triggers attempts on the part of each economy to exploit the other in a largely parasitic, politicised and economically non-competitive manner. (Łoś 1990: 200–19)

To a certain extent, Ossowski's typology resembles the Weberian categorization of legitimacy: traditional, legal-rational, and charismatic. However, it does not deal merely with one element of society (legitimacy), but with the more general composition of social systems. It is thus more general and more all-encompassing.

Spurious Activities

In a society where real activities are often counter-productive and there is a need to act efficiently (praxeologically), in order to avoid anything regarded as negative, bad, or contrary to one's intention, one may develop a tendency to pretend that one's activities mean something (when in fact they are meaningless). This genesis can be found where there is a state of social warpedness—a state of social unresponsiveness, or the social void existing between a general and accepted social framework and a myriad of affiliations to a variety of small groups. From a theoretical point of view, spurious activities are autotelic. They do not lead to any other activities for they are goals in themselves.

The term "spurious activities" is usually attributed to Jan Lutyński, who brought them to the general attention of Polish scholars. According to him,

since the action is always understood as an aim-directed undertaking, and since direct goals are regarded as important, the difference between spurious activities and other activities is seen in the fact that spurious behaviors do not realize direct goals, goals that are supposed to be achieved in accordance with generally accepted ideas in the given society and culture. Therefore, spurious activities are those that—taking into consideration their direct goals or real performances—have a different meaning than appears to be the case. (Lutyński 1990:105)

Lutyński lists various examples of spurious activities, such as activities performed for the purposes of show; those performed as a pretext for entirely different actions; those undertaken for "insurance" purposes; "activities that do not fulfill their functions, but are designed with the knowledge or acceptance of those who have commissioned them, and that are performed counter to the interests of those for whom they are performed, and without their knowledge" (Lutyński 1990: 106); and activities that are performed only on paper and serve as a substitute for the enterprises that were supposed to be performed.

It is obvious that spurious activities in Lutynski's context do not differ essentially from the activities triggered by the all-thumbs attitude. Witold Jarzebowski's understanding of spurious activities, however, cannot be reduced to the notion of "all thumbs." He connects spurious activities with the notion of "organizational fictions" and maintains that the "fabricated" life of an organization (especially under "real socialism") develops as a necessary consequence a further avalanche of spurious activities (Jarzębowski 1976).

Witold Kieżun tried to explain the persistent phenomena of low efficiency, poor-quality work, lack of innovation, and economic stagnation as by-products of "the existence of various forms of spurious activity that is one of the main features of real socialism" (Kieżun 1991: 330) as it appeared under totalitarian domination. He suggests that, while spurious activities exist on the bottom of the social system, they originate at the top.

According to the unanimous opinion of interviewed enterprise directors, a large proportion of these directives are simply never realized because no account is taken of the requirements of material and human resources. This creates a situation of apparent activity by central organs. And again symptoms of autonomization in regulations are observed; regulations are formulated almost for their own sake ("regulation for the sake of regulation"), often with no thought to the practicalities of carrying them out. (Kieżun 1991: 225–6)

Independent of its features, Kieżun's understanding of spurious activities ("purposely construed, not goal-oriented activities") underlines one constant element: the prevalence of personal emotional engagement with activities that have a task-oriented, impersonal character. Indeed, emotional and personal involvement in such circumstances seems to be specific to Poles. Anger, allegiance, a wish to cooperate, envy, annoyance, competition that is not measured by objective standards but evaluated by subjective criteria, "the creation of an atmosphere" of fidelity, and a "missionary" spirit protective of the underdog (or those labelled as underdogs)—these are Polish emotions. So, what is unique about these attitudes is not the ability to work in a group or perform tasks, or assess with impartiality the effectiveness of work already performed, but an emotional density, an irrational blockage of interpersonal relationships, and an accumulation of psychological miasma. In short, a psychological orientation towards the idea of the task instead of the task itself.

In other industrialized, democratic societies, people do quarrel both in small groups and large organizations; they are jealous and they compete on the basis of irrelevant criteria rather than qualifications or skills. Nonetheless, in these societies leaders are chosen through more formal contests (prescribed by definite rules) after a period of informal competition. After the final decision is made, competing participants tend to cooperate with that decision. Among the Poles, however, emotional attitudes tend to prevail. After selecting a leader, the working team splits into factions that fight fiercely with one another. Various data "files" (collection of negative arguments, failures, mistakes) are set up for use against the leader should the possibility of deposing him arise. This happens not only in small circles. According to the press, "Wałęsa, once the hero of the Western world for his defiance of communism and his leadership of the Solidarity labour movement, has become the butt of jokes at home and an embarrassment internationally" (McKinsey 1992: 1). The mechanism whereby a hero falls from grace is complicated here. Traditional Polish attitudes of spectacular principledness led people to expect from their president the highest standards of perpetual theatrical performance (a member of the intelligentsia, Wojtyla—the pope—is able to supply that). Wałęsa, with his working background, did not pass this everyday test.

The foregoing description is, of course, over-stylized, but it nonetheless accentuates one important point: the prevalence of intersubjective relations over objective task-oriented interactions. It demonstrates an inherent inability to translate relevant public issues into soluble tasks. If the Poles are unable or unwilling to cooperate in order to achieve established goals, they are forced to rely on their own individual survival strategies. To cope effectively with the growing bog of social situations that generate insecurity, they have to build (or overbuild) their own egos. A detached observer of Polish society would certainly note the enormous number of unrecognized "geniuses." Everyone, even a "nobody," nourishes this secret hope. Yet it is nourished not as an adequate description of psychological reality, but as a device through which to gain enough strength to overcome the horde of threats surrounding the individual.

It might appear as if the phenomenon of over-personalization shares certain characteristics with Max Weber's concept of rationalization (as a perverse example of anti-rationalization). The resemblance is, however, superficial. Polish society is not so much characterized by a lack of rationalization processes, since rationalization has rapidly occurred in the areas of industrial relations, education (and the application of natural scientific discoveries to social life), and health care and can be seen in the development of Machiavellian schemes for grasping power. What does appear to be unique in this society is an intrinsic inability to pass from the threshold of the inner life of a small group to the inner life of a large social group.

One possible explanation is classical. During the partition period (1795–1918) the state and the law were rejected as representing imposed alien structures. Civil society was only able to generate attitudes that united people in a shared "missionary" stance against the invaders. The world of privileges, pathologically developed under communism, encouraged the existence of spurious activities on Polish "social" soil.

Strategies of Collective Social Action

It is paradoxical that the changes that the real decision makers under real socialism wanted to introduce were based on the use of spurious activities and supported by the recommendations of a sui generis perverse understanding of social engineering (sociotechnics). Four types of sociotechnics can be distinguished. The first is sociotechnics *proper*, that is, a theory of efficient social action, or, more concretely, a theory of applied social science. Sociotechnics proper supplies recommendations for social change, provided that these recommendations do not violate (a) a requirement to eliminate equivocal values (Podgórecki 1975: 36–45) or (b) an existing body of tested social regularities.

The social engineering that was pursued in Polish sociopolitical practice violated both of these principles. At best it amounted to the second type, *quackish* social engineering, which claims to be competent in formulating pragmatic recommendations. In the worst scenario, it was the third type, *dark* social engineering—sociotechnics applied with the knowledge that it would generate, as a by-product, a multitude of social harms.

The fourth type of social engineering is *self-made* sociotechnics, which "presupposes the existence of verified knowledge concerning the effectiveness of social activities but understands this knowledge as an accumulated and generalized professional experience" (Podgórecki, in Kubin 1990: 19–20). It is necessary to add that, although professional experience may sometimes be translated into verifiable propositions, it constitutes nothing more than a pool of directives produced by various types of social or bureaucratic agencies operating in social reality.

The spectacular development of sociotechnics in Poland (the Research Committee of Social Practice and Sociotechnics of the International Sociological Association was established in 1974 as a product of the activities of the Polish Section of Sociotechnics at the Polish Sociological Association and has since published several books on this subject in Poland and abroad) was not stimulated by the planned processes of social change in the country.[58] In fact the reverse occurred. The blossoming of sociotechnics in Poland was generated by an extensive abuse of social planning.

Government use of quackish and dark sociotechnics forced social scientists to unmask or uncover the precise activities of government. This was not an easy task. Sociotechnicians were compelled to invent and employ sociotechnics of a higher order: a type of sociotechnics that could unmask the real intentions of the government without at the same time jeopardizing its own security. As a consequence of these dangerous duels with government, a new paradigm of practical social science was produced. It symbolized a theoretical maturing of the practical social sciences much as logic did for the natural sciences (Podgórecki 1975, 1989, in Kubin 1990).

Party or ex-Party sociologists see this situation in a different way. Stalled within their own cognitive-reference "bewitched circle," they are unable, even in hindsight, to notice significant developments outside this circle. This is the case of Piotr Sztompka. "Their [the experts'] influence was at its peak during the period that Sztompka called 'era of experts' (1970–1980). During that period, they were called upon to act as consultants and to assume positions in governmental bodies. In fact, they were subsequently perceived as too close to the centers of power" (Breton et al. 1990: 365). Ironically, those who were regarded as "too close to the centers of power"—Jan Szczepański, Włodzimierz Wesołowski, and Władysław Markiewicz—represented the very core of this Party center (Wesołowski and Markiewicz, as Party members of a high rank, and Szczepański, whom Wojciech Jaruzelski called a "wonderful man" and "Jan the sage" [Jaruzelski 1992: 105–6], as a personal adviser to Edward Gierek). They served additionally as gate-keepers (censors) who did not allow the undertaking of unbiased research.[59]

Social Change

The social realities of the twentieth century indicate that various societies live under more or less consciously guided social change and continuous, prearranged strategic wars.

One element of the intellectually confusing, unexpected, and disturbing career of Marxism in the 1970s (and its associated modern, neo- or post-Marxist conceptions) was a hunger for theoretical explanation, or at least guidance, to monitor the many social changes. Marxist practice, which shifted with social change, was built on the assumption that in the last instance, social changes were the cumulative result of a variety of *material* factors.

On the other hand, theoretical conceptions that stress nonmaterial phenomena (normative and spiritual) as the decisive factors in macrosocial processes are theoretically weak, as well. "Without any doubt, the confrontation which generated changes in the year 1989 demanded significant presence of mind, restraint, suffering and sacrifice. In a sense, these changes were generated by prayer, and certainly could not happen without an unconditional trust in God, who is the Lord of history, and shapes the human heart" (Papal Encyclical "Centesimus Annus," May 1, 1991). Was Polish society, *nolens volens*, as a macroscale laboratory of social change for more than half a century, finally able to furnish a keen observer with verifiable insights into the underlying nature of these transformations?

According to the Polish macronatural experiment, economic factors are indeed of primary importance at the macrosocial level, not in the context of who owns the means of production, but as a generalized, social expectation of an economic standard of living. This standard of living was (and is) determined not only on the basis of direct internal and intersocietal comparisons (among groups and classes living inside Poland) but also on the basis of studying the relative deprivation resulting from cross-societal comparisons. The identification and introduction of an additional, as yet unrecognized form of relative deprivation—external relative deprivation—is required.[60] Thus, the Poles are strongly motivated by economic factors when they feel themselves deprived of a particular standard of living. They believe that they are entitled to a high standard of living by virtue of their ethos.

The events of 1989, which took place first in Poland and later in the whole of Eastern Europe (including the very source of the Marxist disease, the Soviet Union), clearly showed that it was the collective social *praxis* that unmasked and documented the pretentiousness of the Marxist and post-Marxist way of reasoning. In effect, it was not so much the intellectual criticism from outside that defeated Marxism. Rather, it was the practical behavior of the very targets of Marxist ideology that gave it the final theoretical blow. Thus, the ultimate proof of the falseness of Marxism was furnished by the Polish macrosocial laboratory.

The Intelligentsia

The intelligentsia represents another social phenomenon peculiar to Polish sociology since it is unique to Polish society. In the nineteenth century and the beginnings of the twentieth, the intelligentsia was also to be found in Russia. This social stratum is distinct in that it does not possess the features of a social class. It does not have a common interest (service towards other social classes) or an ideology of its own (Gella 1989; Zajączkowski 1961, 1962). Traditionally, this stratum was not interested in gaining power for itself. The intelligentsia was a social body with a "calling" to represent the goodness of society as a whole; it produced recommendations appropriate to all members of the society that ennobled citizens through certain ritualistic requirements.

These requirements turn the knights' armor outside in, transforming a shield into a vocation. Thus, the intelligentsia of the nineteenth and twentieth centuries was the embodiment of an ancient liturgy. In medieval times, the knight had a pious duty to defend the higher values of his lord, lady, or sovereign. The obligations binding knights created a sacred chain protecting these values. Currently, members of the intelligentsia are guided by internal imperatives that impose upon them the prescribed ethos of the intelligentsia.

One can formulate a general observation: as long as civil society did not exist as an operational body and was unable to defend higher social values, a peculiar social category of secular monks (knights) emerged with a *saintly* obligation to protect these values with their talents and lives. When civil society does gain enough strength on its own, the bourgeois class, through independent organizations and institutions, generates a body to serve this purpose. When the bourgeoisie is underdeveloped, the intelligentsia enters into the picture. This observation, if correct, raises an additional question: why was the intelligentsia as a phenomenon specific only to Polish and Russian society? Is the underdevelopment of the bourgeoisie in these countries an adequate explanation?

Meta-attitudes

For sociologists, the concept of attitude is only one of many existing, though not sharply-defined, concepts. "Opinions commonly refer to topical and short-run judgments, usually dealing with questions of public affairs; attitudes are *somewhat* enduring and inclusive; beliefs are more basic still, having to do with the central values of life" (Berelson, Steiner 1964: 558; emphasis added). For psychologists, an attitude is an "overall, learned core disposition that guides thoughts, feelings, and actions toward specific others and objects. Three components have generally been found to be common to all attitudes: (1) cognitive (or beliefs), (2) emotional (or feelings), and (3) behavioral (or action). A concept is generally considered to be an attitude only if it possesses, at least to some degree, each of these three components" (Middlebrook 1974: 575–76).

By this understanding, an attitude targets concrete persons or objects and displays certain cognitive, emotional, and behavioral properties. Although the degree of "concreteness" is debatable, its object is an important ingredient in the understanding of an attitude. In sociology, this ingredient is not as portentous. What is essential, however, is an indication of how people in larger groups behave in certain situations. To introduce order into various forms of social behavior, a more encompassing concept is required. To satisfy this need, the idea of meta-attitude has been proposed. To repeat the definition given earlier, meta-attitudes "can be defined as a kind of disposition towards a stable reaction in any socially defined way that does not manifest itself externally, but structures externally expressed motivations from the inside. Meta-attitudes are hidden and petrified attitudes" (Podgórecki, in Podgórecki, Łoś 1979: 240).

In harmony with this understanding, meta-attitudes organize the life of an individual from within. A meta-attitude transforms several concrete attitudes into tested, operational reactions to certain life situations. Meta-attitudes do not target specific others or objects (as do attitudes) but instead exhibit *blanket* imagined behavior. They pertain to all objects, individuals, ideas, symbols, and cognitive elements connected to the content of this attitude.

Meta-attitudes, like the principled, instrumental, fiddling-instrumental, survival, spectacular, and all thumbs, have already been discussed. It should be noted that inquiry into this new theoretical field recently brought some additional findings. In 1989, an extensive study was conducted on the "empirically derived typology of the mentality of Poles." It was based on factor-analysis research using fifteen scales of "mentalities." Three basic meta-attitudes were specified:

(1.) a passive-productive anti-individualistic type of thinking ("the hero of socialist work"); the people displaying this trait presented themselves as conformists, accepting central management and full employment;

(2.) a defensive-conservative-soliciting type of thinking ("thieving and begging"); the people thus defined displayed attitudes characteristic of the "ordinary" type of life orientation; and

(3.) an enterprising-autonomous life orientation (the "ideal member of civil society"); the people of this type openly declared themselves supporters of pluralism and tolerance.

The inquiry made an attempt to link these three types of meta-attitudes with the individual's level of education and place in the occupational hierarchy. Thus, meta-attitudes (1) and (2) were found mainly in blue-and white-collar professions, and among unskilled workers and farmers. The higher bureaucrats, military officers, specialists, white-collar workers and craftsmen had a tendency to occupy the opposite positions of category (3), the "enterprising-autonomous attitude" (Koralewicz, Ziółkowski 1990).

Had this study tried to connect more sociologically juicy factors, and had it been less related to universalistic psychological phenomena, it would have led to more potent explanatory findings. For example, the "thieving and begging" life orientation could easily be understood as a version of the "fiddling survival" meta-attitude, whereas the "autonomous-enterprising orientation" could simply be understood as one of the variations of the instrumental meta-attitude.

A given meta-attitude contributes to the *structuring of a social structure* since it funnels a specific constellation of attitudes into a united whole. Meta-attitudes are tested and selected by trial and error. As a result of this cognitive-creative process (which Petrazycki calls "unconsciously ingenuous"), a cluster of co-operating, complementary, and mutually supportive concrete attitudes are bound together. Consequently, these attitudes often appear to be appropriate, functional devices with which members of a given society deal with their particular social problems. For example, meta-attitudes consolidate majorities or minorities (visible or invisible), ethnic groupings, nationalities, and repressed people to deal with issues pertinent to them. Generally speaking, meta-attitudes, whether those specific to Polish society like the instrumental, principled, spectacular-principled, fiddling-survival, and all-thumbs (Podgórecki), or comparative meta-attitudes specific to other societies like the "seniority principle" in Japan (Nakane) or social cooperation based on institutionalized bargaining in the Netherlands—"verzeuling" (Goubtsblom), seem to condense the most significant features of the given society. If this is the case, what is so innovative about this concept?

Meta-attitudes indeed appear in all societies, but *only* certain combinations are typical for a given society as generated responses (functional for some, and dysfunctional for others) to social problems. In order to complete the task of building a general sociology of humankind, all of these, and other, as yet unrecognized, meta-attitudes must be studied. To construct a sociology that deals only with the uniqueness of a given society, one must examine the particular composition of meta-attitudes peculiar to that society. The unique constellation of meta-attitudes may be understood as the *ethos* of a given society.

Ethos

Sociology that deals with legal behavior constitutes a sub-branch of general sociology: a sociology of law. This sub-branch is developing meteorically (Ferrari 1990). There are several reasons for its rapid growth. One reason is that behind the law there is a strong, influential, and self-centered, as well self-interested, lobby of lawyers. They dress in a particular manner, use exotic language, restrict entrance to law schools, and use other means to build artificial barriers between themselves and the rest of the population. But in the case of morality, everyone is competent. Morality is not usually perceived as attached to a specific profession. As a rule, it is treated as an extension of religious beliefs (Catholic, Jewish, Buddhist, Muslim). In this sense, the field of morality is open to all possible evaluations, interpretations, and opinions. Morality *per se* does not have an epistemological lobby.

Maria Ossowska (1896–1974), a Polish Sociologist who was virtually unknown in the international "market of ideas," devoted her entire adult life to the task of building a theory of morality.[61] She was aware of the logical requirements and the need to collect findings of existing investigations and conduct new empirical studies using subdisciplines of the social sciences. She started from the logical-semantic foundations of morality.

In her 1947 book *Podstawy Nauki o Moralności (Foundations of a Science of Morality)*, she tried to analyze the logical meaning of morality. In *Motywy Postępowania (Motives of Behaviour)*, published in 1949, she attempted a panoramic overview of existing concepts of morality presented from the discipline of psychology. *Moralność Mieszczańska (Bourgeois Morality)*, published in 1955, analyzed morality and the way it was understood in a concrete sociological setting (nineteenth-century England). In subsequent books published in 1949, 1970, and 1973, she continued to tackle the problems of moral phenomena from the perspective of a theoretical sociology.

She resolved these Herculean attempts to identify the concept of morality in an astonishingly simple and sharp conclusion: "This fact [that morality is concerned with objects of praise or blame] makes it hopeless to find a definition that would satisfy the intuitions of all"; moreover, "ethos can be ascribed only to a group. An individual may have a morality, but he cannot have an ethos" (Ossowska 1972: 4, 174). This methodological capitulation led, at the same time, to a theoretical victory. Indeed, the concept of ethos that emerged from Ossowska's monumental and solitary inquiry (whose methodology she herself developed step by step) pointed to *a new cognitive category in the sociology of morals*—the category of *ethos* (lifestyle). This category, once applied to empirical and theoretical inquiries, surpasses the limitations of the subjective *Wel-*

tanschauung. When the concept of ethos is enriched by the notion of meta-attitude, an unexpected opportunity emerges. A link is established between the attitudinal world of the individual and society's existing repository of social knowledge.

Polish sociology, if it does not merely repeat or build on the achievements of European and American sociologies, has considerable general value. At the same time, the most interesting concepts are most closely connected to the uniqueness of Polish society and its historical transmutations. One can conclude that the more socially complicated the "laboratory" of the society in question, the higher the probability that theoretical concepts built on this base will have a more encompassing and universal validity. Nonetheless, the task of interpreting the accumulated social and economic experience of Polish society under a politically designed and imposed laboratory is still an open one.

From a traditional epistemological point of view the anthropological concept of "ethos" presents an agglomeration of meanings. Thus, it might be argued that this concept mingles together both the "is" and "ought" points of view, that is, it mixes descriptive and postulatory notions. But from the sociological point of view, the situation appears to be different: the concept of ethos unites the descriptive and normative perspectives, providing the possibility of analyzing social reality both factually and obligatorily. This approach appears to be ep-istemologically possible because ethos, as the prescribed pattern of behavior accepted in the given community, can be dealt with jointly as both graphic and normative.

Ethos, then, is studied as an existing phenomenon, as a set of social facts that have been developed during long periods of social transformation. It is also examined as a network of habits existing *hic et nunc*. Thus, the ethos of the knight, the scientist, the businessman, the monk, and environmentalist—each can be treated as a pattern of expected behavior, and additionally as a model of recommended behavior. If the concept of "agency" was supposed to unite normative and factual aspects of human action, then Cohen's acrobatic attempts (Cohen 1987: 273–308) to grasp the essence of this vague notion (made so popular by Anthony Giddens) was preceded by Ossowska's simpler and more persuasive elucidation.

In sum, one has an impression that the Polish sociologists did not sufficiently ex-ploit the unique chance granted to them. Recent indigenous assessments of Polish sociology seem to corroborate this view. Antoni Sułek came to this estimation of the recent developments in this area: "Disproportion between empirical studies and penury of theoretical thinking is, let's hope, a matter of time and amount of re-search needed for adequate generalizations" (Sułek 1992: 16).

A parable might summarize the achievements of Polish post-war sociology better than an abstract discourse. Thus: "When the well-known sage Si-Tien used to live in Po, a country ruled by a clique of cruel tyrants, everyone was convinced that under conditions of liberty and tolerance he would write books that would shake mankind to its roots with their wisdom," said the student Liu.

"However, when his students smuggled him to Ka, a free country, he was unable to produce anything of great value. Why?" "Wisdom gained in the cage may have some practical value, but that obtained in the world outside is unfit to describe it," said Si-tien.

FOUR THEORETICAL GENERALIZATIONS

Despite this note of skepticism, one can formulate four basic theoretical generalizations concerning modern Polish society.

The thesis that social fear and the missionary attitude were the main factors of social change in post-war Poland emerges as the first main theoretical conclusion of this book.

The processes of transformation that took place in Poland after the Second World War and the internal working of the macrosocial laboratory thus created were deeply influenced by Polish history and the traditional culture of nobility. For several centuries, the ethos of social-neighborly life was at the center of that culture. A social life orientated towards face-to-face interactions, mainly on the family and neighborly levels, was its lasting residuum. The latter led eventually to a peculiar ideology of missionary patriotism as its derivation. Quite early on, it had become an autotelic ideology, transformed, especially by intelligentsia during the nineteenth century, into a supreme, ultimate value. Throughout World War II this lofty patriotic spirit had successfully prevented the Polish population from collaborating with the Germans. Yet the nation, savagely decimated by the war, was not so uniformly resistant to the pressures created by the subsequent imposition of the Soviet-designed sociopolitical system. Bitterly frustrated segments of those populations that had been traditionally and consistently spurned by intelligentsia, members of social groups exposed to an acute "status inconsistency," and some members of the upper strata who were blackmailed into submission by the enforcers of terroristic Soviet ideology, with its menacing spectre of the "dictatorship of the proletariat," started, usually reluctantly, to collaborate with the new system, hiding behind the facade ideas of "social justice." They became partially responsive to the propaganda coming from the system of real socialism that was regarded by the general population as a political model developed within an alien and inferior social context. Nevertheless, the spirit of the intelligentsia, operating still as an integral part of the national culture and constituting a residual background of the collaborators themselves, moved the latter to adopt an exaggerated meta-attitude of insecurity. But attitudes of fear (and the instrumentality produced by it) had also permeated the population at large. They had contributed to a widespread frustration and an attendant moral indignation. This indignation produced a moral imperative to reject the model of real socialism, which in turn (a) had led to a repudiation of the entrapments of the cliquish social infrastructure based on "small establishments," (b) had cemented the widespread self-defensive phenomenon of dirty togetherness, (c) had brought into being the Solidarity movement as a missionary and national critique of real socialism, and (d) with time, had fragmented and decomposed Solidarity. Subsequently, after the abolition of this type of socialist regime, the insecurity-instrumental attitudes manifested themselves in the newly emerging political structures of post-totalitarianism, not only as an internalized defensive social practice of the former collaborators but also as a well-tested and familiar formula for social stability. These attitudes are also responsible for blocking and delaying efforts to release the accumulated social frustration through an efficient and responsible decommunisation (lustration) operation, parallel to denazification. Gradually, the insecurity-instrumental attitudes have become since 1991 the predominant factor in the democratic parliamentary process and in a chaotic war of all against all, in which new sociopolitical visions are lacking and where nobody can be regarded as a reliable and safe partner, except for a handful of the closest and most well-tested friends.

The second theoretical observation is connected with the first. It emerges from a study of Polish society as a whole and can be summarized as follows: *this society is not rich in impersonal types of human interactions.* Polish society, for all its historical turbulence—defensive not aggressive wars, lack of independence for a century and a half, adherence to a code of excessive hospitality, its relatively impoverished society, the presence of the largest alienated Jewish subcommunity in the world, and the imposed Communist macroexperiment—was and is characterized by one constant feature: a reliance on one or another form of social, but personally tainted, togetherness. This emotionally and personally loaded framework of interpersonal relationships is generalized very impressively by Polish romantic literature, which is difficult for outsiders to follow and therefore virtually unknown.

Originally, this togetherness was created by a cohort of the nobility that was based on military units linked by different "coats of arms"; then, it was a brotherhood of nobility (not always friendly), built on neighborly families. A further type of togetherness was sealed by the intelligentsia's insistence on manners and social background (social barriers were supposed to defend the "purity" of the intelligentsia's missionary attitude towards the needy, and against the intrusion of alien elements). Later, it was a unit composed of "us," cemented by suspicion and mutual defense against "they" (occupants, informers). Significantly, this defense block was so effective that, during World War II, Polish society produced no higher-level administrative collaborators. The internal structure of the entire society became so transparent that no attempts were ever undertaken to generate such cooperation.

During the relatively short period of Communist dominance (half a century), due to the sophisticated development of mass propaganda and persuasion, Polish society was strictly polarized into two distinct groups: a minority built on conspiratorial principles that governed the Communist state (interlinked among themselves by their own quasi-society, being divided also into a myriad of Party subcliques), and a large majority community split into smaller groups that, while often hostile towards each other, yet supported each other against a common enemy. At times this support degenerated into an attitude of dirty togetherness, resulting in the fiddling survival strategy.

All these historical experiences of mutuality developed emotional and symbolic forms of communication that reinforced the peculiar social bonds based on face-to-face relationships, but did not breed procedural, impersonal types of social ties. Traditional, patriotic, and high-level devotion to Polish democracy and tolerance (towards other religions and sometimes also nationalities) created a false and misleading impression that grassroots-level democratic institutions were deeply rooted in Polish society as well. A lack of simple procedural and impersonal devices introducing into social reality mutually respected norms of democratic cooperation reinforced an anti-objective tendency. It was the tendency to perceive all social events through glasses tainted by personal interests and emotions, and to attach to them a subjective type of importance. As is well known, the spirit of *Gessellschaft* triggers the advancement of organizational and technical abilities. These abilities help to arrange social matters in an orderly and administratively efficient manner. In consequence, the rules of existing but underdeveloped procedural task-solving organizational arrangements and abilities were undermined. This social background supported an already well-cultivated *Gemeinschaft* community and hampered the development of the socially recognized *Gessellschaft* society. Lack of a traditional Polish bureaucracy played here an additional substantial role.

In Polish society, intuitive law (law based on mutual agreements among parties), not official law (law supported by the state apparatus), is respected. Historical experience taught the Poles not to rely so much on official law since it consistently supported the interests of foreign, nineteenth-century (Austrian, German, or Russian) or modern (Soviet Union) states. This general aversion to state law induces Poles to trust only mutual arrangements among trusted (or at least tested) partners, more than to rely on abstract, impersonal, and often incomprehensible legal settlements.[62]

It is not an accident that "praxeology" (to reiterate, practical science determining how to proceed in a proficient manner), which formulates various recommendations regarding effectiveness, was invented (by Tadeusz Kotarbiński) in Poland.

Thus, one can infer that although the Polish democracy is an old one, and although it has had several significant, sometimes even spectacular, political traditions, it is at the same time not inherently prone towards the development of impersonally structured and procedurally oriented pragmatic institutions.

Nevertheless the historic macroexperiment that affected Polish society before the transition period (1945–1989), and especially during (1989-), shows quite clearly that the law may serve as an independent factor transforming a society as a whole. Of course, the law does not have that potential when it is treated exclusively as an abstract concept; nor does it have that potential when treated solely as an abstract, normatively constructed (based on imperatives) legal system. *Law in order to play the role of an independent macrosocial variable should contain (1) a socially legitimized legal system, (2) a legal system addressed to the basic values of the given society, and, above all, (3) a legal system supported by an elaborated network of established impersonal intuitive legal arrangements existing in this social system.*

Thus the impersonal infrastructure of intuitive law is a sine qua non for instilling into the legal system the potential of introducing real macrosocietal changes.

After the revolution of 1989, the Polish legal system gained its own sui generis legitimacy. Because it was not clearly disentangled from the former totalitarian sociolegal system, this legitimacy was not strong, but seemed to be sufficient as a basis for limited, rational reforms of a mezzo-level. The misleading trap that is hidden here is to assume that such reforms can be introduced by normative fiat. This assumption is encouraged by the fact that Poland has many normatively oriented lawyers who are sophisticated and familiar with other legal systems. Indeed, these lawyers have done spectacular work in transforming many elements of the Polish Communist legal system. Nevertheless they are not skillful in producing the basic *grund norm* (the work on Polish constitution, treated as the highest priority, was even in the middle of 1993 not finalized), and they are not enough prepared to undertake a complicated task of launching a rational legal policy. Policy that would match the pre-designed plans with the responsible and sound diagnostic discerns of the socio-economic character.

Nonetheless the real trap is still ahead. When the relatively simple normative-legalistic work is accomplished (preparation of a new legal system), and when the anticipated future results of the legal reforms that are to be introduced are assessed as positive, this legal system may encounter a green light. Then, the *real* trap will materialize: how to match this legal system with the requirements of the infrastructure of impersonal relations of the intuitive laws.

The third general statement relevant to theoretical sociological knowledge is also furnished by the unique Polish macrosocial historical experience and macrolaboratory experiment. It is connected with an analysis of the ever-present anomie that was growing in Polish society throughout this experiment.

It is well known that Emile Durkheim's concept of anomie can be understood psychologically or sociologically. Its psychological understanding stresses the state of individual alienation and the denial of moral responsibility. Robert M. MacIver captured its significance well (1950: 84–85): "Anomy signifies the state of mind of one who has been pulled up by his moral roots, who has no longer any standards but only disconnected urges, who has no longer any sense of continuity, of folk, of obligation. The anomic man has become spiritually sterile, responsive only to himself, responsible to no one. He derides the values of other men. His only faith is the philosophy of denial. He lives on the thin line of sensation between no future and no past."

The sociological understanding of anomie is not only more ethically sterile than the psychological one but also more attuned to abstract notions of structural human interrelations. According to Merton (1968: 216), "Anomie is then conceived as a breakdown in the cultural structure, occurring particularly when there is an acute disjunction between the cultural norms and goals and the socially structured capacities of members of the group to act in accord with them."

Polish experience, as pointedly articulated in the work of Kwaśniewski (1984), brings an additional perspective to the possible elucidation of anomie. According to his study, Polish society in the 1980s was not totally demoralized since its members were able to distinguish clearly, on a cognitive level, bad from good social behavior. This study reveals the extent to which members of this society were under pressure to behave defiantly during the Communist regime. Additionally, the study revealed that members of Polish society showed high emotional and behavioral tolerance of recognized social plagues (alcoholism, bribery, corruption, private and official mistrust, institutional deviance).

The Polish case clearly indicates that anomie is not necessarily a far-reaching *normlessness*, nor is it a widespread attitude of ethical irresponsibility. Among the Polish population, prevalent patterns of social behavior were recognized as negative and were not socially approved during the reign of communism. Nonetheless, these patterns were followed at the behavioral level.

The concept of "social warpedness" (Podgórecki 1972: 54) assists in the comprehension of this incongruity. When various socialization strategies, such as those determined by the traditional family ethos, those designed by the Catholic church, those introduced and imposed by the new Communist world perspective, were neither fully nor partially in opposition to each other, and when these strategies fought with each other over a prolonged period of time, a growing cognitive and ethical chaos emerged. This new chaotic ethos was generated among the younger generation, which, as a result of mutual nullification, was deprived of authority. This generation started to challenge all visible symbols of prestige and supremacy. The process of value nihilation was also rapidly spreading among workers who, once indoctrinated with the belief that they were the owners and governors of the entire social and economic system, had ample opportunity to see that they were exploited even more drastically than they had been under the capitalist system. This ethos was also growing among white-collar workers (the "new intelligentsia") who, as a consequence of their direct involvement in governmental administrative operations, had many opportunities to observe the cynical manipulations of political decision makers and propagators of Communist ideology.

Yet the genesis of social warpedness does more than furnish a significant object for analyzing the social behavior of Poles living under communism. A far more important factor was that the results of the clashes of divergent strategies became an autotelic (independently existing) social factor, subsequently contributing to the existing pool of predominant social motivations. Disjunction between stimulus and reaction, accidental replay to a given incentive, or a lack of reaction should be regarded as typical warped behaviors. In this manner the chaotic, activated by erratic inducements and irrational social behaviors, spread as a new type of conformity. The present and visible panorama of subsidiary selves, facade selves, and looking-glass selves provides additional argument for a lack of authentic social processes and the prevalence of by-products of uncoordinated social changes.

These chaotic patterns of behavior gave additional impetus to the further development of social instrumentality. In unpredictable warped social surroundings, when it became virtually impossible to foresee patterns of behavior in others, instrumentality reinforced itself as the most suitable survival strategy. Therefore, the fiddling type of instrumental subsistence emerged as the patterned behavior of Poles.

The fourth essential theoretical generalization about Polish society can be summarized by the statement that this society, as part of the "family" of the post-Communist bloc, was unable to break its bonds with this bloc abruptly and inadvertently. Post-fascist societies like Germany, Italy, Austria, or, in some sense, Vichy France rejected their past (including the state) after losing World War II. This happened within the framework of international events that were triggered by the war and the military dictatorships in various countries. Some of them, especially Germany, had been involved in the most horrendous crimes. Fascist or rightist totalitarian countries, thanks to the war, were defeated not only militarily but also ideologically—sometimes, as in Japan, even culturally. In effect, they were compelled not to continue their former existence, or they were interested in discontinuing it.

The case of post-Communist societies was different. Although in this situation one may say that "the Kaiser went; the generals remained," or "*Regierung vergeht, Verwaltung besteht*" (governments come and go, bureaucracy remains)," these well-known statements acquired a different meaning. In the post-Communist bloc the old states did continue their legal existence, although some new states were created. As the result of what Juan Linz (1978: 42) calls "resentiment policies against persons and institutions identified with the old order," some institutions disappeared and some of the traditional state emblems (flag, hymn, state emblems—in the Polish case the eagle's head quickly regained its crown) reappeared, but they did not preclude the existence of the former state. In Poland, the Communist and its semiloyal (Linz's expression) parties were not outlawed.

So, in post-Communist countries after 1989, the former state as a rule continued to exist. There were several reasons for this. Financial reasons seemed to be most important: post-Communist countries could not absolve themselves unilaterally from their heavy debts (especially in situations when they were pressed to seek new loans). Additionally, for pragmatic and moral reasons, it was not easy to dismantle the nomenklatura and the higher echelons of bureaucracy. Notwithstanding the nomenklatura's own resistance, its members monopolized the already gained modern "expertise." In Poland they were also not easily removable due to the Catholic idea of forgiveness (properly or wrongly interpreted). An additional obstacle to obtaining a divorce from the still normatively binding state surfaced when it became clear that the tasks of the top law-enacting institution (the Parliament) of producing a new constitution and changing the whole legal system, and an assignment of coordinating the body of law into a unified frame, were overwhelming, while the pressures of current demands to pass the new laws were urgent. Thus, during the post-Communist period in Poland, the normative legacy of communism has had firm grounds to endure.

Notes

1. By ethos one should understand, in this book, the peculiar interrelation between *declared* values (those not always accepted), *accepted* values (those not always realized, especially under pressure), and values that *motivate actual behavior* (sometimes neither declared nor accepted). Thus, ethos is an aggregate of socially proclaimed, accepted, and consolidated patterns of behavior.

2. Among these new classes were the "red bourgeoisie" (heavily oriented towards the petty-bourgeoisie culture), the nomenklatura (monopolizers of political power), and a widespread Party bureaucracy.

3. With the exception of Petrażycki, no one was able to foresee the development of German and Soviet totalitarianism. During an unrecorded lecture in 1931 (during which the lights went out unexpectedly), Petrażycki discussed the potential for such a development. Professor Stanisław Piętka, who was in the audience at the time, personally communicated this information to me.

4. The following story perhaps best describes the typical background of this new scientific cadre. An officer with the rank of lieutenant colonel enters the Party office and says, "The war is over. My task in the army as a political officer is completed. Thus, I submit myself to the Party's disposal. What should I do?" He was asked, "Comrade B.B., do you know anything about philosophy? Do you recognize the names Ajdukiewicz, Ingarden, Kotarbiński, Ossowski, or Tatarkiewicz?" He replied with some indignation, "No, I don't know them." "Good! Very good! So, you are assigned to an accelerated course for university philosophy teachers." Colonel B.B. responded, "But did I make myself clear that I was totally ignorant in this matter? Before the war I worked as a tailor's apprentice." "Yes, yes. You did. This gives you an advantage. You will not be prejudiced."

5. According to Zuzowski (1992: 159, 167), who appears to be well informed in this type of political matter, this group consisted of approximately 100 followers, half of whom were Party members. Zuzowski confirms that "Experience and Future" was originally supported by Stefan Olszowski and adds that it was later patronized by Mieczysław Rakowski.

6. This notion was essential for an adequate diagnosis of Polish society.

7. The Institute of Social Prevention and Resocialization, after preparing its own report, commissioned someone who was not a sociologist to translate the work into "plain" Polish. This translation was subsequently incorporated into the text of the report, enabling Party *apparatchiks* and bureaucrats to digest its content. This may have been decisive both in spreading the idea that social policy should be supported with well-grounded analysis, and in bringing about the downfall of those who had prepared the initial analysis. The report is attached as an appendix to *A Story of a Polish Thinker* (Podgórecki 1986).

8. Diana Crane is a professor of Sociology at the University of Pennsylvania. Although her model was originally built to describe processes found in democratic societies, it is even more appropriate to totalitarian societies.

9. To facilitate reading, I am using "he" (or "his" or "himself") in this text. To express myself properly, I should, of course, write "she" or "he," "her" or "his," and "herself" or "himself."

10. It is important to note that the exposition of the model(s) of socialist scholar is not a detailed, empirically based description of the average scholar operating inside a system of "real socialism." It is instead a stylized model of such a scholar. It is necessary to remember that a socialist scholar can play the role of a real scholar: he (or she) may possess the abilities of an actor. Finally, the meteoric rise of this type of scholar never underwent the scrutiny of sociological analysis.

11. It would be a grave mistake to assume that the socialist model of scholar disappears with the totalitarian state. The legacy of totalitarianism, its accumulated "psychic poisons," are still very powerful, if invisible. One may venture that the near future in the social sciences belongs to a mixture of Western sly and Eastern post-socialist scholars.

12. The Section of Sociotechnics of the Polish Sociological Association was created in 1966. I was its first chairman; Janusz Gockowski was the first Secretary.

13. Later, a similar work entitled *Raport o Stanie Narodu i Panstwa (An Account of the State and the Nation)*, published in 1979, gained considerable recognition in Poland and abroad, partly because it was published underground (uncensored). It was apparently commissioned by Stefan Olszowski and his political faction.

14. This study was completed by Kazimierz Frieske in 1987 (Frieske 1990: 201–51).

15. Chaired by myself.

16. It is probably worth noting that the story of this institute was published by myself in the Warsaw weekly *Kierunki* ("Directions") in an article called "On the Pathology Track," only a few days before the imposition of martial law in Poland on December 13, 1981. The ex-minister of Justice and professor of criminal law Stanislaw Walczak, invigorated by the imposed martial law, sued the editors of the journal (myself included) who were responsible for the publication of the article "The Unusual History of a Certain Reorganization." To neutralize the testimony of Professor Jerzy Kwaśniewski, potentially the most outspoken witness, the ex-minister sued him as well. He lost this case before the Supreme Court. Living in Ottawa, Canada, I challenged the suit to defend the journalists. Due, however, to the political climate created by martial law, I was unable, in the beginning, to find a lawyer who would agree to accept the case. Eventually Dr. Andrzej Rozmarynowicz of Cracow (who later became a senator) accepted the case before the Warsaw Court. Paradoxically enough, while still under the regime of totalitarian law, the ex-minister lost his case on May 21, 1988 (Warsaw Court, Sygn. Act I C 991/82).

17. This anecdote (derived from a conversation with Professor Zygmunt Rybicki, then

president of the University of Warsaw, who died in 1989) and some of the following true stories are quoted here to display to the reader, especially the Western one, the peculiar atmosphere of intellectual life under "real socialism." To understand these narratives as cryptic cheap shots would point to a lack of empathy, inhibiting comprehension of these dark times and doing a grave injustice to those who suffered under them. Some of these stories were published in the Polish press during the Solidarity period of 1980–1981; later, under martial law, they resulted in law suits (see note 16) which were lost by the plaintiff, the former minister of Justice and professor of Criminal Law Stanislaw Walczak.

18. Notwithstanding the prohibitive professorial salary, some intellectual innovators, like Søren Kierkegaard, seriously consider supporting their own publications financially. But who, then, would be able to discover their precious ideas under the geometrical accumulation of paper piles in the absence of reviews or advertisements?

19. As mentioned in the acknowledgements, I conducted a seminar on Polish society in 1973–1976 at the University of Warsaw. The idea of this seminar was, first, to assemble the relevant data, and then, to stimulate and develop a global theory of such a society. During the seminar several areas of social and political life were consecutively analyzed. The atmosphere of the discussions was turbulent and open-minded. When the problem of attitudes of the younger generation was discussed, Andrzej Celiński (currently a senator) presented on large sheets of paper data collected by himself. Those sheets he had already presented he used to destroy with a theatrical gesture. Commenting on this behavior, Marek Tabin (currently a journalist in Germany) whispered loudly, "Do not wreck this paper, it might be useful for your wife to deliver food to the penitentiary." Nobody realized then (1975) how prophetic this statement was.

20. According to the Statistical Yearbook of 1991, Polish universities in 1990–1991 employed 13,917 professors and associate professors (*Rocznik Statystyczny* 1991: 416).

Of special interest is a study conducted by the Center of Public Research Studies in February, 1993, which shows that the situation has changed drastically. As observed in *Donosy* of March 12, 1993, 81 percent of Poles respected the profession of a physician—the highest percentage. In second position (57 percent) were teachers, and in the third were farmers (51 percent), whereas university professors placed fourth (37 percent, *ex equo* with miners). Since government minister has 13 percent of support and a member of Parliament 7 percent (compare with an average clerk—5 percent), the explanation that suggests itself is a peculiar one. All recent opinion polls show that the so-called political class (all those who currently represent power) is basically composed of professors and various types of "intellectuals" (but not necessarily members of intelligentsia). Since public opinion regards them as responsible for the absence, thus far, of the widespread economic recovery that was predicted after the abolition of communism, and for the constant, almost personal quarrelling over the issue, they are blamed for the current economic situation. Additionally, since this political class, as the "white nomenklatura," did not cut itself off vigorously enough from the former, hated nomenklatura but sometimes took over its habits and privileges and even started to cooperate with it, or to collaborate with the "pink nomenklatura," it was the professors who paid with their prestige for this too-eager marriage with the political class.

21. According to the Statistical Yearbook, the urban population in 1990 was 23,600,000, and the rural population was 14,600,000 (*Rocznik Statystyczny* 1991:xxv).

22. This problem is, of course, much more complicated. It will be discussed in chapter 6, which deals with the post-Communist society.

23. Therefore, the following construction, which uses this method to reveal the ethos of Poles, is subject to the same limitation.

24. The final definition of "meta-attitude" is presented and elaborated in the concluding chapter.

25. Concepts like intelligentsia, traditional intelligentsia, string intelligentsia, instrumental, principled, or all-thumbs attitudes, spectacular principledness (principled heroics) the ingenious survival strategy, and dirty togetherness are elaborated in *Multidimensional Sociology* (Podgórecki, Łoś, 1979). They will be explained in this chapter and the next.

26. An anecdote might give a better understanding of the meaning of this meta-attitude. An American millionaire of Polish origin once told me how he had achieved his remarkable success. As the owner of several helicopter factories, he maintained that his helicopters were better than others since they were tested by Polish pilots. These pilots had a gift for finding minor defects, particularly defects in the helicopters' design that might, under certain conditions, lead to tragedy. Polish pilots, equipped with an incredible will to survive, were better able psychologically to withstand tests and individual strain than other nationalities. Thus, in his opinion, this national characteristic, in combination with American technology, had built his impressive success and wealth.

27. It is interesting to note that Bojar quotes both Ewa Tarkowska (1985)—"unfulfilled expectations connected with the marital life lead to the tendency to *realize oneself through children*" (original emphasis)—and myself "who, in the middle seventies (1976), indicated the characteristic tendency for Polish society to treat children as symbols of prestige, as idols symbolizing the integrity of a small group" (Bojar 1991:63, 53). Recognizing the characteristic legacy of a "socialist" society, the editor of the volume, Mirosława Marody (1991:237), writes, "Finally, sociological research conducted in the eighties suggested a specific combination of development and survival. According to this research, Polish parents, even when young, resign their own aspirations, transferring them to their children according to the principle that 'I was not successful, but they must be' (Tarkowska 1985)." The original statement reads as follows: "Recompensation for all adult adversities is located in children. Hard determination is the decisive force: 'I was miserable, but he will be well' " (Podgórecki 1968 :14).

28. It is interesting to note that those who possessed power in Poland before 1989 were not, of course, eager to reveal that the very basis of their existence was not supported by the public. This is precisely why those occupying official positions decisively curtailed studies that tried to enter into this arena. As a result, there are very serious holes in the research that crippled the diagnostic and synthetic picture of Polish society based on systematically collected empirical data.

29. Ryszard Dyoniziak has noted this point and tried to contribute to a better understanding of Polish society. His main area of interest is the social stratification of Polish society (Dyoniziak n.d.). Upon reading his perceptive paper, Edmund Mokrzycki made the following remark: "So far, Polish sociology has shown great restraint in drawing theoretical conclusions from the empirical materials collected, and has avoided posing the most essential questions, regarding them as not its own" (Mokrzycki 1989:34).

30. Anarchy, violence, and corruption have been other important characteristics in the historical development of Polish society. These features are omitted in this analysis since they are not specific to Polish society alone.

31. It is possible that the ethos of this conviction contributed to a half-acceptance of the equality formulated under "socialism," which proclaimed the equality of all, despite the acute terror spread among the Polish population by the NKVD (Soviet security forces).

32. This phenomenon, inherent in the Polish ethos, was dramatically reinforced when it began to play a defensive and survival-oriented function under "real socialism."

33. Sociology and theories about society perform several functions. The first is diagnostic: their primary task is to provide a reliable synthesis of the existing social situation, obtained through accepted methods of inquiry. The second is theoretical: their task is to explain, by using the most appropriate hypothesis or a set of hypotheses, why the existing situation has emerged. The third is sociotechnical: they must formulate recommendations that would be instrumental in creating the desired social situation. The last is that of unmasking: their task is to reveal, from behind, those social, economic, or political forces that manipulate naive subjects who are unaware of the goals of the hidden players.

In Polish social thought, it was Piotr Skarga (1532–1612) who first undertook to open the eyes of society through persistent questioning of the assumptions held by those in power. In this vein Ossowska, analyzing the role of a scholar, states, "The first [soldier] is expected to be obedient to his superiors, while distrust of any authority is the moral duty of a scientist" (Ossowska 1972: 55). Therefore an accusatory display of social vices, so long as it pertains to impersonal matters and is based on civic courage, is accepted, if not welcomed, in the Polish tradition of public reasoning.

34. The instrumental and principled selves perform the roles of metaselves. They are dominant, structuring the composition and hierarchy of the remaining selves.

35. Envy could have played the role of social guardian; as such, it is a heterotelic, functional instrument designed to maintain the existing social equilibrium. Instrumental envy was generated with social development and the increasing complexity of life. Envy became a value in itself, thereby adopting an autotelic character. This point has been suggestively developed by Scheler. "It is surely obvious that, without exception, the apparently innocuous demand for equality—of whatever kind, whether sexual, social, political, religious or material—in fact conceals only the desire for the *demotion*, in accordance with the selected scale of values, of those having more assets and those who are in some way *higher up*, to the level of those lower down" (Scheler 1955:121; original emphasis). Some authors have gone further, maintaining that envy was an intrinsic element of the human psyche. "Envy is a drive which lies at the core of man's life as a social being, and which occurs as soon as two individuals become capable of mutual comparison" (Schoeck 1969: 1). I have suggested that envy, disinterested envy, was an essential element of the Polish ethos (Podgórecki 1976a; 1978a; 1978b; 1987b). As indicated by Dyoniziak, this idea has been reiterated (but not quoted) by Marody (1988: 102) in Dyoniziak (n.d.: 8).

36. Taking into consideration the recommendations of this strategy, it is a mistake to maintain that the Poles are unable to work efficiently. To work effectively, they need the motivating sociopolitical system. In several Western countries they work better than the average person.

37. Mass deportations of Poles (especially the intelligentsia) to the Soviet Union were carried out in 1939–1941.

38. My own limited research on the intelligentsia (and also "intelligentsia") conducted in Canada during 1979–1992 confirmed this generalization. Many Polish nuclear families in various Canadian cities are structured in a similar way. Women play the traditional male role of family provider in these families. More flexible, more responsible for children (and the entire family), and more adaptable, they seem to be able to adjust better and more quickly to new, culturally alien, and onerous (although financially advantageous) Canadian circumstances. They are eager to undertake any kind of job, even those of a

"primitive" character like cleaning, nursing older people, selling, and others that do not correspond to their higher level of education. They are compelled to do this because it is "beneath the dignity" of their husbands to accept such tasks. Manual work does not fit with the pattern of spectacular principledness. Strangely enough, the wives of Polish gentlemen are socialized even by their counterparts to suffer in their own right rather than allow their husbands to degrade themselves by taking on "primitive work." This yields unique results: women work like oxen, while their husbands, frustrated because they are not appreciated enough, spend their time suffering at leisure, complaining notoriously, and demanding consolation and special attention from their wives.

39. I am aware of the complexity of the problem of Polish anti-Semitism. My main task is not to solve it but to present supplementary sociological factors that may shed some additional light on this apparently unsolvable question.

40. To my knowledge this extremely interesting cultural phenomenon has been neither recognized nor systematically analyzed. Provisional diagnosis of this situation was formulated by Anna Clarke (a Jewish-Polish specialist in the history of Polish-Jewish relations; she lives in Ottawa, Canada).

41. As Gella indicates, this term was first used by the Pole Karol Libelt in 1844; the Russian Peter Boborykin used it in 1860 (Gella 1971: 4).

42. Maria Ossowska disagreed with Chałasiński's characterization (Ossowska 1969). Although Ossowska was right to question some of his arguments (particularly where she showed that some features of Chałasiński's picture are not specific to the Polish intelligentsia), the general tenor of his analysis seems to be well substantiated by historical and sociological data.

43. When I was in Oxford (1971 and 1978–1979), I was struck by the similarity between the Polish intelligentsia's subculture on one side and the amateurish climate of Oxford life on the other. There was, however, one difference: in Oxford, one may find some towering intellectual figures (imported, if not indigenous), whereas in Poland, one drowns in the shallowness of good manners and the emptiness of overabundant verbiage.

44. According to Władysław Kwaśniewicz, "Only about sixty percent of them survived the war" (Kwaśniewicz 1989: 11).

45. Perhaps in order to defend *ex post facto* his dogmatic Communist past, Leszek Kołakowski developed a thesis that communism was attractive for Polish intellectuals after World War II (Kołakowski 1985: 3–10). Jan Drewnowski rejects this "very serious bungle." Drewnowski rightly stressed that the technique of applying pressure to achieve compliance among the intellectuals who were opposed to Marxism was multivariate. Summarizing his arguments, he says, "In a short manner, one may conclude that these methods consisted of placing intellectuals into a trap without an exit, subsequently introducing various forms of pressure, including terror against dissent, and privileges and perks to motivate the obedient to compliance. These methods have been diversified: different for different groups, flexible in various historical periods, and flexible in various individual cases" (Drewnowski 1991: 28–29).

46. "I remember that when I attended the meeting of the Club [*Logofagi*] I saw there Adam Podgórecki, Zygmunt Skórzynski, Jacek Woźniakowski, Andrzej Rozmarynowicz, Benedykt Łubienski, Zbigniew Marek, Henryk Markiewicz, Grzegorz Leopold Seidler. I was then preparing my habilitation thesis, so I attended the meetings, only when the progress of my work allowed me to do so" (Studnicki 1992).

47. "In 1951, or perhaps 1952, Andrzej Ciechanowiecki was arrested by the security organ. The charge was, from the Communist point of view, a serious one. It was claimed

that he was active in the underground political or military organization. Shortly after his arrest, the mother of Andrzej Ciechanowiecki came to Dr. Skąpski, who did not yet have his Ph.D., and asked him to destroy the "book" of *Logofagos* [Skąpski was the caretaker of this book]. This was fully justified, since that was the time of constant searches, arrests, 'kettles,' and other types of events. If the security organs found any personal documents, and especially lists of names, or even worse, a list of names with addresses, then these documents immediately became 'proof' of conspiratorial organizations'' (Studnicki 1992).

48. Now is the last moment to prepare the history of these (and other) groups, which were active after War World II and which then prepared the ground for the forthcoming development of the dissident movement in Poland.

49. It would take a separate study to describe the kaleidoscopic variety of the membership of these groupings and the ideological ferment that existed therein. The main goal of this analysis is to show the *continuous line of ideological inquiry* developed by various representatives of civil society, and, more specifically, by the alumni of the Jagiellonian and Warsaw universities; their continuous readiness to confront the changing sociopolitical reality in Poland with a comprehensive diagnosis of the existing situation; and their attempts, based on this diagnosis, to enlarge and achieve political freedom should such possibilities emerge. In *A Story of a Polish Thinker* (1986), I tried to present, in daily sequence, the predicaments that constituted the lot of those who continued this legacy in the mid–1970s.

50. The main architects of this diagnostic center were Czesław Czapów, Jerzy Kubin, Wacław Makarczyk, Aleksander Matejko (now a professor in Canada), and Andrzej Rażniewski.

51. Though one would expect it to have been substantive, the contribution of the Polish army and the Home Army (the largest European underground army during the Second World War) in preparing the climate for Solidarity is virtually unknown. What is recorded is that under martial law, people read books about the struggle of the Home Army during the war (Łopinski et al. 1990).

52. These facts are unknown. Several people who have been more active in these developments than I are still silent. A special book should be devoted to this movement. In particular, a detailed monograph should be attached to the heroic and meticulous work of Jan Józef Lipski. I am deeply convinced that these historical events should be revealed, especially in light of the well-publicized, highly (and, I think, unintentionally) misleading book by Adam Michnik, *Kościół, Lewca, Dialog* (*Church, Left, Dialogue*, Paris, Instytut Literacki, 1977). According to Michnik, the real opposition in Poland began with the activities of various atheists and social-democratic pre-war professors and post-Marxists— his friends, activists in March, 1968 (some claim that this student revolt was provoked and triggered by the secret police)—and the activities of certain former Party activists (many of whom were former officers in the Polish army created in the Soviet Union, others colonels in the secret service—but all of whom were disillusioned with the new tendency within the Party to rely more on indigenous Communist underground activities). Having high regard for the historical and journalistic abilities of Timothy Garton Ash (the author of *The Polish Revolution: Solidarity*), I approached him once, giving him the addresses of people who could furnish him with first-hand data to develop his point of view. To my knowledge, he did not try to approach these actors and creators of this still-unknown chapter of modern Polish history.

53. Jan Olszewski became prime minister of the third democratic government of Poland after 1989.

54. The principle of reciprocity underscores the extent to which one could, or should, use one's official position to arrange private matters for oneself, one's family, and, most important, for those who would later reciprocate with similar favors. The most important feature of this partnership is that, while illegal, it leads to a social cohesion based on the continuous threat of blackmail, exposing the beneficiary of the partnership.

55. The legacy of post-totalitarianism seems to be eternal. At the beginning of 1992, I submitted to the Polish authorities a plan for the ousting of the worst Communist-totalitarian heritage—the nomenklatura. The essence of this plan was simple: all former members of the nomenklatura would have a duty to declare, and subsequently return to the state treasury, all financial gains acquired during their tenure. Criminal sanctions and an obligatory loss of property were to be imposed on those who did not comply with the law. This plan was discussed in May at the forum of a Polish scientific association. The chairman of the meeting summarized the discussion for me in a letter of May 15:

The general conclusion based on the discussion of your project was: the solution of this problem will never materialize. "Combined" nomenklaturas (old and new) will not allow it to be resolved, as they did not permit in the past the disclosure of the names of Security agents [this was changed at the beginning of June, 1992]. The quest for accountability of the old nomenklatura is needed mainly as a test of the openness and purity of *present* public life. The new nomenklatura is not interested in revealing its texture, contrary to its declarations. The new nomenklatura collects forces to defend its freshly acquired position against growing social rage. Step by step, people come to the conclusion that the essence of past sociopolitical change boils down to a change of promise, in the name of which the government ("they") orders its subjects to renounce their rights and well-being; the utopia of the socialist heaven is replaced by a utopia of the capitalist heaven. This is only one step from the restriction of existing liberties, civil rights, and workers' rights. The perpetual postponement of the enactment of a new constitution, and the continuous enlargement of the State Protection Agency are favorable conditions for it."

56. The following statement, tragic in its content, may illustrate the strength of this attitude. "I was behind bars in PRL [Communist Poland] for eight and a half years. Observing the development of events after "our" victory, I am not free of the fear that, sometime in the future, I will be compelled to regard this time as lost" (Modzelewski 1992:7).

57. This chapter deals exclusively with the achievements of Polish sociology after World War II. Thus, contributions to the field of sociology by the anthropologist Bronislaw Malinowski and Florian Znaniecki are omitted. Also omitted is the meteoric appearance of Leon Petrażycki (discussed, along with Malinowski and Znaniecki, in chapter 1), although, due to the exigencies of his life (his scientific work in Russia, his illuminating publications in Germany, his major scientific discoveries in Russia again, and, finally, his publications in post-World War I Poland), his work did gain some recognition in Poland, but only after World War II. This appreciation was peculiar: some scholars hid themselves from Marxism behind his genius; some struggled to reveal the inventiveness hidden within his own obsolete language—a task that is still not finished despite the monumental editorial work of his selective writings (Petrażycki 1985); others tried to translate his grand ideas into modern achievements of the social sciences.

Ironically, it was Robert Merton who showed the Poles the originality of Ludwig Fleck, a major figure in the sociology of knowledge (Merton 1982: 10–14). Despite the worldwide popularity of the feminist movement, the Poles remained blind to the fact that it was Stanislaw Schanter who elaborated—not in a literary way like Henrik Ibsen (1828–1906) in *A Doll's House* but in a systematic, sociologically mature manner—most of the basic ideas later debated by this movement around the world (Schanter 1947).

58. See especially Podgórecki (ed.) 1968, 1970, 1972, and 1974; and Kubin 1990.

59. It is symptomatic that some hard-working and evidently empirically oriented Western scholars, especially those deprived of the guidance of emphatic entrance into the Polish "soul," could come to such shocking conclusions as this: "In short, intellectuals close to the Party were essential to Solidarity" (Laba 1991: 4). Elsewhere, this author makes the sharp observation that "especially in oppressive situations, intellectuals act as gatekeepers who interpret their own societies for foreigners. But intellectuals occupy a particular niche in their societies and have categories of thought and deep ideologies shaping their presentations" (Laba 1991: 7). Nonetheless he writes, "A rare exception is Jan Malanowski, a senior Polish sociologist and member of Solidarity and the Party's Central Committee in 1981. In his book on Polish workers, Malanowski lamented that ideological pressure had pushed social investigations into designated areas known as 'safe problems' " (Laba 1991: 8). Why did the author not realize that, if Malanowski, who died in 1992, was a member of the Central Committee of the Party, he was also the "gatekeeper who pushed social investigations into the areas of safe problems"?

60. If a Polish peasant thinks she is deprived in comparison with an urban Polish woman, she remains within a societally relevant reference circle. But if her activities are motivated by a negative evaluation of her socioeconomic position in comparison with a woman living in a Swedish city, then she is trespassing beyond her societal frame of reference. This relative deprivation could be called *external relative deprivation*.

61. It is intriguing to note that Maria Ossowska's achievements are not discussed in the book on Polish masters of sociology edited by a former Communist (Sztompka 1984). Nor does the book mention Ludwik Fleck and Stanislaw Schanter. Yet one can find in this volume an influential Marxist who produced only one book in his life. This is a collection of political pamphlets united by the grammatical error in the title.

62. The results of disentanglement decisions have not been noticed by lawyers—theoreticians travelling around the globe in search of inspiration—but by a practitioner animated by an Australian-Polish specialist, Martin Krygier. Then the head of the Polish administration, Jan Rokita, chairman of the Council of Ministers, summarized the pressures of everyday occurrences thus: "So we—Poland—are paying a high price for these two circumstances, that we used law as the means for transformation and we decided to build on the basis of Communist law. For these two things we are paying an enormous price—in the form of a complete disintegration of the legal system; its much-extended internal incoherence; very few rules that are stable, particularly in economic life—very few; unheard-of confusions in the political system of the state where laws create overlapping spheres of competence of various organs" (Krygier 1993: 15).

References

ABBREVIATIONS AND DEFINITIONS

BGW   a Warsaw publishing house

CRZZ   Centralna Rada Zwiazkow Zawodowych (General Council of Trade Unions)

Donosy   electronic newspaper sent daily gratis from Warsaw to international subscribers

IFIS   Instytut Filozofii i Sociologii (Institute of Philosophy and Sociology)

PAN   Polska Akademia Nauk (Polish Academy of Sciences)

PIW   Panstwowy Instytut Wydawniczy (Governmental Literary Publishing House)

PTS   Polskie Towarzystwo Sociologiczne (Polish Sociological Association)

PWN   Panstwowe Wydawnictwo Naukowe (Governmental Scientific Publishing House)

UW   Uniwersytet Warszawski (University of Warsaw)

Allart, Erik, and Włodzimierz Wesołowski, eds. *Social Structure and Change in Finland and Poland: A Comparative Perspective.* Warsaw: PWN, 1978.

Ash, Timothy Garton. *The Polish Revolution: Solidarity.* New York: Charles Scribner's Sons, 1984.

———. "Poland After Solidarity." *New York Review of Books*, 37, no. 11 (1991): 13.

Barzini, Luigi. *The Europeans.* London: Weidenfeld and Nicolson, 1983.

Bendix, Reinhard. *Max Weber.* Berkeley, CA: University of California Press, 1977.

Berlin, Isaiah. *Four Essays on Liberty.* London: Oxford University Press, 1969.

Beskid, Lidia. *Warunki i Sposób Życia Społeczenstwa Polskiego w Czasie Regresu (Conditions of Life in Poland during Regression).* Warsaw: PAN, 1987.

Bojar, Hanna. "Rodzina i Życie Rodzinne" ("Family and Family Life"). In *Społe-czeństwo Polskie u Progu Zmiany Systemowej*, edited by Mirosława Marody. London: Areks, 1991.

Breton, Reymond, Gills Houle, Gary Caldwell, Edmund Mokrzycki, and Edmund Wnuk-Lipiński, eds. *Social Change in Canada and Poland*. Ottawa: Carleton University Press, 1990.

Canetti, Elias. *Crowds and Power*. New York: The Noon Day Press, 1962.

Chałasiński, Józef. *Społeczna Genealogia Inteligencji Polskiej (A Social Genealogy of the Polish Intelligentsia)*. Warsaw: Czytelnik, Polski Instytut Sociologiczny, 1946.

Cohen, Albert. *Delinquent Boys: The Culture of the Gang*. New York: The Free Press, 1955.

Cohen, Ira. "Structuration Theory and Social Praxis" In *Social Theory Today*, edited by Anthony Giddens and Jonathan Turner. Stanford: Stanford University Press, 1986.

Committee in Support of Solidarity. *Reports*, no. 20, December 10, 1983. London.

Chambers, Mary. "The Identity Crisis and Decomposition of Solidarity: Poland 1989–1990." Unpublished M.A. Thesis, Carleton University, Ottawa, 1992.

Cíupak, Edward. "Podstawy Światopogladowe Społeczenstwa Polskiego" ("Worldviews of the Poles"). *Człowiek i Światopoglad*, 1975, no. 3.

Collins, Randall. *Weberian Sociological Theory*. Cambridge: Cambridge University Press, 1986.

Crane, Diane. *Invisible Colleges*. Chicago: University of Chicago Press, 1972.

Czapów, Czesław. *Sociotechnika w Zakładzie Pracy (Sociotechnics in Enterprise)*. Warsaw: CRZZ, 1977.

Davies, Norman. *God's Playground. A History of Poland*. Volume II. Oxford: Clarendon Press, 1981.

Domanski, Henryk. "Od Profesora do Handlarza" ("From Professor to Merchant"). *Polityka*, July 20, 1991, no. 29

Drewnowski, Jan. *Rozkład i Upadek Sowietyzmu w Polsce (Decay and Fall of Sovietism in Poland)*. Lublin: Norbertinum, 1991.

Dyoniziak, Ryszard. "Społeczenstwo Polskie - Przyczynek do Teorii" ("Polish Society - Contribution to Theory"). Unpublished manuscript, n.d.

————. "Potrzeby Konsumpcyjne a Problem 'Fałszywej świadomości'" ("Consumptive Needs and the Problem of 'False' Consciousness"). *Kultura i spoleczenstwo (Culture and Society)* 11, no. 2 (1967).

———— Krystyna Iwanicka, Anna Karwińska, and Zbigniew Pucek. *Spoleczenstwo w Procesie Zmian (A Society in the Process of Change)*. Krakow: Universitas, 1992.

Ferrari, Vincenzo, ed. *Developing a Sociology of Law*. Milan: Guiffrè, 1990.

Fredro-Boniecki, Tadeusz. *Zwycięstwo Księdza Jerzego (The Victory of Father Jerzy)*. Warsaw: Niezależna Spółka Wydawnicza, 1990.

Friedrich, Carl, ed. *Totalitarianism*. Cambridge, MA: Harvard University Press, 1954.

Friedrich, Carl, J., and Zbigniew K. Brzeziński. *Totalitarian Dictatorship and Autocracy*. Cambridge, MA: Harvard University Press, 1965.

Frieske, Kazimierz. *Sociologia w Działaniu: Nadzieje i Rozczarowania (Sociology in Action: Hopes and Disillusionment)*. Warszawa: Uniwersytet Warszawski, 1990.

Fuller, Lon. *The Morality of Law*. New Haven: Yale University Press, 1969.

Gałęski, Bogusław. *Sociologia Wsi (Rural Sociology)*. Warszawa: PWN, 1966.

Galtung, Johann. "Structure, Culture, and Intellectual Style . . . ." *Social Science Information* 20, no. 6 (1981).

———. "A Structural Theory of Imperialism" in *Journal of Peace Research* 8, no. 2 (1971).

Gella, Alexander. *Development of Class Structure in Eastern Europe*. Albany: State University of New York Press, 1989.

Gella, A., ed.. *The Intelligentsia and Intellectuals*. London: Sage Publications, 1976.

Giedymin, Jerzy. *Science and Convention*. Oxford: Pergamon, 1984.

Goldfarb, Jeffrey C. *Beyond Glasnost: The Post-Totalitarian Mind*. Chicago: University of Chicago Press, 1989.

Gomulka, S., and A. Polonsky, eds. *Polish Paradoxes*. London: Routledge and Kegan Paul, 1990.

Hann, C. *A Village without Solidarity*. New Haven: Yale University Press, 1985.

Havel, Vaclav. *Summer Meditations*. Toronto: Alfred A. Knopf, 1992.

Herz, John H., ed. *From Dictatorship to Democracy*. Westport, CT: Greenwood Press, 1982.

Holtzer, Jerzy. *Solidarność (Solidarity)*. Paris: Instytut Literacki, 1984.

Jaakkola, Magdalena, and Wacław Makarczyk. "Social Networks." In *Social Structure and Change in Finland and Poland: A Comparative Perspective*, edited by Erik Allart and Włodzimierz Wesolowsk, ch. 11. Warsaw: PWN, 1978.

Jain, Ajit, ed. *Solidarity*. Baton Rouge: Oracle Press, 1982.

Janicka, Krystyna. "Ruchliwosc Miedzypokoleniowa" ("Intergeneration Mobility"). In *Struktura i Ruchliwość Społeczna (Social Structure and Mobility)*, edited by Kazimierz Słomczynski and Włodzimierz Wesółowski. Wroclaw: Ossolineum, 1973.

Janik, Wojciech L. "Konferencja: Wieś i Rolnictwo w Latach 1970–83 ("Conference on Countryside and Agriculture in 1970–83"). *Studia Sociologiczne* 97, no 2 (1985).

Jaruzelski, Wojciech. *Stan Wojenny, Dlaczego . . . (Martial Law, Why . . .)*. Warsaw: BGW, 1992.

Jarzębowski, Witold. "Fikcje Organizacyjne i Dzialania Pozorne" ("Organizational Fictions and Spurious Activities"). Halia: Sociotechnics Section, PTS, 1976.

Jasiński, Jerzy. "Punitywność Systemów Prawnych" ("The Punitiveness of Legal Systems"). *Studia Prawnicze*, 1973, no. 35.

Kałużynski, Zygmunt. "Jak Uciec od Życia" ("How to Escape from Life"). "*Polityka*, 1992, no. 52.

Kamiński, Antoni, Z. *An Institutional Theory of Communist Regimes*. San Francisco: C Press, 1991.

Karpowicz, Ewa, and Krystyna Lelinska. "Percepcja Sejmu X Kadencji" ("The Diet's Image in 1991"). Warsaw: Diet Research Bureau, 1991.

Kersten, Krystyna. *Narodziny Systemu Władzy Poland 1943–1948 (The Emergence of a New System of Power 1943–1948)*. Paris: Libella, 1989.

———. *Żydowski Pogrom w Kielcach w 1946 (The Jewish Pogrom in Kielce in 1946)*. Wroclaw: Bellona, 1992a.

———. *Polacy Żydzi Komunizm (Poles, Jews, and Communism)*. Warsaw: Niezależna Oficyna Wydawnicza, 1992b.

Kiciński, Krzysztof. "Postawy Młodego Pokolenia wobec Wartości Społecznych i Indywidualnych" ("The Younger Generation's Attitudes towards Individual and Social Values"). Warsaw: IPS: R, 1972.

Kieniewicz, Stefan. *Historyk a Swiadomość Narodowa (The Historian and National Awareness)*. Warsaw: Czytelnik, 1982.

Kieżun, Witold, ed. *Style Zarządzania (Styles of Management)*. Warsaw: Ksiazka i Wiedza, 1977.

————. *Management in Socialist Countries*. Berlin: Walter de Gruyter, 1991.

Kinzer, Steven. "The Nightmare's Roots: The Dream World Called Serbia." *New York Times*, Section 4, May 16, 1993.

Kłoskowska, Antonina. "The Ambiguity of Cultural Development." *Polish Sociological Bulletin* 96, no. 4 (1991).

Kocowski, Tomasz. "Portrzeby a Wartości" ("Needs and Values"). Unpublished paper. N.d.

Kojder, Andrzej. *Przymus w Społeczenstwie (Oppression in Society)*. Warsaw: Polskie Tow, Sociologiczne, 1989.

————. "Limited Potentialities of Humanistic Sociotechnics in the Monocentric Social System." In *Dilemmas of Effective Social Action*, edited by Jerzy Kubin. Warsaw: Centre for Science Advancement, PAN 1990.

Kołakowski, Leszek. *Szkice o Filozofii Katolickiej (Essays on Catholic Philosophy)*. Warsaw: PWN, 1955.

————. "Komunizm jako Formacja Kulturalna" ("Communism as Cultural formation"). *Kontakt*, 1985, no. 11.

Konrad, Georg, and Ivan Szelenyi. *The Intellectuals on the Road to Class Power*. New York: Harcourt Brace Jovanovich, 1979.

Koralewicz, Jadwiga, ed. *Społeczeństwo Polskie przed Krysysem w Świetle Badań Sociologicznych z lat 1977–1979 (Polish Society before the Crisis in the Light of Sociological Studies of 1977–1979)*. Warsaw: PWN, 1987.

————. *Autorytaryzm, Lęk, Konformism (Authoritarianism, Insecurity and Conformity)*. Wroclaw: Ossolineum, 1987.

Koralewicz, Jadwiga, and Marek Ziółkowski. *Mentalność Polaków (The Polish Mentality)*. Poznań: Wydawnictwo Naukowe, 1990.

Koralewicz-Zębik, Jadwiga. *System Wartości a Struktura Społeczna (System of Values and Social Structure)*. Wroclaw: Ossolineum, 1974.

Kowalski, Sergiusz. *Krytyka Solidarnościowego Rozumu (Critics of Solidarity's Wisdom)*. Warsaw: PFN, 1990.

Król, Marcin. "Measures against Solitude." Interview with Wiesław Władyka in *Polityka*, 1992, no. 43.

Krygier, Martin. "Four Visions of Post-Communist Law." Paper presented in Chicago during the annual meeting of The Law and Society Association, May 29, 1993.

Krzemiński, Ireneusz. *Czy Polska po Solidarności? (Poland: After Solidarity?)*. Warsaw: Instytut Sociologii UW, 1989.

Kubin, Jerzy, ed. *Dilemmas of Effective Social Action*. Warsaw: Center for Science Advancement, PAN, 1990.

Kuroń, Jacek. *Moja Zupa (My Soup)*. Warsaw: BGW, 1991.

Kurczewski, Jacek. "Co to jest Klasa Średnia w Polsce?" ("What is The Middle Class in Poland?"). *Więź*, 1989, no. 2.

Kurczewski, Jacek, ed. *Prawo w Spoleczenstwie (Law in Society)*. Warsaw: PWN, 1975.

Kwaśniewicz, Władysław. "Sociological Dilemmas of Intelligentsia: The Case of Poland." Conference paper presented in Radzyna, November 27–29, 1989.

Kwaśniewski, Jerzy. "Social Problems in Poland." In *Social Control and The Law in Poland*, edited by Jerzy Kwaśniewski and Margaret Watson. Oxford: Berg, 1991.

———. *Society and Deviance in Communist Poland*. Leamington Spa: Berg, 1984.

Laba, Roman. *The Roots of Solidarity*. Princeton: Princeton University Press, 1991.

Le Carré, John. *The Secret Pilgrim*. Toronto: Penguin Books, 1991.

Łebkowski, Tadeusz. "O Problemie Rewolucji w Polsce w Latach 1944–1989" ("About the Revolution in Poland in 1944–1989"). Unpublished paper, N.d.

Łętowska, Ewa. *Baba na Świeczniku (Woman on the Candelstick)*. Warsaw: BGW, 1992.

Letocha, Daniele. "The Dialectics of Tolerance in Sixteenth-Century Poland." *Proceedings of the Unitarian Universalist Historian Society* 20, pt. 2 (1986).

Linz, Juan. *The Breakdown of Democratic Regimes: Latin America*. Baltimore. Johns Hopkins University Press, 1978.

Lipski, Jan Józef. *KOR*. London: Aneks, 1983.

———. *Tunika Nessora (Nessor's Tunic)*. Warsaw: PFN, 1992.

Lopinski Maciej, Marcin Moskit, and Mariusz Wilk. *Konspira: Solidarity Underground*. Berkeley: University of California Press, 1990.

Łoś, Maria. *Aspiracje a Środowisko (Aspirations versus Environment)*. Warsaw: PWN, 1972.

Łoś, M., ed. *The Second Economy in Marxist States*. London: Macmillan, 1990. New York: St. Martin's Press, 1990.

Łukasiewicz, Piotr. "The Non-Formalized Communication Circuit as a Social Institution." *Polish Sociological Bulletin* 83, no. 3 (1988).

Lutynski, Jan. "Apparent Activities." *Polish Sociological Bulletin* 2, no. 1 (1978).

———. *Nauka i Polskie Problemy (Social Sciences and Polish Problems)*. Warsaw: PWN, 1990.

Makarczyk, Wacław. *Czynniki Stabilizacji w Zawodzie Rolnika, i Motywy Migracji do Miast (Elements of Stabilization in the Farmer's Occupation and Motives of Migration)*. Wroclaw: Ossolineum, 1964.

Makarczyk Wacław, and Zdzisław Szpakowski. *Przemiany Życia Społeczno-Kulturalnego Ludnosci Wiejskiej (Changes in the Social Life of the Peasant Population)*. Warsaw: Ośrodek Badania Opinii Publicznej i Studiow Programowych (Centre of Public Opinion Studies), 1972.

Marody, Mirosława. "Antinomies of Collective Subconsciousness." *Social Research* 55, nos. 1–2 (1988).

Marody, Mirosława, ed. *Społeczeństwo Polskie u Progu Zmiany Systemowej (Polish Society Facing Social Change)*. London: Aneks, 1991.

Matejko, Aleksander, *The Well-Being of Population: Comparison Between Post-Industrialism Canada and Post-Communism Poland*. Forthcoming in Guro Nanak *Journal of Sociology*, vol. 13, no. 2.

Merton, Robert K. *On the Shoulders of Giants*. New York: The Free Press, 1965.

———. *Social Theory and Social Structure*. New York: The Free Press, 1968.

———. *Teoria Sociologiczna i Struktura Spoleczna*. Warsaw: PWN, 1982.

Misztal, Bronisław. "Between the State and Solidarity: One movement, Two Interpretations—The Orange Alternative Movement in Poland." *British Journal of Sociology* 43, no.1 (1992).

———. *Eastern Europe in Transition*. Westport, CT: Greenwood, forthcoming.

Modzelewski, Karol. "A Letter." *Polityka*, 1992, no. 2.

Mokrzycki, Edmund. "Polish Sociology of the Eighties: Theoretical Orientation, Meth-

ods, Main Research Trends.'' In R. Scharf, ed. Sozialwissenschaften in der Volks-
    republic Polen, IGW, Erlangen, 1989.
Mróz, Bogdan. ''Poland's Economy in Transition to Private Ownership.'' *Soviet Studies*
    43, no. 4 (1991).
Narojek, Winicjusz. *Społeczeństwo Planujące (Planning Society)*. Warsaw: PWN, 1973.
Nosowski, Zbigniew. ''Triumf i Niepewność: Polski Katolicyzm Lat Osiemdziesiątych''
    (''Triumph and Uncertainty: Polish Catholicism in Eighties''). *Więź*, 1991, nos.
    7–8.
Nowak, Krzysztof. ''Covert Repressiveness and the Stability of a Political System: Poland
    at the End of the Seventies.'' *Social Research* 55, nos. 1–2 (1988).
Nowak, Leszek. ''Man Vis-à-Vis Others.'' *Polish Sociological Bulletin* 96, no. 4 (1991).
Nowak, Stefan. ''Psychologiczne Aspekty Przemian Struktury Społecznej i Ruchliwosci
    Społecznej.'' *Studia Socjologiciczne* 21, no. 2 (1966).
————. ''Społeczenstwo Polskie Drugiej Połowy Lat Osiemdziesiatych—Próba Diag-
    nozy Stanu Świadomosci Społecznej'' (''Polish Society of 1980s—Tentative Di-
    agnosis of Social Awareness''). In Polish Sociological Association. *Materialy*.
    Warsaw, 1987.
————. *Ciągłość i Zmiana Tradycji Kulturowej (Continuity and Change in Cultural
    Tradition.)* Warsaw: PWN, 1989.
————. ''Values and Attitudes of the Polish People.'' *Scientific American* 245, no. 1
    (1981).
————. *Studenci Warszawy (Warsaw Students)*. Warsaw: Wydawnictwo Uniwersytetu
    Warszawskiego, 1991.
Olszewski, Jan. *Przerwana Premiera (An Interrupted Première)*. Warszawa: Tygodnik
    Solidarność, 1992.
Ossowska, Maria. *Podstawy Nauki o Moralnosci (Foundations of a Science of Morality)*.
    Warsaw: Czytelnik, 1947.
————. *Motywy Postępowania (Motives of Behavior)*. Warsaw: KIW, 1949.
————. *Moralność Mieszczanska (Bourgois Morality)*. Wrocław: Ossolineum, 1956.
————. *Sociologia Moralności (Sociology of Morals)*. Warsaw: PWN, 1969.
————. *Normy moralne (Moral Norms)*. Warsaw: PWN, 1970.
————. *Social Determinants of Moral Ideas*. Philadelphia: University of Pennsylvania
    Press, 1970.
————. *Ethos Rycerski (The Ethos of Knights)*. Warsaw: PWN, 1973.
Ossowski, Stanislaw. *O Nauce (About Science)*. Warsaw: PWN, 1967.
Petrażycki, Leon, (eds. Licki Jerzy, Andrzej Kojder) *O Nauce Prawie i Moralnosci
    (About Sciences, Law and Morality)*. Warsaw: PWN, 1985.
Podgórecki, Adam. *Założenia Polityki Prawa (Principles of Legal Policy)*. Warsaw:
    Wydawnictwo Prawncze, 1957.
————. *Zjawiska Prawne w Opinii Publicznej (Legal Phenomena in Public Opinion)*.
    Warsaw: Wydawnictwo Prawnicze, 1964.
————. *Prestiż Prawa (Prestige of Law)*. Warsaw: Ksiazka i Wiedza, 1966a.
————. ''Rozmaite Rozumienia Sociotechniki (''Various Understandings of Sociotech-
    nics''). In Adam Podgórecki. *Zasady Sociotechniki (Principles of Sociotechnics)*.
    Warsaw: Wiedza Powszechna, 1966b.
————. *Zasady Sociotechniki (Principles of Sociotechnics)*. Warsaw: Wiedza Pow-
    szechna, 1966(b).
————. *Law and Society*. London: Routledge and Kegan Paul, 1974.

————. "Osobowość Polaka" ("Polish Personality"). *Odra*, 1976.

————. "Spoleczeństwo Polskie w Świetle Badań i Prognóz" ("Polish Society in Research and Prognoses"). *Odra*, 1978a, no. 6.

————. "Całościowa Analiza Społeczenstwa Polskiego" ("Global Analysis of Polish Society"). *Prace Instytutu Profilaktyki Spolecznej i Resocjalizacjii*. Warsaw: UW, 1978b.

————. *Program polityczny dla Polski* (*A Political Programme for Poland*). Unpublished, privately distributed. Ottawa, 1982.

————. *A Story of A Polish Thinker*. Cologne: Verlag für GesellschaftArchitectur, 1986.

————. "Polish Society." *Praxis International* 7, no. 1 (1987)a.

————. "Całościowa Analiza Społeczenstwa Polskiego" ("Global Analysis of Polish Society"). In *VII Ogólnopolski Zjazd Sociologiczny*, edited by Edmund Wnuk-Lipinski. Warsaw: PTS, 1987b.

————. "Totalitarian and Post-Totalitarian Law." Ottawa: Carleton University, Department of Sociology and Anthropology Working Paper Series, 1990.

————. *A Sociological Theory of Law*. Milan: Guiffrè, 1991.

Podgórecki, Adam, ed. *Sociotechnics - Practical Applications of Sociology*. Warsaw: KIW, 1968.

————. *Sociotechnics - How to Act Efficiently*. Warsaw: KIW, 1970.

————. *Sociotechnics - Styles of Action*. Warsaw: KIW, 1972.

————. *Sociotechnics - Functionality and Dysfunctionality of Institutions*. Warsaw: KIW, 1974.

Podgórecki, Adam, and Andrzej Kojder. *Ewolucja Świadomosci Prawnej i Postaw Moralnych Społeczeńtwa polskiego* (*Evolution of The Awareness and Moral Attitudes of Polish Society*). Warsaw: Polish Radio and Television Committee Poll, 1972.

Podgórecki, Adam, and Jacek Kruczewski, Jerzy Kwasniewski, and Maria Łoś. *Poglądy Społeczeństwa Polskiego na Prawo i Moralność* (*Polish Social Attitudes towards Law and Morality*). Warsaw: Ksiazka i Wiedza, 1971.

Podgórecki, Adam, and Maria Łoś. *Multidimensional Sociology*. London: Routledge and Kegan Paul, 1979.

Post, Barbara. "Ethos Warszawskich Pracowników Nauki" ("The Ethos of Warsaw Scientists"). In Nauka w Kulturze Ogólnej (Science in General Culture). Wroclaw: Zaklad Narodowy im. Ossolinskich, 1985.

Przegląd Rządowy. Published by The Government Press Bureau. Warsaw, 1980.

Psomiades, Harry. "Greece: From the Colonels' Rule to Democracy." In John H. Herz. *From Dictatorship to Democracy*. Westport, CT: Greenwood Press, 1982.

Reszke, Irena. "The Meaning of Occupational Prestige Scales." *Polish Sociological Bulletin* 69–72, nos. 1–4 (1985).

Ritzer, George. *Contemporary Sociological Theory*. New York: Alfred A. Knopf, 1988.

Rocznik Statystyczny (Statistical Yearbook). Warsaw: Glowny Urzad Statystyczny, 1991.

Ruane, Kevin. *The Polish Challenge*. London: British Broadcasting Corporation, 1982.

Sadowski, Lesław. *Polska Inteligencja Prowincyonalna i Jej Ideowe Dylematy Na Przełomi xixi Wieku*. Warsaw: PWN: 1988.

Sadowski, Zdislaw, ed. *Społeczenstwa Post-Totulitarne* (*Post-Totalitarian Societies*). Proceedings of a Conference Sponsored by The Polish Association of Cooperation and The Club of Rome, Warsaw, 1991.

Sarapata, Adam. *Studia nad Uwarstwieniem i Ruchliwościa Społeczna w Polsce* (*Studies in Social Stratification and Mobility*). Warsaw: Ksiazka i Wiedza, 1965.

————. *A Portrait of Bureaucracy: The Bankruptcy of the System in Poland*. Delft-Poznan: Eburon Publisher, 1992.

Schapiro, Leonard. "The Role of the Jews in the Russian Revolutionary Movement." *East European Review* XL, 1961.

Schatz, Jaff. *The Generation: The Rise and Fall of the Jewish Communists of Poland*. Berkeley: University of California Press, 1991.

Scheler, Max. "Das Ressentiment im Aufbau der Moralen." in *Gesammelte Werkes*, Bern, Vol. 3, 1955.

Schoeck, Helmut. *Envy*. London: Secker and Warburg, 1969.

Siciński, Andrzej, ed. *Style Życia w Miastach Polskich* (*Styles of Life in Polish Cities*). Wroclaw: Ossolineum, 1988.

Skotnicka Iłłasiewicz, Elżbieta. "Poland in Europe." in *Poland in Europe*. Warsaw: Diet Press, 1992.

Słomczyński, Kazimierz. *Zróżnicowania Społeczno-Zawodowe i Jego Korelaty* (*Socio-Professional Differentation and Its Correlation*). Wroclaw: Ossolineum, 1977.

Słomczyński, Kazimierz, and Władyslaw Wesołowski, eds. *Struktura i Ruchliwość Społeczna (Social Structure and Mobility)*. Wroclaw: Ossolineum, 1973.

Staniszkis, Jadwiga. *Patologia Struktur Organizacyjnych* (*Pathology of Organizational Structures*). Wroclaw: Ossolineum, 1972.

Steczkowski, Jan. "Niekochana Elita" ("Unloved Elite"). *Dziennik Polski*, January 10, 1991, no. 8.

Studnicki, Franciszek. Talk given on Polish Radio, April 2, 1992.

Sułek, Antoni. "Zmiana Ustroju w Polsce a Zmiany w życiu Polskiej Sociologii" ("Social Changes in Poland and Changes in Polish Sociology"). In *Spoleczenstwo Polskie (Polish Society)*, edited by B. Synak. Gdynia: Victoria, 1992.

Synak, Brunon, ed. *Spoleczenstwo Polskie* (*Polish Society*). Gdynia: Victoria, 1992.

Szacki, Jerzy. *Historia Myśli Sociologicznej* (*History of Sociological Thought*). Warsaw: PWN, 1981.

————. In *Spoleczenstwa Post-totalitarne* (*Post-totalitarian Societies*). Proceedings of a conference sponsored by The Polish Association of Cooperation and The Club of Rome, Warsaw, 1992.

Szanter, Stanislaw. *Sociologia Kobiety*. Warsaw: B. Kadziel, 1948.

Szczepański, Jan. *Elementarne Pojęcia Sociologii* (*Elementary Notions of Sociology*). Warsaw: PWN, 1969.

————. *Przemsył i Spoleczeństwo w Polsce Ludowej* (*Industry and Society in People's Poland*). Wroclaw: Ossolineum, 1969.

————. *Polish Society*. New York: Random House, 1970.

Szczepański, Jan Józef. *Malenka Encyklopedia Totalizmu* (*A Tiny Encyclopedia of Totalism*). Crakow: Znak, 1990.

Szczypiórski, Andrzej. *The Polish Ordeal—The View from Within*. London: Croom Helm, 1982.

Sztompka, Piotr. *Masters of Polish Sociology*. Wrocław: Ossolineum, 1984.

Sztompka, Piotr. "The Theory of Cultural Becoming." *Polish Sociological Bulletin* 96, no. 4 (1991).

————. *Robert K. Merton: An Intellectual Profile*. London: Macmillan, 1986.

Torańska, Teresa. *Oni* (*They*). London: Aneks, 1985.

Touraine, Allain, François Dubet, Michel Wieviórka, and Jan Strzelecki, *Solidarity*. Cambridge: Cambridge University Press, 1983.

Tymowski, Andrzej. *Minimum Spoleczne* (*Social Minimum*). Warsaw: PWN, 1973.
Voslensky, Michael. *La Nomenklatura*. Vienna: Fritz Molden, 1980.
Walicki, Andrzej. "The Three Traditions in Polish Patriotism." In *Polish Paradoxes*, edited by Stanisław Gomulka and Antoni Polonsky. London: Routledge and Kegan Paul, 1990.
Warzywoda-Kruszynska, Wanda. "Zbiezność Cech Spolecznych Współmałżonkow" ("Congruency of Social Characteristics of Spouses"). In *Struktura i Ruchliwosc Spoleczna*, edited by Kazimierz Słomczynski and Włodzimierz Wesołowski. Wroclaw: Ossolineum, 1973.
Wasilewski, Jacek. "Kontraktowy Sejm Jako Miejsce Formowania się Elity Politycznej" ("Contractual Parliament as a Formation Forum for the Political Elite"). In *Początki Parlamentarnej Elity* (*Beginnings of Parliamentary Elite*), edited by Włodzimierz Wesołowski and Jacek Wasilewski. Warsaw: IFiS PAN.
Wedel, Janine. *The Private Poland*. New York: Facts on File Publications, 1986.
Wesołowski, Włodzimierz. "Weber's Concept of Legitimacy: Limitations and Continuations." *Sisyphus - Sociological Studies*. Warsaw: PWN, 1989.
Wesołowski, Włodzimierz, and Adam Sarapata. "Hierarchie Zawodów i Stanowisk" ("Hierarchies of Professions and Positions"). *Studia Sociologiczne* 1961, no. 2.
Wnuk-Lipinski, Edmund, ed. *VII Ogólnopolski Zjazd Sociologiczny*. Warsaw: PTS, 1987.
Wojciechowski, Jerzy. "Solidarity: Its Scope and Meaning." In *Solidarity*, edited by Ajit Jain. Baton Rouge: Oracle Press, 1982.
Wyka, Kazimierz. *Życie na Niby* (*Limbo Life*). PIW, 1957.
Wyrwa, Tadeusz. "Historia lat siedemnastu." *Aneks*, 1986, nos. 41–42.
Zajączkowski, Andrzej. *Z Dziejów Inteligencji Polskiej* (*Some Elements of the History of the Polish Intelligentsia*). Wrocław: Ossolineum, 1990. Written in 1962.
Zajączkowski, A. *Główne Elementy Kultury Szlacheckiej w Polsce* (*Main Elements of the Nobility's Culture in Poland*). Wrocław: Ossolineum, 1961.
Znaniecki, Florian. *The Social Role of the Man of Knowledge*. New York: Octagon Books, 1965.
Zuzowski, Robert. *Political Dissent and Opposition in Poland*. Westport, CT: Praeger, 1992.

Index

About the Author

ADAM PODGÓRECKI is Professor of Sociology at Carleton University and Warsaw University. He is the author of many articles and more than 20 books published in Poland, Britain, and the United States, including the recent *Social Oppression* (Greenwood, 1993).